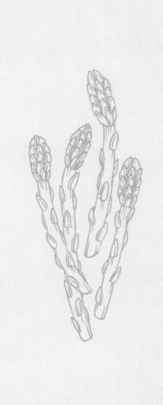

ruffage

ruffage

A PRACTICAL GUIDE TO VEGETABLES
100+ RECIPES AND 230+ VARIATIONS

by abra berens

PHOTOGRAPHS BY EE BERGER
ILLUSTRATIONS BY LUCY ENGELMAN
FOREWORD BY FRANCIS LAM

CHRONICLE BOOKS
SAN FRANCISCO

Library of Congress Cataloging-in-Publication Data available.

ISBN 978-1-4521-6932-3

Manufactured in China.

Prop styling by Lee Berens and Mollie Hayward

Food styling by Mollie Hayward

Design by Sara Schneider

Typesetting by Frank Brayton

10 9 8 7 6 5 4

Chronicle books and gifts are available at special quantity discounts to corporations, professional`associations, literacy programs, and other organizations. For details and discount information, please contact our premiums department at corporatesales@chroniclebooks.com or at 1-800-759-0190.

Chronicle Books LLC
680 Second Street
San Francisco, California 94107
www.chroniclebooks.com

foreword

One of the first things I remember Abra Berens cooking was a mistake. It was a post-college dinner party at a friend's apartment. She'd spent some time in professional kitchens, and so she was welcomed like an ambassador from Restolandia, her moves at the stove studied and admired. As she braised pork in milk, she told everyone that by the time it was done, the milk would have reduced and caramelized into a thick, ribbony, savory dulce de leche. It didn't happen. The sauce remained stubbornly fluid, separated, in fact. We were promised magic and ended up with meat, curds, and whey. Were she perfectionist, ego-driven, the kind of showy cook who cooks at her guests more than *for* them, she would have been mortified. Happily, Abra is none of those things, and she happily served the different-yet-delicious dish to her friends. (Everyone loved it.)

Fast forward 10 or 12 years, and I'm having lunch at the restaurant she was running, an unassuming counter inside a produce market. I confess I can't remember everything on the menu, but I do remember that the food was delicious, real, mostly vegetables; there were eggs and, I think, a baked potato—with a mushroom ragù and all kinds of delicious things on top that made it somehow transcend the profoundly plain fact of its existence as a baked potato.

Anyway, I ordered far too much food because the cooking was so damned good. I remember that the sauces were bright and saucy, and the beans creamy and beany, but most of all I remember the feeling of it. That this was cooking that was simple because it was confident. You hear about chefs having "respect" for their ingredients all the time, but usually that's just code for "I can get really expensive stuff that you can't." Abra's cooking is influenced by her time as a farmer, which means that she has an instinct and techniques for what to do with tomatoes that are perfect, heavy orbs of juice, along with the ones that got picked a little hard by mistake. Hers is a smart way of cooking, a curious, thoughtful way of cooking, but most of all, a cooking of good spirit. At that lunch, everything was made flawlessly, but there was still a clear, direct, shining, smiling line between the spirit of woman who made this food and the spirit of the woman who gladly served her closest friends a big pile of meat that looked absolutely nothing like the way she intended.

So here is this book. It's full of that good spirit and those techniques. It's a cookbook that's an idea book, a learning book, a live-with-you-in-the-kitchen book. I've dog-eared so many pages: creamed mozzarella, charred green beans and fat chunks of tomato drizzled with tuna mayo, mustard braised potatoes with chicken thighs. I mentioned the creamed mozzarella, right?

I was afraid, getting ready to write this foreword, that I would be hamstrung because I get to know Abra as a person, and that I would infer all kinds of magical things from the book because of that. But I'm happy to say that, in these pages, you will also get to know her, and the things she knows. She's a dirt-nailed philosopher and a cold-beer storyteller. You'll learn about the life and life-giving properties of plants the way a farmer sees it. You'll never see a cucumber the same way again. You'll start using the phrase "science feels." It's heartrending, beautiful, sly, funny, and dear. One page feels like a prose poem and the next feels like your bestie slipping you notes in school.

But maybe I am overstating it. (I'm not.) Maybe, in the end, this book is a brassica. There's a great line in it: ". . . it is cabbage I come home to. She is a reliable and hard-working friend." For all the cooking smarts it contains, all the knowledge, stories, ideas, warmth, and good spirit, let this book be your cabbage.

FRANCIS LAM

This, like everything, is for Erik.

Should we do the dishes?
Let's go to bed.

CONTENTS

eggplant 181

braised: stewy eggplant and
tomato coddled eggs 184

oven roasted: crispy eggplant
w/fresh mozzarella, tomatoes,
pickled raisins, and mint 187

puréed: smoky eggplant pasta w/ pounded
walnut relish, mozzarella, and basil 191

fennel 195

raw: shaved fennel salad w/apricots, chili oil,
parsley, mint, and lamb chops 199

braised: braised fennel 204

garlic 207

raw: grilled pork chops w/garlic
and kale relish 211

sautéed: garlic and spinach pasta 214

confit: garlic confit 217

confit: garlic marinated white beans
w/celery and parsley salad 218

green beans 221

pan roasted: blistered green beans
w/tomatoes, pounded walnuts,
and raw summer squash 225

grilled: charred green beans w/crispy
chickpeas and curry yogurt 227

braised: green beans w/tomatoes, lentils,
and onions 230

greens, delicate:
arugula, leaf lettuce, head lettuce,
spinach, baby bok choy 233

raw: perfect salad 238

braised: braised lettuce 241

grilled: charred whole romaine
w/hard-boiled egg, anchovy vinaigrette,
and garlic bread crumbs 244

greens, hearty:
chard, collards, kale, radicchio
and other chicories 247

raw: massaged kale w/tomatoes,
creamed mozzarella, and wild rice 251

sautéed: sautéed greens w/garlic
and chili flakes 255

braised: braised kale w/jowl bacon,
onions, and parsley 256

oven roasted: oven-roasted kale chips
w/grated raclette 259

kohlrabi 261

baked: kohlrabi potato gratin 266

raw: kohl-slaw w/apples, black lentils, sherry
vinaigrette, and seared salmon 269

leeks 273

raw: marinated leek salad w/wheat berries,
carrots, and seared salmon 277

braised: slow-cooked leeks
w/thyme and cream 281

onions 285

raw: shaved onion salad w/cucumber, yogurt,
and mint over lamb chops 289

braised: vinegar-braised onions w/seared
whitefish and arugula 291

caramelized: caramelized onion and
goat cheese toasts 295

parsnips 299

oven roasted: roasted parsnips w/fresh goat
cheese, pecans, and pickled apricots 303

puréed: parsnip purée w/duck breast,
radicchio, and cranberry relish 307

peas 311

marinated: marinated peas w/yesterday's roast
chicken, baby onions, and lettuce 315

puréed: sweet pea toasts 317

pan roasted: peas w/parsley, thyme,
butter, and onions 319

peppers, sweet 323

grilled: grilled peppers w/eggplant and
tomato over couscous 327

braised: peperonata w/poached eggs and
paprika potatoes 331

potatoes 335

boiled: simple boiled potatoes w/sweet butter
and herbs 339

oven roasted: roasted potato salad w/egg,
celery, herbs, and bread crumbs 342

braised: mustard braised potatoes
w/chicken thighs 345

baked: jacket potatoes w/shaved vegetable
salad and tuna mayo 349

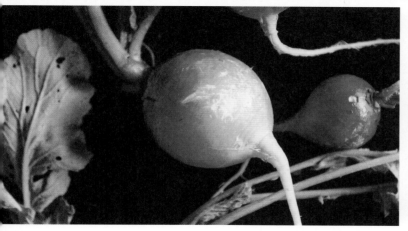

introduction

In 2009, my friend Jess Piskor and I started Bare Knuckle Farm in Northport, Michigan. I was a young cook, only a year and a half out of cookery school, but knew I wanted to make food that was representative of a place. Seemed like the best place to start was by growing it. Jess's family graciously let us take up residence in a frost valley between two of their cherry orchards. We gave it a go.

At the end of my first year of farming, I was as poor as I've ever been, having plunged my savings into starting a business. I had two weeks before returning to Chicago, to a job that paid me in greenbacks instead of leafy greens. Trying to save my pennies, I was eating the last of our farm's vegetables that hadn't sold at the final market. There were carrots still in the ground to overwinter and harvest in the spring. The kale plants, which we had chopped down because they were covered in aphids, had unfurled little baby leaves, all tender and green. The chickens had been relocated to another farm for the winter, but I still had eighteen eggs from their last few layings.

Every day, I went out to the farm and pulled a stash of carrots from the ground. I shivered at night, but the carrots only got sweeter with every passing frost. The tiny kale greens sprouted anew each day, photosynthesizing every faded hour of fall sunlight. The eggs were almost obscenely orange-yolked. I couldn't have bought food in the store of this quality even if I had had dollars instead of pennies. I was broke as hell but was eating some of the best meals of my life.

Each night was something new from the same primary ingredients. Roasted carrots with cumin and a hard-boiled egg. Shredded carrot and kale slaw with scrambled eggs. Poached egg with carrot latkes and kale salad. Spicy roasted carrots with sautéed kale and hollandaise. I was more than satisfied but still dreaming of all the meals I would eat back in the city. I pictured cakes and pies and meat and fish and great big pieces of cheese and salami.

I packed up my stuff and moved back to Chicago to work at a pie shop for the holidays—gobbling slices of pie and free coffee with abandon. After two weeks I felt like garbage and craved the carrots and kale I thought I had been eating out of austerity alone. I went to the store, feeling a little silly for not having packed up some of those perfect (and perfectly free) carrots, and bought a basket of vegetables. I ate a big bowl of leafy greens and root vegetables dressed in a lemony garlic mayo; I felt whole again. Popeye after a can of spinach never came back so strongly.

The fall of 2009 changed me. It taught me that ingredients can be repetitive, but meals need not be. It taught me to identify what my body actually needs (vegetables) versus what it just wants (sweets). Though I say this with some hesitation; there is an unhelpful danger in equating decadent foods with sinfulness and vegetables with moral fortitude, and this is not a diet book. It isn't about right or wrong; it is about the practical and daily choices we make. Since that time, vegetables have become the chosen cornerstone of my diet. I love meat and dairy and sweets, but I know that it is the vegetables that keep me together.

Farming changed the way that I cook, beyond cultivating a love and desire for vegetables. I learned of the plant's needs and how those needs shape how the vegetable is flavored and textured, and when it is at its prime. It may seem silly to say, but plants are sensible creatures. Their whole goal is to create seed, protect that seed, and ensure germination the next season, thus continuing the plant's existence. Even the most rudimentary understanding of what a plant does has made me a better cook because I am playing to

the strengths of the vegetable instead of trying to conform it to my desires. I hope that you, too, with the help of this book, start to be able to read the landscape of the food you are cooking. It is true, you are in charge, not the cauliflower. It is also true that by playing to the inherent strengths of a particular ingredient, you can coax out the most delight with the least amount of fight.

This book stems from my experiences as a former farmer and chef. My goal is to share what I've learned and practiced so that you feel empowered to shop for, store, and cook vegetables every day and in a variety of ways. I hope that you will then be even more excited to make dinner trying new preparation techniques and flavor combinations. My biggest dream is that as you build experience and confidence you feel excited about trying your own original variations—effectively cooking beyond the page.

how to use this book

This book is organized alphabetically for ease of looking up the vegetable that you want to cook. I find that my best cooking happens when I go to the market without a planned menu or shopping list, allowing myself to be swayed by what looks best and then tailoring my menu to those items instead of the other way around.

In short, go to the store, go to a farmers' market, or sign up for a weekly farm share. Get your hands on some vegetables to cook, and with this book as a resource, write your menu.

At the start of each chapter is a collection of notes on what to look for in a vegetable when you're shopping, how to store the garnered vegetable, and other tips and tools of the trade that I thought would be helpful or interesting. Each chapter also starts with an essay inspired by that chapter's vegetable. These stories are wide-ranging and include information about the plant's growth cycle, how the vegetable fits into our larger food world, and some tales of how food has shaped my life personally. These essays are not essential to execution of the recipes but aim to give you a deeper appreciation of that vegetable and how it fits into the garden, the kitchen, my mind, or our broader food culture.

Then each chapter is broken out by the various preparation techniques—raw, grilled, oven roasted, pan roasted, braised, etc.—that I favor for preparing these vegetables. There's certainly more than one way

to peel a carrot, but in each chapter, I tell you what *I* do, why, and exactly how.

Each technique is presented with one complete recipe followed by two to four variations. By using the same cooking technique but different flavor accessories, you can make several dishes that are structurally the same but present very differently on a plate. Preparing a beet salad with smoked whitefish, sour cream, and dill is effectively the same as making a beet salad with oranges, feta, mint, and pecans, or a beet salad with apples, Cheddar, walnuts, and parsley. The framework is the same, but each dish is dramatically different.

The variations illustrate (literally) how you can either swap ingredients in and out from the base recipe or how to evolve the original recipe into a totally new meal. Extra information is noted for clarity.

These recipes and variations are also made with a circumscribed list of pantry ingredients because one of my biggest hurdles to making dinner is having to go to the store for something I'll use only once. A strongly stocked pantry of a few stalwart components ensures that whatever vegetable I have on hand that day can be assembled into a dish, quickly and deliciously. I've chosen pantry staples that are common and widely available, to minimize your having to order anything online days before making dinner.

A note on the measurements in this book: the recipes are written in the units in which vegetables are sold at the market or store. I have added rough equivalents in weight or volume, but know that these recipes are flexible. If you have two extra ounces of cauliflower in the purée, it will be just fine. Again, you are the boss, not the cauliflower.

Similarly, I use the term "glug" a good deal in these recipes—a holdover from my grandmother's recipes. Like "glug," many cooking terms in this book make sense to me but might be obscure to you. For clarity, there is a glossary of terms to help define them in your mind. Words listed in the glossary are denoted later in the book to remind you to look them up if you have a question.

Unless otherwise noted, recipes in this book are scaled for four servings. Some of the recipes make a classic vegetable side dish. Others are a meal unto themselves. The recipe notes will guide you. One of my all-time favorite recipes is a response to the question *What goes with that?* The recipe is: the best-looking vegetables you can find, tossed with olive oil, salt, and pepper, then roasted until crispy. My response to *What goes with that?* is that a roasted chicken thigh, seared piece of fish, or hard-boiled egg are good add-ons to just about any vegetable recipe in this book.

One more note: the final step in most of these recipes is to "taste and adjust the seasoning as desired." I find it annoying when a chef tells you to cook something until it is "done" giving no indication how to tell when it's done. Well, the same could be said of seasoning "to taste." Seasoning is intensely subjective, and as a cook you need to learn what level of seasoning and acidity you like in a dish. Again, you're in charge.

To do so, please perform the following experiment at least once; it is, hands down, one of the best things you can do for your cooking. Make the following recipe in this exact order and don't stray from it.

ADVENTURES IN SEASONING

1 egg

10 fl oz (300 ml) oil (any kind except olive)

½ tsp (3 g) salt

1 Tbsp (15 ml) apple cider vinegar

Whiz the egg in a food processor.
Slowly drizzle in the oil to make a mayonnaise.
Taste it.
Gross, right? It tastes fatty, one-note, not great.
Add the salt and whiz again.
Tastes pretty good, right?
Add the vinegar.
"Hallelujah" chorus!

This demonstrates how salt and acid balance food. The salt unlocks the flavor. The acidity lifts it to the rafters.

To continue the experiment, add another ½ tsp of salt and whiz again.

To me, it tastes even better. To you, it may be too salty. You have to regulate the finished dish to your preference and now you can taste the difference and see how to fine-tune everything you make from here on out.

These recipes are written with a light touch on the salt so that you have the opportunity to add more if you like it that way. The recipes were developed and have been tested with Morton's kosher salt, which is saltier than other brands. Other kinds and brands of salt will have different levels of salinity, and you will need to calibrate accordingly.

It's disempowering to feel constrained to follow a recipe precisely. I hope that, with these tools to ease shopping for and storing vegetables and introducing the foundational techniques of preparation, you will feel confident cooking and adjusting the recipes to your preference, and motivated to cook beyond the page, improvising new combinations of your own to delight in. When you do, I hope that you will write to me about it; there's always another way to eat a carrot.

glossary of terms

This section presents three types of information: straight definitions, techniques you may reference, and mini-recipes you'll want to come back to.

general vocabulary

ACIDULATED WATER
Water with an acid diluted in it and used to either keep vegetables from oxidizing or poaching eggs (vinegar makes the whites firm up faster). The traditional ratio is 1 qt (1 L) water to the juice of 1 lemon (1½ oz | 45 ml), 2 Tbsp (30 ml) vinegar, or 1 cup (240 ml) white wine.

BUNCH
Standard unit of sale at a store or market. Approximate weights or volume measures follow these in all recipes.

FOND
The browned bits left in the pan after frying or searing and released during the deglazing process.

GLUG
The amount of liquid poured from a container before air is pulled in past the "seal" formed by the flowing liquid in the neck of the container, creating a glug sound. An average glug measure is about 2 tablespoons to ¼ cup (30 to 60 ml). It doesn't need to be exact—just splash some oil in a pan. If you need more, add it. I've yet to need less oil in my life.

MIDRIBS
The thick, fibrous central stem of hearty greens.

NAPPÉ
Consistency of a liquid that will coat the back of a wooden spoon—think the thickness of custard. In roasted tomatoes, the spoon or spatula should leave a clean line across the baking dish without the juices running in.

PARCHMENT LID (CARTOUCHE)
A circular piece of parchment paper that covers a slowly simmering liquid, used when you want to evaporate some but not all of a liquid and prevent a skin from forming. Using a metal lid keeps all of the liquid in. (Tip: save old butter wrappers for this; they are free and work well.)

SCIENCE FEEL
Term that my friends Heidi and Molly use for when you think there might be some science behind your opinion but you don't have the facts to prove it but it seems logical so you really *feel like it is true*.

TOSS
To gently stir ingredients (with a spoon or hand) until coated with a dressing or well combined.

techniques

BLOOM
To toast dried spices, usually in a bit of warm oil or fat, to activate their fragrance and flavor. Heat the oil until shimmering, remove from the heat (avoid the potential of burning), add the spice, and toast until fragrant. I like to have the next ingredient to be added on hand to add to the bloomed spice, to drop the pan temperature and stop the spice cooking.

BLISTER
To cook an ingredient over high heat with a bit of hot fat to sear, develop color, and create little bubbles on the skin.

BOILED EGGS
Place eggs in a saucepan in which they fit snugly at the bottom and add cold water to just cover the eggs. Bring to a boil. Remove from the heat and cover. Allow to cook to desired doneness: 5 minutes—soft but not runny; 7 minutes—medium;

10 minutes—hard but not flaky yolk; 12 minutes—pale, flaky yolk but no gray ring around the yolk. I also like to gently tap the wide end of the egg on a hard surface before placing it in the water to create a hairline crack in the shell, making it easier to peel.

BRAISE

To cook at a low temperature in a moist environment after first searing to caramelize the outside crust. This traditionally renders tough cuts of meat tender (think pot roast or brisket). For vegetables it is a gentle way of cooking with little fat and flavorful liquid to yield very silky finished dishes. For meat I never braise above 300°F (150°C). Vegetables don't have the same connective tissue to break down and can handle a higher temperature (generally about 350°F [180°C] or so).

BROWN BUTTER

This method separates and cooks the milk proteins in the butter until golden brown with a nutty flavor. Heat the butter in a saucepan (preferably not black, for ease of seeing the butter darken) until melted and foamy. (Skim the foam and stop here for clarified butter or ghee.) Allow the foam to settle and it will eventually fall to the bottom of the saucepan and slowly caramelize. Cook the butter until the flecks of milk solids become golden brown. When brown, remove from heat and allow to cool. If you think you might have taken the butter too far, before cooling, pour the butter into a different container, leaving the dark flecks in the pan.

CLEANING MUSHROOMS

For cultivated mushrooms, brush the dirt away with a dry towel. For wild mushrooms, especially morels (which can be very inhabited with crawlers), soak in heavily salted water to kill or at least make the bugs detach from the mushroom. Then lift the mushrooms from the salty water and dry on towels before cooking. Washing mushrooms does *not* cause them to absorb water, making roasting difficult. Just give them a good dry.

CONFIT

Result of slow cooking in fat at a low temperature—like frying and poaching having a love child. Submerge the ingredient in some form of fat (generally oil) and cook at a low temperature until the vegetable is tender and yielding. The flavor of the fat will permeate the vegetable and, in the case of garlic or onion, vice versa. I generally confit around 300°F to 325°F (150°C to 165°C). Don't pitch the fat after cooking; use it in other applications, like frying other ingredients, in vinaigrettes, or to garnish a dish.

DEGLAZE

To loosen browned bits of food from the pan bottom after searing or sautéing. Pour off any excess fat, add ¼ to ½ cup (60 to 120 ml) of wine or hard cider to the pan, and with a flat wooden spoon vigorously scrape up the bits from the pan and continue cooking to reduce the liquid volume. This triple-duty method uses those very flavorful bits, adds acidity to a dish, and cleans the pan before washing.

ESCABÈCHE

A Spanish technique of cooling a just-cooked ingredient in an acidic marinade. As the ingredient cools, the flavor of the marinade is pulled into the center of the ingredient's cells.

GRILLING OR SEARING CHOPS

Bring the meat to room temperature. Heat the grill to high heat. Pat the meat dry, brush lightly with neutral oil, and season liberally with salt and pepper. Place the meat on the grill and allow to sear and develop a nice crust. Flip and sear the other side. The cooking time for each side depends on how thick your meat is and how cooked you want it to be. When in doubt, I generally allow the first cooking side to sear thoroughly to achieve a good crust, and then look for uncooked meat at the center. If it looks like it is getting close to being cooked to medium rare, I flip the meat and sear the other side for only 3 to 5 minutes just to mark the meat but not overcook. Allow the cooked meat to rest in a warm but not hot place for 5 to 10 minutes before serving, to allow the juices to redistribute within the meat. If you don't have (or don't want to use) a grill, a broiler is effectively an upside-down grill, or a screaming-hot pan will give a similar level of char (though it will smoke up the house).

POACHING

To gently cook an ingredient in simmering water. For meat and fish, I bring everything (the flavorful cooking liquid and the meat) to a simmer together; when the meat is 80 percent cooked, I turn off the heat and allow the protein to finish in the hot cooking liquid. For vegetables, I heat the liquid and then add the vegetables and cook until just cooked through or even leaving a touch of crunch in the center. For eggs, acidulate the water and bring to a simmer. The acid in the water helps the egg white proteins coagulate more quickly and evenly, ensuring a nice shape of the egg. Cook until the white is set but the yolk is soft, about 3 minutes. Lift the egg from the water with a slotted spoon and touch the center to be sure that the white is opaque and firm.

ROASTING

To cook ingredients in a high, dry heat, so the internal moisture evaporates away, concentrating the flavor and creating a textural difference between the outside and inside. Best practices: Coat the ingredient in a fat, which raises the outer temperature of the ingredient, ensuring a faster and more even cooking time; allow enough space between the ingredients to allow the evaporating moisture room to escape. Overlapping ingredients trap the evaporating moisture and steam the ingredient, preventing a nice crusty exoskeleton.

ROASTING MUSHROOMS

Slice the mushrooms to the desired thickness. In a large frying pan heat a large glug of oil (either neutral or olive) over high heat until starting to smoke. Add the mushrooms and season with salt and pepper. Allow to brown and crisp and any released liquid to evaporate. Stir to flip and brown the other side. A pan extremely full of mushrooms will take a very long time to brown; for more even and consistent cooking, fry the mushrooms in batches, or just be prepared to let them go for longer than you think. Conversely, you can also roast mushrooms in a hot (350°F to 425°F [180°C to 220°C]) oven. Fill a roasting dish with mushrooms cut to the desired thickness, dress with a very big glug of oil, and season with salt and pepper. Place in the oven and bake until

golden brown and cooked through, stirring every 10 to 15 minutes.

SEARING FISH OR CHICKEN

Allow the fish or chicken to come to room temperature. Pat the fish dry with a paper towel (the drier the skin, the less it will stick and the crispier it will be). Heat a glug of neutral (high heat) oil in a large frying pan over high heat until smoking hot. Season the fish or chicken liberally with salt. Place the skin-side down and press it into the pan, ensuring good contact between the skin and the pan as the proteins constrict. Allow the meat to sear until it moves easily when gently nudged with a spatula (meaning the skin is fully crisped and released from the pan). If the skin doesn't release, add a bit more oil and continue to fry the skin. Either transfer the pan to a 350°F to 425°F (180°C to 220°C) oven to finish cooking or flip the piece (boldly, with the courage of your convictions) and cook the other side to desired doneness. Serve skin-side up and encourage your guests to try it. Many people pull the skin off, but it adds textural contrast to the flesh and is both delicious and packed with omega-3 fatty acids and micronutrients.

STRIPPING GREENS

To strip the tough, unpalatable stems from hearty greens, you can either cut away with a knife or remove by hand. If doing by hand (my preferred method), hold the base of the stem in your nondominant hand, place your dominant thumb and index finger on opposing sides of the stem, and pull downward, ripping the greens from the stem. Alternatively, fold the front sides of the leaf together and with your nondominant hand strip the stem from the back of the folded leaf. If there is a bit of thin stem left with the leaves, it's OK.

SWEAT

To gently cook (usually onions and garlic) on low heat until soft and translucent but without coloring, generally 5 to 7 minutes.

TOASTING NUTS

As with dry spices, toasting nuts before use activates their flavor (and adds crunch). Oven toasting yields a more even toast but takes a bit longer. Heat the oven to 350°F to 425°F (180°C to 220°C), spread the nuts evenly across a baking sheet, and bake until lightly browned and fragrant, about 7 to 10 minutes. Pan toasting is faster but less even. Heat a dry pan over medium heat, add the nuts, and toast until browned, 2 to 3 minutes, then flip and continue toasting for another 2 to 3 minutes.

cutting techniques/phrases (from thick to thin)

TIP AND TAIL
To cut off both ends of a vegetable, generally the stem and root end. This is usually the first step in preparing a vegetable.

CHUNKS
Large, irregular pieces, cut for cooking, not for appearance. Generally about 1 inch (2.5 cm) thick or so.

OBLIQUE CUT
To cut the vegetable into sticks with an angled edge, giving a nice look and more surface area for browning. Place the vegetable on the cutting board running left-right (parallel to the counter edge). Cut the end of the vegetable at a 45-degree angle. Give the vegetable a quarter turn and cut again (at any length) at a 45-degree angle. Repeat until you reach the other end.

DICE
To cut into small(ish) squares by slicing in one direction, turning the slices 90 degrees and slicing across at the same thickness. Small dice is generally ¼ inch by ¼ inch (6 mm by 6 mm); large is ¾ inch by ¾ inch (2 cm by 2 cm).

BATON
A cut traditionally ¼ inch by ¼ inch by 1 to 2 inches (6 mm by 6 mm by 2.5 to 5 cm) long. Makes small sticks by slicing one direction, flipping the slices, and slicing the other way to make long, thin rectangles. I use this cut over matchsticking when I want a bit more chew in the dish.

MATCHSTICKS (JULIENNE)
Like a baton but a smaller cut, traditionally ⅛ inch by ⅛ inch by 1 to 2 inches (4 mm by 4 mm by 2.5 to 5 cm). I use instead of a baton when I want a subtler mouthfeel.

RIBBONS (WIDE CHIFFONADE)
Cut at irregular lengths about ⅛ inch (4 mm) thick. For greens, strip out the midribs, stack, and roll into a log, and slice thinly, allowing the ribbons to unfurl as you go.

THINLY SLICE
To cut into thin ¹⁄₁₀-inch (2.5-mm) ribbons. Most commonly used for onions—tip and tail the onion, set the cut-side down, and then cut the onion in half from north to south pole. Peel and place each half, cut-side down, with one pole facing you, and cut across the onion very thinly from right to left (or opposite if you are left-handed), making thin ribbons or petals.

SHAVE
To cut into the thinnest possible slices with either a sharp knife or a mandoline. Think finely cut cabbage for coleslaw or very thinly sliced radishes for a salad.

EGGPLANT
POTATOES
CARROTS
GARLIC

PART 1
strong pantry

A pantry is like a quiver of arrows, at your back and at the ready. Having a shelf of even a few dependable staples is the single best thing you can do to ensure that you can always make a quick, varied, and delicious meal at home. This chapter is dedicated to what I keep in my pantry and reflects the majority of ingredients used in the recipes outside of the primary vegetables. This list, intentionally, can be sourced from a neighborhood corner store or small-town grocery. There are a few ingredients that I love using that aren't available in all stores; I've noted substitutions by each one in the recipe.

Relying on a stalwart set of supplies improved my cooking for three reasons.

One, by keeping key ingredients on hand, you'll never be dissuaded or disappointed by a recipe because you don't have something you need. You will always have a good substitution on hand. If a recipe calls for feta, you can either go to the store, give up, or use the Parmesan you already have instead. It won't be the same, but it will be similar enough. Understanding how each ingredient functions within a dish gives you an immeasurable amount of control to transform a recipe to your own tastes.

The single change that has made me utilize my pantry is to look regularly at what I have there. I transfer the grains from their packaging to clear jars and store those jars on open shelves. I also label most things, because the one time I grabbed sushi rice instead of risotto rice was enough. Seeing the ingredients not only reminds me of what I have on hand but also that I was excited enough to buy them. So I should use them.

Two, you will be able to make faster meals because your tools are in place (with less time spent shopping). Similarly, dinner is always partially prepped because you can mix and match from a handful of condiments and sauces. Having these on hand is great; making them regularly enough that it doesn't feel like a chore is even better. It will take some time, but developing a new skill always does. The secondary benefit is that when it seems like you really don't have anything in the house and are tempted by takeout, you can always whip up something—like pasta dressed with chili oil and garnished with sunflower seeds. Your quiver is full of quick fixes.

Three, by cooking faster, easier, and more delicious meals regularly, you'll increase the likelihood of making meals you enjoy at home—meaning you're more likely to continue to do it and increase your appetite for experimentation. This has a positive effect on your budget, relationships, and health. As a society, we will never stop going out to eat, because restaurants serve an important social function as a third space to develop community outside of the home and work. That said, I do believe that there has been an undermining of home cooking to sell a packaged food product or push the idea that you must be trained as a chef to know how to cook. Yes, our time is valuable, and outsourcing our food preparation is reasonable as long as it is a deliberate choice and not one made out of fear or ignorance of the process. When you know you can use your precious time to make good food, it restores the luxury of bringing people together **or** celebrating the ease of letting a restaurant do it for you.

This pantry list is a lot to go out and buy in one fell swoop. Instead, I urge you to simply read through this book and find the recipes that use ingredients you already like and have on hand. Start there, then add more items as you go. I found that I initially spent more to stock my pantry, but then spent less on average because I wasn't buying random ingredients scattershot at the whim of a recipe I found online.

My golden rules for buying ingredients are: buy only what you are excited about, use it up, and if you can't remember if you have it on hand, don't buy more—you probably have something you can use in its place.

oils

I try to always buy oil in glass containers, because when oil is in plastic it seems to go rancid more quickly. This is not scientifically proven, so it's a **science feel** on my part, but I really think it is true! Plastic and clear bottles allow oxidization as well. Dark glass or metal containers will help preserve the integrity of the oil. If you have very old oil, smell it before using. If it has gone rancid it will smell flat and musty. Throw it out. Moral of the story: if you don't cook often or prefer butter to oil, buy small amounts and store them in the refrigerator.

When considering which oil to use and when, think about flavor and smoke point—the temperature at which the oil will begin to burn. Neutral oils have less inherent flavor but a higher smoke point, making them well suited to high heat cooking like roasting or grilling. Oils with more delicate flavor, like nut or fine olive oils, generally have a lower smoke point, and the hotter the oil gets the less nuanced the flavor. Also note that unrefined oils tend to contain more particulate matter, making them more flavorful, but with a lower smoke point. Save nut and other high-quality oils for finishing vegetables or a salad.

I also think about whether the flavor of the oil is important to the dish. If the other ingredients are strong, like herbs or spices, I use neutral oil because it is generally cheaper than the others. Use olive oil if you want its added depth of flavor. That said, if you want to make chili oil and all you have on hand is olive oil, feel free to use it. These are all rough guidelines and things that make a difference in the high volume/low margin world of restaurants—less important to a household budget.

NEUTRAL OIL

I use this term to include any sort of high smoke point, flavorless oil. I use grapeseed, rice bran, or safflower oils because they are not grown as a monoculture in our country. If you have access to these I encourage you to do the same because it creates demand in the market. If you don't have access, you can use any vegetable oil.

I also use neutral oils when making something with very strong flavors like herb or chili oils. I used to use olive oil for these but didn't taste the olivey-ness and so couldn't justify the cost.

OLIVE OIL

Look for extra-virgin and cold-pressed. There is fraud in the labeling practices of olive oil, so if you can get a taste of it before you buy it, all the better; if not just keep trying them until you find one you like. I look for an oil that tastes buttery and doesn't have a bitter harshness at the finish. I like Colavita and the Turkish Zaytun brands.

I use a lot of oil in my cooking, so I buy the big tins. If you do too, use a can opener to cut a small air hole on the nonspout side of the oil tin—it will make the oil pour more evenly.

If you have access to very good olive oil from a specialty shop, use it to dress salads and over fresh cheeses. Heat kills the delicate flavor of oils, so it is a waste to use it for frying. I don't generally buy flavored olive oils, but if you like them, go for it.

NUT OILS

Walnut and hazelnut oils are increasingly available. I use these as finishing oils to add a delicate nut flavor to a finished dish. As with olive oil, heat will kill the flavor, so don't cook with these. Nut oils are also very volatile and should be refrigerated.

COCONUT OIL

Only recently has coconut oil become more available. You can use it in place of any of the oils in this book, but it will lend a distinctly buttery and tropical flavor note. I love it for roasting cauliflower but didn't include it in any recipes because I had trouble finding it in all stores.

acidity

Second to seasoning, acidity is the most important flavor to balance a dish. Each recipe has some form of acidity. Remember the mayo experiment in the introduction? A dish lacking acidity may taste good but can become great with a squeeze of lemon or dash of vinegar. Beyond vinegar and citrus, wine, pickley things, and fermenty things can add the same level of brightness and feel new and exciting when you are expecting the traditional splash of lemon. Bottom line: if it makes your mouth water or pucker, it can be used to brighten up a dish. Add a touch, taste it, and decide for yourself.

VINEGARS

APPLE CIDER	This is my most used vinegar because it is versatile and more commonly made in the Midwest than the others; look for smaller batch production. It should taste tart but still appley.
SHERRY	This is my favorite vinegar because it tastes of the wood casks that age sherry, a fortified wine from Spain. If you can't find a good sherry vinegar, mix up 2 parts white wine vinegar with 1 part balsamic, or just use white wine vinegar.
WHITE WINE	I tend to buy Champagne vinegar, but any sort of small-batch production will work well. Just look for one with bright color and a super tangy flavor.
RED WINE	This should have the same acidity as white wine vinegar but with some notes of oak. If you don't have it on hand, use white wine vinegar.
BALSAMIC	Most major brand supermarket balsamic is crappy vinegar with caramel-flavored syrup stirred in. Unless it's a good balsamic, which is expensive, I tend to avoid it. A couple of recipes in this book call for balsamic vinegar because the sweetness works well in the dish. For these, feel free to use whatever you found in the store. I save my fancy, chi-chi balsamics for pouring directly over berries or panna cottas.

LEMONS + LIMES + ORANGES

Citrus is regularly available at even the smallest store. If you don't have access to fresh citrus, substitute 2 Tbsp (30 ml) white wine vinegar for each lemon. It won't be the same, but it is way, way better than using the presqueezed, metallic-tasting citrus juices.

If you can get your hands on organic citrus, buy that. Conventional citrus holds pesticides and herbicides in its skin even after washing.

To zest, I use either a Microplane grater (for fine pieces) or a vegetable peeler (for large strips) depending on how the zest will be used.

WINE + HARD CIDER

Vinegars are a sour version of these drinks. The milder versions add a gentle level of acidity to the base of a recipe. You won't taste it and think, *Oh, white wine!* but it will make the finished dish taste brighter and lighter than if you'd skipped it.

The "cooking wines" at the grocery store are mediocre and won't add nearly the level of complexity that a cheap drinking wine will add. I tend to buy boxed wine and keep it in the kitchen. I want it to be inexpensive but of decent enough quality that if someone dropped in and I had nothing to offer them, I could offer a glass of the wine I cook with and not be too embarrassed.

FERMENTED THINGS

There has been a huge rise in small-batch, artisan-fermented products in the market the past few years—which is great! Long gone are the days of poorly made sauerkraut that smells like dirty sponges.

Fermented products (be they cabbage, carrot, pickles, beets, and the like) should taste tangy and bright and not at all astringent. The acidity comes from the creation of lactic acid as bacteria ferment the sugar in the vegetable.

I add sauerkraut or fermented carrots or pickles to rich dishes for bright pops of acidity. Kimchi or curtido (a Latin American fermented cabbage relish) can be used anywhere you would use sauerkraut, but remember that they're spicier.

CAPERS

Capers are the bud of the caper plant, harvested before they flower, then pickled or salted to preserve them. They lend foods a briny, salty, herby flavor.

I keep a jar of the brined ones on hand; I find them easier to use than the salt-packed ones that are more floral in flavor but must be rinsed of excess salt before use. I don't use capers often, but have found myself roughly chopping and adding them to a dish that I can't make taste just right.

PICKLES

Pickles—vegetables preserved with salt and acidity (usually in the form of vinegar or through fermentation)—are a great way to inject brightness into a dish. Add a splash of pickle liquid or a roughly chopped handful of pickles into a dish. All of a sudden what you're making feels new and interesting. Pickles keep for a long time on the shelf, so there's no reason to not have a jar on hand in case you find yourself without a lemon or good vinegar.

To pickle your own vegetables requires a whole 'nother book, but for pretty decent results you can always bring 1 cup (240 ml) vinegar (except balsamic), 1 cup (240 ml) water, 1 Tbsp (21 g) sugar, and 2 tsp (12 g) salt to a boil, then pour it over 1 qt (1 L) of vegetables.

I'm also a big fan of boiling the pickle liquid left in the jar after all the pickles are gone and of pouring it over fresh vegetables. You will have some weird flavors, but it is a great way to get a quick pickle, avoid wasting any of that liquid, and not have to measure anything.

spices and seasonings

To be honest, I have always been a little scared of spices. Always afraid I would add a skosh too much and everything would be ruined. Instead I've relied on herbs, which add a less dangerous punch of flavor (see page 37 for their fanfare). But hey, caution to the wind, there are myriad spices out in the world; these are the ones I use the most. Once you get a handle on the flavors you like, you can add spices with more abandon, but start slowly so as not to overpower.

Blooming spices is critical to unlocking their full scent and flavor profiles evenly. There are two methods: One, heat them in a dry frying pan over medium-high heat until they smell fragrant, then add them to whatever you are cooking. Two, heat a **glug** of oil until just about smoking hot, remove from the heat, then add the spices. I often burn spices when toasting in a dry pan because

I never let myself stand there and watch them, so I tend to use the second method.

SALT (KOSHER, CRUNCHY)

The type of salt that you use will dramatically affect your finished dish. All of these recipes were tested with Morton kosher salt. I like kosher because it is coarser than iodized and contains fewer additives (including the iodine, which can taste metallic). I like Morton because it is easier to find than other brands.

Morton salt tastes "saltier" to me than other salts, so if you are using another brand or a fine sea salt, know that you will probably need to add more salt. I often double the amount of salt if using something other than Morton. Add it at the end, a pinch at a time, until it tastes good to you.

I also keep a large-crystal sea salt on hand to finish dishes—I like Maldon or the salt from JQ Dickinson Salt-Works of West Virginia. These can take some work to source, but even small grocery stores are starting to carry coarse sea salt. Buy a few and give them a try to see if you like them. If you don't, you can always use the salt to season pasta water or soups, or to de-ice the driveway (JK: don't do that).

BLACK PEPPER

Always grind your pepper freshly. Just as fresh-ground coffee beans make the best cup, this is the single best thing you can do to have flavorful pepper. Freshly ground Tellicherry black pepper tastes a world apart from the tins of dry, preground pepper dust of my childhood.

I have had trouble finding a great pepper mill that won't break with a few weeks' worth of heavy use. My family finally found that Turkish coffee grinders work very well and last longer than any other mill I've found. Plus, they are generally copper or brass and beautiful to look at even when not in use. Luckily whole peppercorns (and their mills) are more and more ubiquitous. I've seen little plastic pepper grinders in grocery stores (and even gas stations); these are a good option if you don't want to invest in a permanent mill.

CHILI FLAKES AKA CRUSHED RED PEPPER

I love all sorts of hot peppers, but it can be difficult to find the more esoteric peppers. If you can find chile de árbol, Aleppo, Urfa, or bird of paradise pepper, by all means use them. All of the recipes here were developed with chili flakes like the ones on the tables in pizza joints (in jars with the lid left unscrewed as a prank).

Chili flakes are the spice with the greatest variation in spiciness from one jar to the next. The fresher the flake, the spicier it tends to be. If the chili flakes are soft and moist, they are probably fresher and spicier. If you find your jar is particularly spicy or mild, write that on the label to remind you the next time you use them.

CUMIN

Cumin seeds lend an unmistakable earthy depth of flavor to many a dish. Buy whole seeds for recipes that call for them; they are small enough to tenderize in cooking.

CURRY POWDER

Curry powders vary widely from brand to brand and blend to blend. Some are sweeter than others, some spicier.

I find I use curry powder more if I buy a blend I like rather than trying to make my own. In general, I look for one that is yellowish-orange and contains some form of hot pepper. If you want to make your own, I'm sure it will be delicious—and if that makes you want to use it more, all the better.

PAPRIKA

Paprika is a fine powder of dried pimenton peppers. There are many types: smoked, sweet, and hot. The sweet is really just the same peppers, unsmoked. The hot is spicy but not as hot as cayenne. I tend to use smoked paprika; try either and use whichever you prefer.

herbs

When people ask me, "What is the secret to being a good cook?" I always say: salt, acid, and herbs. All three add an intensity of flavor, elevating an average dish to sublime. Most of the recipes in this book call for a fresh herb of some sort. They are not a must, but their flavors and their fragrance improve the dish immensely. If you have any sort of growing space, including window sills, plant some herbs. They are generally easy to grow and are cheaper options than store-bought. Here are my go-tos:

PARSLEY

One component of the classic French *fines herbes* blend; the others are chervil, chives, and tarragon. I buy flat-leaf because I prefer the texture. If you have access to only curly, use that, but always chop it. I don't generally grow this herb because I use so much that my plants can never grow enough. I instead use the space for herbs I use in smaller quantities.

CILANTRO

You can chop the tender stems along with the leaves—this means you are throwing away less of what you have purchased. Note: some 5 to 20 percent of humans have genetic taste receptors that make cilantro taste anywhere from unpleasant to revolting. When entertaining guests, it's good to check with them. If you're preparing a dish that calls for fresh cilantro, offer it on the side so they can eat the dish without it, and those who love cilantro can absorb the extra.

TARRAGON

Another component of the French fines herbes blend, its leaves are tender and lend a slight anise flavor to dishes. It pairs especially well with eggs, fish, and chicken. Tarragon is perennial even in the northernmost climates, making it a good option for an outside garden.

CHIVES

Yet another French *fines herbes* component, chives add a mild onion acidity to dishes. They are perennial in most growing zones and can easily take over. I keep them in pots to prevent too much spreading. The purple flowers are also tasty and can be added to any dish you would add chives to.

BASIL

One of the most commonly grown herbs, it's a summer pleasure that won't survive the first frost of fall. Consider planting lemon or Thai basil for slightly different flavor profiles. When you are harvesting, cut the center stem, just above the two little sucker leaves, to encourage the plant to branch out and grow bushier. When you find yourself with too much basil toward the end of summer, harvest as much as possible and blend it into oil with salt for winter use.

MINT

Mint is known to spread and take over anywhere it is planted. You can control it in planters or plant it in a place where you don't mind its going berserk. Mint is normally associated with sweet flavors and berries; I find it pairs well with anything spicy and feels like a new twist when used in place of basil with things like tomatoes and carrots.

OREGANO

Oregano or marjoram are stronger, late summer flavors. They taste herby and green and can easily take over a dish, so use them sparingly when you want something not as bright as basil or as wintery as sage. A perennial in cold environments, oregano does well in a garden, though it will spread like mint. Use the delicate purple flowers in salads or to garnish dishes. I also love grilling oregano stems and adding the charred leaves to late summer dishes or to lightly smoke fish on the grill.

SAGE

The herb of Thanksgiving can be used any time throughout the year, though it pairs best with the hearty flavors of fall. Like oregano, it is perennial in northern gardens and does well indoors. In the spring the plant will flower with delicious little edible purple or yellow flowers. Beyond turkey day stuffing, the leaves fry well in butter and lend a mild herbal quality to the oil and a delicate crispness to a dish when the leaves are crunched over the top.

ROSEMARY

I can't keep a rosemary plant alive to save my life, so I use less rosemary than other herbs, but it has its place and pairs well with other flavors of the Mediterranean—lemon, tomatoes, olives, capers, and the like. I also love it with honey. Use it sparingly or the dish can become medicinal. Consider trying to bring it inside for winter—some people manage this, though it's never worked for me.

THYME

The more ubiquitous woody herb, thyme is, unlike rosemary, a perennial, with a less intense aroma. I really like lemon thyme as a resource for adding a citrus note to recipes.

BAY

Most dried bay leaves don't taste of much and so I generally leaf (ha ha) them out. If you happen to grow your own bay plant or know someone who does, that is a horse of a different color. The leaves (fresh or recently dried) lend a delicate floral flavor to all things. If I have them I will use them in a way that shows off their flavor (like adding three leaves to a pot of rice). If I don't, I don't sweat it.

EDIBLE FLOWERS

Most edible flowers are aesthetically pleasing alone, and I like using them in salads and to garnish something and make it pretty. The only flowers that add a lot of flavor are tangerine marigolds—which, honest to goodness, taste of tangerine— and nasturtiums, which are peppery. Use them with abandon, but don't break your neck or bank to get your hands on them.

WEIRD HERBS

I love all herbs, and one of my favorite garnishes is a picked herb salad made of twenty-plus different ones adding a million different flavors to each bite. Short of growing them yourself, it is hard to find these herbs, so thank the farmer who is crazy enough to grow them, or make yourself a garden of little pots and many herbs some spring. I love lemon balm, sweet geranium, lemon verbena, borage, chervil, anise hyssop, lavender, pineapple weed (wild chamomile), and on and on.

grains

Grains are the easiest way to make a side dish a full meal. Several are good sources of protein and fiber. Grains also store very well after they have been cooked, about a week covered in the fridge. One of the biggest differences between restaurant and home cooks is that restaurant cooks make more than one serving at a time. It takes about as much time to make 4 cups (800 g) of rice as it does to make 1 cup (200 g). Try making more than you need, cooling it, storing it, and then using it for a fast meal later in the week. They will be the cooked arrows in your quiver.

LENTILS

Lentils are legumes, like beans, and a good source of protein. Unlike beans, they cook quickly and don't need to be soaked in advance.

There are four broad categories of lentils: red, green, brown, and black. I rely on green and black in this book because they hold their shape the best, but brown is more readily available and can be substituted in any of the recipes. The red ones are the softest and break down during cooking, making them great for soup or spooned over rice, but not great for the recipes in this book.

COOKED LENTILS	Base recipe yields 1 cup (200 g) cooked lentils. Heat a <u>glug</u> of neutral oil in a saucepan. When hot, add ¾ cup (150 g) lentils with ½ tsp (3 g) salt and <u>toss</u> to toast briefly. Add 1½ cups (360 ml) water or stock, bring to a boil, reduce the heat so the liquid simmers, and cook until the lentils are tender but not mushy, about 25 minutes. The liquid will mostly evaporate. If you taste and the lentils aren't tender, add more water, ½ cup (120 ml) at a time. If they are tender and there is still liquid, drain away the excess and save for a soup or something like that.

RICE

Rice is a good way to bulk up a vegetable salad, making it more of a meal than a side. Beyond the traditional warm rice side dish, I like cooling rice and using it in a salad the same way cold pasta is used in pasta salads.

LONG-GRAIN RICE

Rice absorbs other flavors well. Once cooked, consider dressing it with a good **glug** of olive oil, vinaigrette, or herb oil to make it more flavorful when cool. Please note that brown rice will take significantly longer to cook than white, as the heat has to soften the fibrous bran. In general, the thicker the grain, the longer rice will take to cook.

I've stopped cooking rice with a specific proportion of water to grain. Instead, I heat as much water as I would for pasta, cook until tender, and then drain the water away. As with pasta, heat enough water to maintain a heat mass after the grain is added. This ensures that the water comes to a boil again quickly and that the grains will cook evenly. Cooking rice this way minimizes variables: no measuring, no rinsing, no burning.

COOKED RICE	Base recipe yields 1 cup (180 g) cooked rice. Bring a large pot of heavily salted water to a boil. The water should taste salty like the sea—roughly ½ tsp of salt per 1 qt (960 ml) of water. Add ½ cup (100 g) of rice, return to a boil, reduce the heat so the liquid simmers, and cook until tender, about 12 minutes. Drain the water away, fluff with a fork, and serve.

RISOTTO RICE

More and more grocery stores are stocking Arborio rice; if you can't find it locally, it can be ordered online. Risotto rice has a shorter grain and different starch structure from traditional long-grain rice. To achieve a creamy texture (without adding cream or cheese), risotto must be stirred nonstop, and the hot cooking liquid must be added a ladleful at a time so it helps draw the starch out of the grain. The agitation from the stirring releases the starch from the grain's center. The cooking liquid should be hotter than the rice to avoid dropping the temperature of the rice when it is added (making it cook more slowly and get mushy). If the grains drown in liquid, there isn't a smooth transfer of the starch from grain to surrounding liquid. This sounds complicated, but it isn't in practice; just try it a couple of times.

From start to finish, risotto takes about 20 minutes, so it is my go-to I-need-to-make-dinner-as-fast-as-possible solution. Serve it with a salad or fold a **bunch** of hearty greens into the hot risotto, and you're done. I generally make more risotto than needed because it fries up well as a crispy rice cake or the Italian *arancini* (stuffed rice balls). Feel free to add any other aromatics to the base: bacon, sausage, garlic, chili flakes, celery, thyme, etc.

Risotto can be made in advance and then finished just before dinner. Cook the rice to 80 percent doneness and then chill. To finish cooking, simply rewarm, adding more warm liquid until the rice is tender and creamy.

COOKED RISOTTO	2 qt (2 L) water or stock	1 onion, _sliced thinly_	2 cups (200 g) risotto rice
	½ cup (120 ml) olive oil	1 tsp (6 g) salt	½ cup (120 ml) white wine

Base recipe yields 4 servings. Bring the cooking liquid to a boil in a soup pot. In a large frying pan, heat the oil, add the onion and salt, and sweat the onion until tender, about 7 minutes. Add the rice and briefly toast. Add the wine and begin stirring. When the wine has evaporated, add a ladleful of hot cooking liquid and continue stirring until all the liquid is absorbed. Add another ladleful. Continue stirring and adding more water after each absorption until the rice is tender and creamy (about 20 minutes).

WILD RICE

Wild rice is not a grain, but a grass seed, a traditional Native American food from Minnesota—grown in wet bogs, harvested by hand by farmers floating in canoes, then dried in reed baskets over a fire, giving it notes of smoke and tea. It is dark in color, rich in texture, and deeply flavored.

It will cook without being soaked but can be soaked overnight to speed cooking time. Wild rice holds its texture after being cooked. I generally cook more than needed; the extra can make a fast salad the next day or be crisped and served with scrambled eggs for breakfast. On a sweeter note, wild rice makes a tremendous rice pudding for breakfast or dessert.

COOKED WILD RICE	Base recipe yields 1 cup (165 g) cooked rice. Either boil like pasta and drain when tender, or sweat 1 sliced onion, 3 garlic cloves, and ½ tsp (3 g) salt in a glug of oil. Add ½ cup (90 g) wild rice and ½ cup (120 ml) white wine and toast briefly. Add 2 cups (480 ml) water, bring to a boil, reduce to a simmer, and cook until the rice is tender, 30 to 45 minutes, depending on whether it was soaked. Drain off any excess water as needed.

WHEAT BERRIES

Wheat berries are the whole-grain seed of the wheat plant, similar in size to green lentils, with a slightly nutty flavor and chewy texture. They are ground to make flour or left whole to be used as a cooked grain. Wheat berries are getting easier to find, especially in the bulk section of grocery stores. Substitute barley or farro if you can't find wheat berries.

COOKED WHEAT BERRIES	Base recipe yields 1 cup (180 g) cooked wheat berries. In a saucepan, heat a glug of oil, add ½ cup (90 g) wheat berries and ½ tsp (3 g) salt, and briefly toast. Add 2 cups (480 ml) water and bring to a boil, reduce to a simmer, and cook until the grains are tender, about 30 minutes. Drain any excess water and serve.

beans

More and more heirloom beans are being grown by local farmers, and you can find a rainbow of offerings at many farmers' markets. Each bean has a different texture and cooking time. Ask your farmer or vendor about a particular bean's characteristics if you're not familiar with it. Record any of those notes and store with the beans for a reminder when you do end up cooking them.

I keep both dried and canned beans on hand. I generally soak beans overnight for more even and faster cooking. You can cook dried beans without soaking; it will just take longer.

There are a lot of myths around cooking beans. I find the length of cooking time and texture of the cooked bean depend on the bean's variety and age—the older the bean, the longer it will take to cook and the tougher the skin. If you have particularly old beans, add a ¼ tsp (2 g) of baking soda to the soaking liquid to soften the skins.

I don't like the flavor of the liquid surrounding canned beans; I rinse the beans thoroughly before using.

COOKED BEANS	Base recipe for medium-size beans such as black, great northern, or cranberry yields 1 cup (160 g) cooked beans. Soak ½ cup (90 g) of beans overnight in water, heat a glug of oil in a saucepan, and add any aromatics (onion, garlic, thyme) or spices (chili flakes, cumin, coriander, paprika) to bloom. Add the drained beans and 2 cups (480 ml) water, bring to a boil, reduce to a simmer, and cook until tender, skimming away any foam that bubbles up. When fully tender, transfer from the heat and add ½ tsp (3 g) salt and 1 Tbsp (15 ml) vinegar. Let cool in the cooking liquid and refrigerate overnight, giving them time to soak up the salt and vinegar.

CHICKPEAS

Like beans and lentils, chickpeas are legumes and a good source of protein. I tend to buy canned chickpeas, as dried chickpeas take about 2 hours to cook to tender creaminess, and they produce a lot of foamy scum, requiring more watchful cooking and skimming of said foam. If buying dried, cook with the same method as for dried beans (facing page). If using canned, rinse well before using.

Crispy chickpeas add a lot of texture to vegetable salads and are nice to have on the counter for a snack.

CRISPY CHICKPEAS	Heat the oven to 350°F to 425°F (180°C to 220°C)—the hotter the oven, the faster they'll cook. Drain a can of chickpeas and rinse well.
	Dress the chickpeas with ½ cup (120 ml) olive oil, ½ tsp (3 g) salt, and ½ tsp (2 g) chili flakes (optional).
	Spread on a foil-lined baking sheet in a single layer and bake until crispy and deep golden brown, about 20 minutes. Remove from the oven and let cool, keeping in a single layer or they will steam and soften. Keep at room temperature until ready to use. If they get soft, recrisp in the oven (a few minutes).

---

pasta

I keep three types of pasta on hand at all times: long (spaghetti or linguine), short (penne, fusilli, or orecchiette), and pearl (also known as Turkish couscous).

I like long pasta with sauces, short pasta with chunky ingredients, and pearl pasta for pasta salad or any dish in which you want little pops of texture.

| **COOKED PASTA** | Bring a large pot of salted water to a boil. Use more water than you think is necessary; the higher the volume of water, the faster it will return to a boil (because the temperature will rebound after having the cold pasta added), and the faster it will cook, improving the texture. The water should be salty like the sea (1 tsp to 1 qt [1 L] of water) because it makes the pasta taste more like its primary ingredient—wheat.

Add the pasta, stir, and return to a boil, then reduce to a simmer and cook until just tender, testing regularly after the first 7 minutes of cooking. Drain. |
|---|---|

COUSCOUS

Couscous is a tiny pasta with the texture of quinoa. There's no need to boil it like pasta; it is small enough to cook by simply pouring hot liquid over it. Bulgur (steamed, dried, and crushed wheat berries) is a good substitution but should be soaked for longer (an hour in some cases), until tender. It is a whole-grain option if you aren't eating pasta, though note that like all wheat products, bulgur contains gluten.

COOKED COUSCOUS	Base recipe yields 2 cups (280 g) cooked couscous. Bring 1½ cups (360 ml) water or stock to a boil, pour over 1 cup (135 g) couscous, cover, and let sit for 7 minutes, then uncover and fluff. When in doubt, follow the directions on the side of the box.

grits

Grits, polenta, and cornmeal are all ground corn of varying coarseness. Grits are the largest grind and my preferred version.

Feel free to substitute polenta for any grit recipe. I find cornmeal too fine for the dishes in this book. If you can only get cornmeal, bake cornbread instead and happily serve it with recipes that call for grits or polenta. Cornbread will be as good a vehicle for getting sauces into your mouth.

I never add dairy or cheese to grits until after they are cooked because I tend to burn it with annoying ease. Add any sort of dairy after the grits are cooked and it will slowly absorb, but be forewarned, if you use buttermilk be careful upon rewarming, as it will want to separate.

Grits can be made well in advance and then warmed or kept warm in a slow cooker.

COOKED GRITS	Base recipe yields 1 cup (245 g) grits. Bring 2 cups (480 ml) water with ½ tsp (3 g) salt to a boil. Whisk the water into a swirl, pour ½ cup (70 g) grits into the water, and whisk vigorously. Reduce the heat to very, very low and bring to a boil. At this point I turn off the heat and let the grits absorb the water at the back of the stove for at least 20 minutes but up to 3 hours. If you need it ready faster, keep cooking, whisking regularly to ensure it doesn't stick, burn, or spit.

bread

I try to always have a good quality loaf of bread on hand (preferably sourdough, preferably whole wheat). I don't always manage this, but when I do, I always have a meal in no time, either by piling a salad on top of a thick slice of toast, browning croutons, or making bread salad (panzanella) by <u>tossing</u> the bread with any number of vegetables and a good amount of dressing.

Bread freezes really well. Double wrap in plastic wrap and then place it in the freezer. If you will want only a slice or two, slice it before freezing.

Save all heels of bread or leftover pieces and either freeze to make a batch of stuffing or bread pudding or let dry out on a baking sheet and then grate to make bread crumbs.

Bread crumbs, especially garlic bread crumbs, add immediate texture and interest to a dish. If you ever taste something and think, *This is a little boring*, sprinkle a heaping spoonful of toasted or garlic bread crumbs over the dish and taste again.

GARLIC BREAD CRUMBS

¼ cup (60 ml) neutral oil

4 garlic cloves (28 g), minced

½ tsp (3 g) salt

1 cup (140 g) bread crumbs or panko

In a large frying pan, heat the oil until shimmering hot and add the garlic and salt. Remove from the heat so the garlic doesn't burn, and let sit for 10 minutes (or cook the garlic on low for 5 minutes, keeping a sharp eye out to prevent burning). Add the bread crumbs and stir to combine. Return to the heat and toast the oily bread crumbs until golden brown and fragrant, about 3 minutes. Remove from the heat and let cool. Store in an airtight container and sprinkle on any and all savory dishes.

I often use the oil left from garlic confit to make these. Simply replace the neutral oil with the garlic oil and skip the garlic cloves, unless you want a stronger garlic flavor.

CROUTONS

Croutons are like bread crumbs' bigger sister. To make them, I use two- to three-day-old bread so there is still some softness on the inside, cut into cubes.

Heat the oven to 350°F to 425°F (180°C to 220°C). Heat a glug of olive oil in a large frying pan over medium heat. When hot, add the bread cubes, season with a pinch of salt, and toast until golden brown, turning to brown evenly. Add about 2 Tbsp (30 g) butter and let it melt. Transfer to the oven and let the croutons bake until golden brown, 7 to 10 minutes. Remove from the oven and let cool.

dairy

CREAM

Internationally, cream has different amounts of fat. Assume that cream in the recipes here means heavy or whipping cream if in the United States and double cream in England and Europe.

BUTTER

I buy unsalted butter and keep an extra pound (455 g) in the freezer. There are more and more dairies making small-batch butters so delicious that I buy them to save for my morning toast. If you avoid butter altogether, you can substitute coconut oil in most recipes. Please don't use margarine—it doesn't taste the same, and your money is going to a food processor, not a farmer.

YOGURT

This cultured dairy product is available in most corner and grocery stores. Buy plain yogurt; the fruit flavors are packed with sugar and don't pair well with vegetables. I favor Greek yogurt because I like the texture, but all of the recipes can be made with regular plain yogurt.

You can also use yogurt in place of sour cream. If you miss the texture of sour cream, add 1 part cream to 4 parts yogurt for more richness.

If you have a lot of cream around and some buttermilk or sour cream, mix 4 parts cream with 1 part cultured buttermilk or sour cream, whisk, and let sit at room temperature for two days or until thick. The cultured bacteria will feed on the lactose sugar in the cream and make sour cream.

If a recipe calls for buttermilk but you have only yogurt, thin it with milk as a substitute.

SOFT CHEESE

These are hard to keep on hand because they will go bad more quickly than butter or hard cheese, but having one or two types makes it easy to add nice salty, creamy dollops to your food. For the most part you can use them interchangeably.

Feta is the hardest to replace because of its dry texture and salty finish. It will last the longest if kept in its brine.

Fromage blanc, quark, or ricotta are fresh farm cheeses, creamy and mild. Ricotta is the easiest to find and to make. If you find quark or fromage blanc, buy it and thank the producers for going through the paces, because there aren't many of them.

Fresh goat cheese (chèvre) is a good alternative for those who don't eat cow dairy. It is also becoming more available. I generally buy the plain version and add my own herbs if I want to, rather than buying the ones with an herb mixture already added.

Cottage cheese is readily available across the country, but in the Midwest it is a true staple. I prefer the large-curd version but will use any kind of cottage cheese available because few other dairy products can truly replace its unique texture.

HARD CHEESE

There are thousands of hard cheeses, and for the most part you can use one in place of any of the others. They will taste different, of course, and will change the dish, but all will add a dry salty texture. Again, in general the better the quality, the more expensive. I don't use the finest hard cheese in my cooked dishes—I save those for a cheese board or eating for lunch with some bread. When cooking with hard cheeses, I aim for the middle of the road. Please buy the cheeses from your area to support your local producers; a good cheesemonger will help you find a local version of an internationally recognized cheese. Please don't ever buy imitation cheeses, because you are buying mainly vegetable oils chemically treated to taste of cheese with the texture of velvet. That said, there is a growing list of vegan-friendly products that mimic the texture and flavor of cheese and are derived from plant-based foods like nuts or legumes if you aren't eating dairy at all.

cheddar

Cheddar is a traditionally English cheese that also has deep roots in Midwestern cheese culture, especially in Wisconsin. I look for one about a year old—one that I wouldn't mind eating on its own. The older the cheese, the less moisture in the paste and therefore the less likely to melt smoothly. Save the three-, five-, and seven-year Cheddars for your holiday party.

parmesan

The Italians know what they are doing. You can tell the real deal by the "Parmigiano-Reggiano" spelled out in pin pricks on the rind—Italian law requires this. There are many domestic versions of the original, which can be very good, again especially those from Wisconsin. Please decline any pre-grated "Parmesan" that has vegetable oil on the ingredient list. To be sure you get actual cheese, buy it as a piece; then you can choose whether to grate it, make <u>ribbons</u> with a vegetable peeler, or <u>**chunk**</u> it into pieces for a heartier texture. Save the rind; you can add it to soups and stews to use every bit of what you paid for.

raclette

A traditionally made Alpine-style cheese prized for its even texture when melted and nutty flavor. I started replacing most hard cheeses in my fridge with the raclette from Leelanau Cheese in Suttons Bay, Michigan. Anne and John Hoyt make incredible cheeses—raclette, fromage blanc, and ricotta. If you are able to get some, buy as much as you can. Short of that, replace raclette with something like Gruyère or Emmental.

dried fruit

I love using fresh fruit when it is available but rely on dried year-round. Dried fruit offers a pleasant chewy texture and a sweet-tart flavor. Avoid buying dried fruit that has been preserved with additional sugar. I tend to lightly pickle dried fruit to bump up the acidity level, balancing the sweetness, and making it more suitable for savory applications. Feel free to substitute a fresh version of any dried fruit in the recipes—except cranberries, which are not pleasant to eat raw.

nuts and seeds

I love having nuts on hand to add texture and richness to any dish. If you can't find the nuts you're after in the baking aisle, try the snack aisle. Many are also available in the bulk section, but give them a sniff to be sure that they smell enticing. It is harder to rotate products in a bulk section, so they can sometimes be stale. Most nuts are available raw or untoasted. As with **blooming** spices, **toasting nuts** is critical to activate the oils in the pulp and release the flavor volatiles. To toast, give them a quick bake in an oven (any heat from 325°F to 400°F [165°C to 200°C]) or over a burner in a frying pan. The former will yield an even toasting but it takes a bit longer; the latter produces uneven toasting but is far quicker. Cook until you can smell them, then let them cool. Nuts do go rancid, so I tend to buy in any sort of quantity only the ones I use the most. You can stave off the rancidity by storing in the refrigerator or freezer, but if you do you'll need to toast them to refresh the flavor. If you find them grown locally they will be a world apart from store-bought in flavor and will be priced accordingly. Nuts of any variety can be expensive, so I also tend to use seeds in their stead to provide crunchy, salty texture.

WALNUTS
Easy to find; just be aware that the walnuts generally found in supermarkets are English walnuts. Black walnuts are different from English walnuts; they have a much more perfumey and polarizing flavor.

PECANS
Also easily found, often grown in the South; probably my favorite nut.

HAZELNUTS (FILBERTS)
The nuttiest of the nuts. I love the slightly bitter flavor of the skins so I often leave them on. I have had a hard time finding them in my smaller town grocery store. Sadly, Nutella is not an even substitute.

ALMONDS

Those sold in the snack aisle will probably be salted but are a great option. I also like the harder-to-find Marcona almonds from Spain. Any recipe in this book can be made with either and taste perfect.

PISTACHIOS

Pistachios are the creamiest of the nuts and lend a touch of sweetness to any dish. They are my go-to replacement for any nut I'm out of—they're different, but equally good. If you can't find them, try cashews.

SUNFLOWER SEEDS

These are technically the kernels of the seed, within the black-and-white shell. More sunflowers are being grown to produce non-monoculture crop cooking oils. That also means that the seeds are more available. I love these because they are texturally delightful and cheaper than most nuts. Grind them in a food processor until coarse to replace bread crumbs or add texture to anything at all.

PUMPKIN SEEDS

These are available especially in Central and South American groceries, where they will be labeled pepitas. They are creamy, with a texture similar to cashews, and a great, economical option. I am most apt to replace almonds and pistachios with pumpkin seeds.

preserved and tinned fish

SMOKED WHITEFISH AND LAKE TROUT

Smoked fish are a huge part of the food culture in the northern Midwest. These fish are the hot smoked version, not the traditional cold smoked salmon of lox-and-bagels fame. The heat applied during smoking cooks the flesh, which shortens the protein molecules in the meat, making it easier to flake into dishes.

Although smoking does preserve the fish somewhat, it isn't made shelf-stable like canned or frozen fish. Small grocery stores often have smoked fish in their freezers, so check there, too.

Sadly, there are fewer and fewer fish-smokers out there. If you can't find it, use canned tuna in its place. It won't have the smoky flavor but will have the texture and protein content.

If you want the smoky flavor in a recipe, consider using a smoked cheese in place of the fish. It will be different but still tasty.

TUNA

Thankfully, canned tuna is widely available and a great protein source.

I buy tuna packed in oil, not water, because it tastes better. The water dilutes the flavor of the meat; the oil improves it. Plus, you can use the oil in dressings and vinaigrettes, making use of more of the product. If you can't find oil-packed, buy the water-packed, but ask your grocer to see if they can order oil-packed for you.

As is true of so many things, the better the quality, the more expensive the product. If you have access to an American-caught-and-packed tuna or line-caught tuna, it will be more expensive but worth it, if you have the funds.

ANCHOVY

Anchovies often get a bad rap for being the stinky, super fishy add-ons to Caesar salad and pizza in dingy supper clubs. They are a strong flavor—salty and packed with omega-3 fatty acids—but they are far from stinky. Better and better anchovies are available in even the smallest of grocery stores. I tend to buy oil-packed because they can be used straight from the jar. If you buy salt-packed be sure to give them a thorough rinse to remove the excess salt. I also buy the average dark anchovies for their rich brininess, saving the pristine (and expensive) white anchovies for eating on their own with crusty bread.

condiments

Having these on hand will speed your prep time for meals immeasurably. My husband Erik and I have made many a meal around a big platter of vegetables, a couple of these sauces, and some bread. We have made even more by boiling pasta and **tossing** it with chili oil, ricotta cheese, and garlic bread crumbs (page 48). It used to feel like cheating; now it feels like good planning.

CHILI OIL

2 cups (480 ml) neutral oil

¼ cup (20 g) chili flakes

1 tsp (6 g) salt

You can make this more complicated by adding other spices, like star anise, citrus peel, and other peppers, but I find the most basic form works well for me and is so easy to make that I will whip it up at the last minute. It also lasts for ages so there is no reason to not make a double or triple batch.

Heat ½ cup (120 ml) of the oil until it shimmers. Remove from the heat and add the chili flakes and salt. Let sit until fragrant, about 3 minutes, then add the rest of the oil to cool it and keep the pepper flakes from burning. Let cool and store in a jar on the counter. It will get more nuanced as it ages.

HERB OILS

I make a lot of herb oil with the abundant herbs of summer. I used to make pesto but found that too often I had plenty of basil but no garlic, Parmesan, or pine nuts on hand, so a lot of herbs went to waste. Plus, you can always add the garlic and cheese later. These herb oils last best in the freezer but will keep for weeks in an airtight container in the refrigerator—consider freezing them in smaller containers and pulling one out as you need it. These oils are easiest made with a powerful burr blender, though a regular blender will work well, too. The heat from a regular blender motor will sometimes make the herbs taste bitter immediately after blending. This will dissipate as it cools. If you have a ton of herbs, blend them in batches, making a paste with the salt and oil and then adding more herbs and oil as you go.

PARSLEY OIL

1 bunch parsley (2.4 oz | 1½ cups | 68 g), yellow leaves removed but stems included

1 tsp (6 g) salt

2 cups (480 ml) neutral oil

This is a good way to add an herby flavor when you don't have any fresh parsley in the house. It is also the most forgiving oil to make and a good place to start experimenting.

Roughly chop the parsley. Put the herbs in a blender with the salt and half the oil. Blend until fairly smooth, then add the rest of the oil and blend.

BASIL AND/OR MINT OIL

Use the same proportions as the parsley oil but know that basil will sometimes go black if gets too hot in blending (often the case with a lower-powered blender). If you've had trouble with this *before* you start blending give the basil a 3-second dip in boiling water. This quick blanch will help preserve the color. Sadly, there is no way to regreen blackened basil. I generally use blackened basil in something where it won't show, like ravioli filling or in stuffed tomatoes.

OREGANO OR THYME OIL

For woody herbs like oregano, rosemary, thyme, or sage, blending yields a medicinal flavor. Instead, I leave the sprigs whole and <u>confit</u> them in oil in the oven and then lift the sprigs out after their flavor has been imparted into the oil. I make this oil when I have a huge amount of these herbs and want to preserve them. You can make it with just a few sprigs to hundreds. The oil will be more intense with a higher proportion of herbs to oil. Use the smallest baking dish that will hold your herbs, and add just enough oil to cover the sprigs.

Heat the oven to 200°F (95°C). Arrange the sprigs loosely in a baking dish with tall sides and cover with neutral oil. Bake until fragrant, about 1 hour. Remove from the oven and let cool. When cool, remove the sprigs from the oil and discard them.

SALSA VERDE

1 small red onion (¼ lb | 115 g), finely <u>diced</u> (about ½ cup)

3 garlic cloves (0.6 oz | 20 g), minced

¼ cup (60 ml) freshly squeezed lemon juice or white wine vinegar

1 tsp (6 g) salt

10 grinds of black pepper

2 cups (480 ml) olive oil

Unlike the herb oils, this is a fresh and chunky mixture that is best used within a few days of making. It takes a bit more work but is bright and herby and makes any pile of vegetables or rice feel restaurant fancy. Use as many herbs in any amounts as you have on hand, but avoid the woody herbs like thyme and rosemary unless in very small amounts.

Combine the onion, garlic, lemon juice, salt, and pepper and let sit 10 minutes. Roughly chop the herbs, then add the herbs and oil to the onion mixture and stir to combine. Store in an airtight container in the refrigerator.

VINAIGRETTE

Traditionally vinaigrettes are 1 part acid to 3 parts fat (read: 1 Tbsp | 15 ml vinegar to 3 Tbsp | 45 ml olive oil). To make a punchier salad, I prefer 1:2 (read: 1 Tbsp | 15 ml vinegar to 2 Tbsp | 30 ml olive oil) or even 1:1 in some cases of richer foods. You can add anything you like to vinaigrettes, like onion, garlic, or mustard.

BASIC VINAIGRETTE	1 lemon (1½ fl oz | 45 ml), zest and juice, or ¼ cup (960 ml) vinegar (apple cider, sherry, red wine, etc.)	½ cup (120 ml) olive oil	½ tsp (3 g) salt
	Whisk or shake to combine.		

MUSTARD VINAIGRETTE	2 Tbsp (30 g) whole-grain or Dijon mustard	1 small onion or shallot, minced	½ tsp (3 g) salt
	¼ cup (60 ml) apple cider vinegar	½ cup (120 ml) olive oil	
	Whisk or shake to combine.		

PICKLE LIQUID DRESSING ½ cup (120 ml) pickle liquid—any type except something particularly sweet ½ cup (120 g) mayo ½ tsp (3 g) black pepper Pinch of salt	My friend Laura Piskor first introduced me to this dressing, and I use it all the time. It is lightning-fast to make and tastes like more than the sum of its parts. It will also keep in the refrigerator for ages, so feel free to mix up a larger batch to have at the ready. You can also use the liquid from sauerkraut and kimchi with good results. Whisk all the ingredients together and serve.

BROWN BUTTER VINAIGRETTE

4 Tbsp (60 g) butter

1 lemon (1½ fl oz | 45 ml), zest and juice

1 orange (3 fl oz | 90 ml), zest and juice

1 Tbsp (15 ml) white wine or sherry vinegar

Salt

¼ cup (60 ml) olive oil

This dressing needs to be served warm or on warm or hot food, because when it gets cold the butter congeals and has an unpleasant mouthfeel. Adding olive oil helps mitigate this, but not entirely.

To brown the butter, place it in a stainless steel sauté or saucepan over medium-low heat until it foams; the foam will eventually sink to the bottom and brown. Hold your nerve and let it get toasty and brown. It will smell amazing.

Brown the butter and let cool to not screaming hot. Combine the citrus zest and juice, vinegar, and salt to taste. Whisk in the brown butter, scraping the bottom of the pan to get the brown bits, and the olive oil.

WARM BACON VINAIGRETTE

½ lb (230 g) bacon

1 small onion or shallot (about 2 oz | 55 g), thinly diced or sliced

¼ cup (60 ml) apple cider vinegar

Salt

2 Tbsp (30 ml) olive oil

Like the brown butter vinaigrette, this dressing needs to be either warm or served with warm or room-temp food; on cold food it will congeal. This makes a bit more than you need for an average dish, but it will hold in the refrigerator for a good while; gently warm it to liquefy before serving.

Cut the bacon into ¼-inch (6-mm) pieces and render in a frying pan until crispy. Combine the onion, vinegar, and salt to taste.

Whisk the bacon, bits and fat and all, into the onion mixture.

Add the olive oil and taste; add more vinegar as desired.

ANCHOVY VINAIGRETTE

2 garlic cloves (0.4 oz | 14 g), minced

1 small onion or shallot (2 oz | 55 g), minced

4 anchovy fillets (1.4 oz | 40 g each), roughly chopped

2 Tbsp (30 ml) any sort of vinegar except balsamic

¼ cup (60 ml) olive oil

¼ tsp (2 g) salt

Like the bacon vinaigrette, this dressing has a deep, meaty flavor because of the protein and salt in the anchovies. It will be chunky but can also be blended if you prefer it smooth and emulsified.

Whisk all the ingredients together.

BAGNA CAUDA

1 cup (8 fl oz | 240 ml) olive oil

10 anchovies (1.4 oz | 40 g)—skip the fancy white ones and go for your average grocery store anchovies packed in oil

6 garlic cloves (1.2 oz | 34 g), minced

2 tsp (12 g) salt

1 lemon (optional)

1 sprig rosemary (optional)

8 oz (230 g) unsalted butter

Bagna cauda translates to "warm bath" in Italian, and it is quite possibly one of my favorite foods because it is rich, salty, garlicky, and buttery and makes a party of eating a plate of raw vegetables in the middle of winter. The difference between anchovy vinaigrette and bagna cauda is that the bagna cauda is warm and must be kept warm or the butter will congeal and not be pleasant. The bagna cauda is also richer because of the proportion of butter, so I tend to serve it in the cooler months and rely on the vinaigrette in the warmer ones and when serving on a cold salad. The rosemary and lemon peel are optional but add significantly to the flavor complexity.

In a medium saucepan over medium-low heat, heat the olive oil. Add the anchovy fillets, garlic, and salt. Turn the heat to low and slowly let the anchovies melt and the garlic soften. With a vegetable peeler, cut 2 or 3 large strips of peel from the lemon (if using). Add the lemon peel strips and rosemary sprigs (if using) and fry until fragrant, about 3 minutes, then add the butter. When the butter has melted, remove from the heat, remove the lemon peel and rosemary, and whisk to blend. Serve warm in a dish alongside a large platter of vegetables or any other recipe where indicated in this book.

RANCH DRESSING

½ cup (120 g) sour cream

½ cup (120 g) mayo

½ cup (120 ml) buttermilk

3 garlic cloves (0.6 oz | 21 g), minced

10 sprigs chives, minced

½ bunch parsley (2.4 oz | 68 g), minced

4 sprigs tarragon, minced

2 Tbsp (30 ml) apple cider vinegar

½ tsp (3 g) salt

I love ranch so much. It is creamy and tangy and everything I want. With enough ranch, I could eat 10 pounds of lettuce in one sitting. I wish I had some right now. It calls for some ingredients that aren't always on hand, but this is worth the trip to the store.

Whisk everything together and serve.

BROWN SUGAR–VINEGAR SAUCE

½ cup (100 g) brown sugar

½ cup (120 ml) apple cider vinegar

½ tsp (3 g) salt

This truly feels like a secret sauce. It makes everything taste great. I like to keep it on hand to punch up another sauce (like tomato sauce for pasta or a glaze for roast chicken), roasted vegetables, or a purée. It keeps forever, so keep a little jar on hand and add its goodness, a spoonful at a time, to any dish that tastes a little flat. It also makes a very tasty drink: 2 Tbsp (30 ml) sauce with 8 fl oz (240 ml) sparkling water (and if you're into bourbon, 1 fl oz [30 ml] bourbon).

Whisk all the ingredients to blend.

MAYO

I love mayo, and making it at home produces a far tastier result than store-bought, but like all things in this book, if the hurdles of making it prevent you from cooking, use store-bought. I make mayo with whole egg because I find it more stable.

MAYO

1 whole egg	1 Tbsp (15 ml) white wine vinegar	10 fl oz (300 ml) neutral oil
½ tsp (3 g) salt		

In a food processor, whiz the egg, salt, and vinegar until well blended. Slowly drizzle in the oil until the mixture is thick. If it is too thin, add more oil.

Will keep in the refrigerator for up to one week.

FLAVORED MAYOS

Add the following to the base mayo recipe or to 1½ cups (120 g) store-bought mayo and blend.

Garlic Mayo: Add 3 garlic cloves (0.6 oz | 20 g) and use the juice and zest of 1 lemon (45 ml) in place of the vinegar.

Tuna Mayo: Add one 5-oz (150-g) can tuna in oil to the base recipe.

Smoked Whitefish Mayo: Add 4 oz (115 g) smoked whitefish picked from the bone.

Lemon-Caper Mayo: Add 2 Tbsp (18 g) capers, 2 garlic cloves (0.4 oz | 14 g), and the zest and juice of 1 lemon (45 ml) as acid.

COMPOUND BUTTERS

There is little more enduringly decadent than a dollop of salty, creamy butter slowly melting over a pile of warmed vegetables—except maybe that same butter punched up with bright or salty or herby hits of flavor. That is compound butter. You can make any version by creaming soft butter with your favorite flavors. Some of my favorites are lemon, parsley, Parmesan, caper, and anchovy.

LEMON PARMESAN BUTTER	4 oz (115 g) butter, softened	½ tsp (3 g) black pepper	¼ bunch parsley (¼ cup | 10 g), finely chopped
	½ tsp (3 g) salt	2 oz (55 g) Parmesan, grated	Zest of 1 lemon (1 Tbsp | 5 g)

Combine all the ingredients and blend well. Transfer to a dish or roll into a round in plastic wrap and chill.

ANCHOVY-CAPER BUTTER	4 oz (115 g) butter, softened	1 oz (30 g) capers, roughly chopped	Zest of 1 lemon (1 Tbsp | 5 g)
	½ tsp (3 g) salt	¼ bunch parsley (¼ cup | 10 g), finely chopped	4 anchovy fillets (1.4 oz | 40 g), roughly chopped (optional)
	½ tsp (3 g) freshly ground black pepper		

Combine all ingredients and blend well. Transfer to a dish or roll into a round in plastic wrap and chill.

NUT RELISHES

Scattering chopped nuts onto a dish instantly adds textural complexity, richness, and (usually) salt. These relishes provide extra dimensions of flavor by lending spice, bright herby notes, and/or acidity—making even the simplest platter of crisp greens or roasted root vegetables shine anew.

DUKKAH

½ cup (60 g) hazelnuts

½ cup (70 g) almonds

½ cup (70 g) pistachios

½ cup (70 g) sunflower seeds

1 tsp (3 g) cumin seed

1 tsp (3 g) coriander seed

1 Tbsp (7 g) smoked paprika

1 tsp (6 g) salt

This spice and nut mixture originated in Egypt and is now common throughout the Middle East. It adds a subtle spice, crunchy texture, and richness to any dish. The variety of nuts is less important than the volume, so if you can't find hazelnuts, add more almonds and pistachios.

Toast all the nuts (page 24) until fragrant and let cool. In a dry frying pan, combine the spices and toast over medium heat until fragrant, in a food processor or by hand chop the nuts until they are the texture of Grape-Nuts cereal. Add the spices and salt and blend. Store in an airtight container on the counter.

POUNDED WALNUT RELISH

1 cup walnuts (120 g)

2 lemons (1½ fl oz | 45 ml), zest and juice

¼ cup (60 ml) sherry or red wine vinegar

1 tsp (6 g) salt

1 <u>bunch</u> parsley (2.4 oz | 1½ cups | 68 g), roughly chopped

This relish came from wanting to pickle everything and wondering if you could pickle a nut. Turns out you can! Sort of. It doesn't help preserve the nuts the way that pickling a vegetable will keep it through the winter. But it does pull the acidity into the center of the creamy nut and make for a very interesting garnish that is tangy, creamy, herby, crunchy, and surprising.

Toast the walnuts (page 24) until fragrant, about 10 minutes. Combine the lemon juice and zest with the vinegar and salt in a medium bowl. Transfer the toasted walnuts to a zip locking bag and bash with the back of a frying pan until coarsely chopped. Immediately add the walnuts to the lemon-vinegar mixture and stir to combine. Just before serving, add the parsley, stir, taste, and adjust the seasoning as desired.

PART 2

vegetables

AND HOW I COOK THEM

Jim Harrison, northern Michigan's favorite son and food lover, once told me, "One of the main causes of premature death is fretting about your diet." He then topped up my glass of wine.

His words stuck with me. At the time, he was talking about calorie counting and being overly concerned with gluten, white foods, too much protein, too much sugar, the day in and day out bombardment of what we should be eating, and observing that the bulk of those "shoulds" are divorced from the land and our bodies. It was the fret that rang in my ears. I think about food (and by extension my diet) for more than eight hours every day—it is my work and my home life.

I fret about how food is produced in our country—conventional versus organic versus local. Does the lack of pesticides used on an organic strawberry offset the carbon footprint of its refrigerated transport to the Midwest? I don't know.

I agonize about food insecurity. Can I delight in a box of perfect fava beans that cost $6 and will barely make an appetizer when there is a family a few miles away wondering where their next meal is coming from? I try, but the worry is always there.

I think about the overplanting of corn and soy, because monocultures are often fallible and bad for the environment. I simultaneously worry that the farmers who grow them are being squeezed financially from all sides. Is there a way that they can keep farming but farm something more sustainable? Corn and soy are historically profitable. Who am I to dictate their business?

I buy the most humanely raised meat on the market, but I also eat at old-school mom-and-pop restaurants that do not. Does that make me a hypocrite? Should I care if you think I am?

It's enough to make my head spin. Here's what I do know: we all need to make the best food choices we can, given our circumstances. There are very few black-and-white choices—just a lot of gray.

I try to buy local food as often as possible. The food is fresher, and farmers selling directly are generally farming more sustainably and get a better price for their product. I also buy avocados, because I love them, despite not knowing who grew them.

I try to buy organic. The environmental benefits of organic farming are important to me. I also believe that organic production makes economic sense for farmers and therefore is a more viable career choice. I also shop at a small, independent grocery store where neither local or organic are reliably available because I fear what consolidation into a handful of big stores is doing to our distribution networks.

I also delight in McDonald's hotcakes and shamrock shakes full of monoculture, nonorganic corn, soy, dairy, and wheat. How does Ronald make them so soft and so green? My choices don't always true up.

I want food to be expensive, so farmers can make a good living. I also want everyone to have access to that food regardless of income. I volunteer with food pantries, and we donate surplus produce from our farm to them. Knowing all the while that, while that work is important, it is also a bandage on a symptom of a larger problem. I don't know how to solve hunger and pay inequity, so I help give handouts and hate the fact that, in the richest nation in the history of the planet, we don't value the lives of everyone enough to be sure that no one goes hungry.

These issues are heavy. If I'm not careful they will eclipse the undeniable fact that food is a pleasure to be delighted in. You'll have to make your own choices about the foods that you buy, but don't overthink it and miss the party. Those choices might not be the same each day; you can change your mind. Or, to quote Stephen Sondheim in his hit musical *Sunday in the Park with George*, "The choice may have been mistaken. The choosing was not. You have to move on." (Make the best choice you can but try not to fret about it.)

Jim Harrison passed away recently. He spent his life eating food with gusto as a sensory experience. With every death I remember there's no time to waste. Don't fret your life away, because it's too short as it is. Please pass the local, organic asparagus and the shamrock shakes.

asparagus

Yesterday, the first boxes of asparagus grown by Mick Klug and his daughter, Abby, arrived in the kitchen. Elation. I snatched a slender stalk from the box and shoved it into my mouth, sand and all.

This is my ritual. I love asparagus. I love that it tastes of sweet spring grasses. I like that the grittiness reminds me that asparagus grows best in sandy soil—ground often not always well suited to other crops. It always makes me think about the fact that we never planted it on our farm because it takes three years to put out a decent crop, and we never made the investment. We should have planted it years ago. Ah well. Maybe this year. Tonight, my pee will smell. Spring is here.

I eat lots of things out of season and out of region—eggplant, I love you even in the snow. But there are some foods that I never do this with: asparagus, ramps, summer squash, winter squash, strawberries (berries of all sorts actually), cherries, corn, fava beans. Why? Because, like the asparagus anecdote just offered, I have similar rituals for each of those ingredients. When they arrive back on my scene, it feels as if I'm visiting with old friends who are in town for a long weekend.

Also, these ingredients are simultaneously replaceable and irreplaceable. I don't buy asparagus from elsewhere because there is no mimicking the grassy sugar of fresh-snapped stalks, and because by the time asparagus is gone, green beans are on the scene. Ya know what I mean?

I feel differently about potatoes and carrots. They are sturdy storage crops that travel well from faraway farms and require less energy (not needing refrigeration) to do so. Of course, I celebrate when the very first of the season's new potatoes are dug from the ground—their tender skin so easily rubbed from their creamy flesh and practically shining under a layer of dirt. My celebration takes the form of chucking them into a pot of water, boiling with salt until just tender, and **tossing** them with sweet butter and a big handful of herbs. I eat them with glee, my bare feet delighting in the July grass. Bliss. But boiling, smashing, and dressing with cream in the middle of February is no less joyful.

What's a pity is when the local option isn't having a great year. When the asparagus is woody from drought; when the strawberries taste of water because it won't stop raining. We rarely talk about this in the local, seasonal movement, but all of these ingredients are agricultural products at the mercy of Mother Nature's whim. Sometimes they suck, and that's just how it is. Deflation to that expected elation.

Thankfully, some salt, a splash of vinegar, or a pat of butter makes most things pretty good. There's always tomorrow. There's always next year. We'll make do; good company makes even the worst-tasting meals a celebration.

HOW TO BUY

- Even coloring. Dark spots indicate age or disease. Yellowing shows age and that the asparagus is starting to break down.

- Even skin texture. Pock marks or shriveling show age and moisture loss.

- Budding stalks tend to be woody.

HOW TO STORE

- Store in a vase of water in the refrigerator so the stalks will continue to wick up water.

- Or store wrapped in a damp paper towel in a plastic bag.

- Before preparing, look at the ends. If they look dry, snap them as close to the bottom as you can. Where they snap cleanly shows where they are tender enough to eat. If they are tough and fibrous, they won't snap. (Which is also why I don't cut the stalks. A sharp knife will cut even what is too tough to chew.) If they are not dry or have just been harvested, no need to snap off the ends.

- Avoid cutting or snapping if you don't need to; be sure that you are wasting as little as possible.

NOTES

- I have found no real flavor difference between the thick and thin stalks—this is more a matter of preference and usage. I use the thick stalks for shaving raw or grilling so they can get a good char without going squishy. I like the thin stalks for a quick sauté in butter.

- No matter the thickness, seek out stalks that are the same size. Farmers that take the time to sort by size display the level of attention to detail that can grow very special produce.

- Asparagus tends to be sandy, so give it a good soak in a lot of water and agitate to get the grit out.

W/LEMON, DILL + PARMESAN

W/YOGURT +
SHAVED RADISHES

W/BROWN BUTTER VINAIGRETTE

PAN ROASTED

My mother was a wonderful cook, mastering everything from spit-roasted woodcock to the perfect cream sauce. But she cooked asparagus all to hell. The asparagus of my childhood was microwaved until it turned the color of 1970s bathroom tiles—and was simultaneously limp and stringy—naturally I looked askance at any mention of asparagus on a menu. The first bright green, just-cooked, and still-crisp stalks, rolled in butter and salt, stole my heart; I've never been the same since.

asparagus stalks w/anchovy-caper butter and fresh herbs

This is the finest and arguably the fastest way to get asparagus onto your plate. The key to a good pan roast is to give it the time and space to cook. Overcrowding the pan will steam the vegetable or at least make it cook unevenly. Caramelization won't happen if you insist on stirring every 5 seconds. Trust yourself and your pan. Allow it to brown a bit, then give it one good turn to sear the other side. Transfer to a plate, garnish, and eat.

Using a compound butter here adds surprising depth to this simple dish. If you don't have compound butter on hand, regular butter will be delicious, too.

Neutral oil

2 bunches asparagus (2 lb | 910 g) (any thickness)

3 Tbsp (45 g) anchovy–caper butter (page 62)

Crunchy salt

¼ cup (10 g) mixed tender herbs (parsley, lemon thyme, tarragon, chives, chervil, and so on), roughly chopped

Heat a glug of oil in a skillet over high heat until just about smoking. Add the asparagus so that they all lie in a single layer; this may mean roasting the asparagus in batches. In that case, remove the first batch and let it rest on a warm platter while the other batch roasts, then toss them all together.

Allow the asparagus to get a good sear on one side. Roll the spears over and brown the other side. Turn off the heat. Add the butter and let it melt. Roll the stalks in the butter until coated.

Remove from the pan to a serving platter and sprinkle with crunchy salt and chopped herbs.

variations

w/lemon, dill + parmesan

1 lemon (¾ fl oz | 22 ml), zest and juice	8 dill sprigs, roughly chopped	1 oz (30 g) Parmesan, grated

<u>Toss</u> the pan-roasted asparagus with the lemon zest, juice, and chopped dill, tossing to coat. Garnish with the grated Parmesan.

w/yogurt + shaved radishes

¼ cup (60 g) plain yogurt	1 <u>bunch</u> radishes (1 lb | 455 g), <u>shaved</u> on a mandoline or with a sharp knife

Transfer the pan-roasted asparagus to a serving platter and garnish by drizzling the yogurt (or dotting if it is thick) over the asparagus and then topping with the <u>shaved</u> radishes.

w/brown butter vinaigrette + mint

½ cup (120 ml) brown butter vinaigrette (page 59)	10 sprigs mint, torn

<u>Toss</u> the pan-roasted asparagus with the vinaigrette and garnish with the torn mint.

GRILLED

As with all asparagus cooking, aim to get good color on the outside fast enough that the inside still has a bit of bite. I like to grill asparagus just before eating on the hottest part of the grill so that the feathery tops singe and crisp.

If you find yourself with a boatload of asparagus (as happens with these feast-or-famine vegetables), cook the stalks, then dress immediately and let cool in an acidic vinaigrette. The spears soak up the dressing and make a nice slightly pickley snack later on.

asparagus w/smoked whitefish, pea shoots, and mushrooms

Though this recipe says to pan roast the mushrooms, feel free to grill them as well as the asparagus. I like the difference in color and flavor, but it is an extra step, not a must.

¼ lb (115 g) mushrooms (any variety)

Neutral oil

Salt

2 bunches asparagus (2 lb | 910 g)

¼ lb (115 g) smoked whitefish (substitute tuna or fresh, fully cooked fish)

1 bag (2 oz | 55 g) pea shoots or other sprouts (substitute arugula or spinach or kale in a pinch)

Olive oil

Freshly ground black pepper

Cut the mushrooms into ½-inch- (12-mm-) thick pieces.

Heat a large frying pan over high heat with a glug of neutral oil until shimmering hot. Add the mushrooms with a pinch of salt and toss to coat with the oil. Pan roast the mushrooms until golden brown and crispy (see page 24), 10 to 15 minutes. Stir to flip and cook until the other side is crispy, about 5 minutes.

Heat the grill until smoking hot. Toss the asparagus in a glug of neutral oil and pinch of salt. Grill until charred but still with a little structure in the stalk. Transfer to a serving platter.

Scatter the whitefish, pea shoots, and mushrooms over the top. Drizzle with olive oil, sprinkle with salt and pepper, and serve.

variations

w/lemon, mint + lemon parmesan butter (page 62)

w/pickled beets + feta

w/grated cheddar + garlic bread crumbs (page 48)

RAW

Asparagus takes well to most treatments, but cooking less is more, and sometimes even not at all is best.

The first time I ever ate raw asparagus was in a sunny field at the start of spring. My farmer friend snapped off a stalk, gave it a wipe, and chomped away. As with eating sushi for the first time, it had never occurred to me to eat it raw. I quickly followed suit.

Raw asparagus is sweet and slightly starchy, a bit like raw corn. I like it best when sliced very thinly with a knife or <u>shaved</u> into <u>ribbons</u> on a mandoline or with a vegetable peeler. Large-stalked asparagus is the easiest to shave, but asparagus of any thickness is tasty raw. I find large chunks distracting in a finished dish, but if you like it, cut it as large as your heart desires.

salad of asparagus, arugula, egg, and radish w/mustard vinaigrette

Tasting for salt before serving is key to all recipes but especially so here because the asparagus can soak up the seasoning. Be aware that the salt will leach water from the asparagus, so don't dress more than 30 minutes before serving.

1 <u>bunch</u> thick asparagus (1 lb | 455 g)

1 <u>bunch</u> radishes (1 lb | 455 g) (Easter Egg is the most colorful variety)

2 hard-boiled eggs (page 22)

1 shallot (0.2 oz | 6 g)

¼ cup (60 g) whole-grain mustard

1 Tbsp (20 g) honey

½ tsp (3 g) salt, plus more for seasoning

2 Tbsp (30 ml) apple cider vinegar

½ cup (120 ml) olive oil

1 bag (4 oz | 115 g) arugula

Freshly ground black pepper

With a sharp knife, vegetable peeler, or mandoline, <u>shave</u> the asparagus and radishes as thinly as possible. For the asparagus, cut either on an acute diagonal or in <u>ribbons</u> down the length of the stalk.

Pass the hard-boiled eggs through a fine-mesh sieve or finely chop with a knife.

Finely <u>dice</u> or thinly <u>shave</u> the shallot.

In a bowl, whisk together the mustard, honey, salt, and vinegar. Whisk in the olive oil.

Dress the arugula with 3 Tbsp (45 ml) of the mustard vinaigrette. Season with salt and pepper. Taste and adjust the seasoning—use more vinaigrette as needed. Arrange the greens on a serving platter or individual plates.

Scatter the asparagus, radish, and shallot over the top, sprinkle the egg over the whole lot, and drizzle with a touch more vinaigrette.

variations

w/pickle liquid dressing, spinach + sunflower seeds

½ cup (120 ml) pickle
liquid dressing
(page 58)

½ bag (2 oz | 55 g)
spinach, washed

¼ cup (25 g) sunflower
seeds, toasted (page
24)

Combine the <u>shaved</u> asparagus with the dressing and spinach, and <u>toss</u> to coat. Taste and adjust the seasoning. Sprinkle with sunflower seeds.

w/carrot, kale, bread crumbs + anchovy vinaigrette

3 carrots (¼ lb |112 g)
<u>shaved</u> into <u>ribbons</u>
with a vegetable peeler

1 <u>bunch</u> kale (½ lb | 4 cups |
230 g), massaged
(page 251)

½ cup (70 g) garlic bread
crumbs (page 48)

½ cup (120 ml) anchovy
vinaigrette (page 59)

Combine the <u>shaved</u> asparagus with the kale, bread crumbs, and vinaigrette, and <u>toss</u> to coat.

w/marinated peas, baby lettuce + buttermilk

1 cup (150 g) marinated
peas (page 315)

½ bag (2 oz | 55 g) baby
lettuce greens

½ cup (120 ml) buttermilk

Combine the <u>shaved</u> asparagus with the peas, greens, and buttermilk, and <u>toss</u> to coat. Taste and adjust seasoning as desired.

beets

Someday I will achieve full kitchen domination, where there is always a sweet and a savory compound butter in the freezer (just in case a friend drops in and craves a crêpe), always a balanced three-course meal partially prepared and ready to be garnished, and nothing ever gets thrown away because nothing has been made too far in advance and certainly has never been forgotten in the back of the fridge.

But until then, there are beets. Beets make me feel like a profound planner. They are one of the few fresh ingredients that I buy in large quantities and cook in one big go. This stems from my inherent love of efficiency; if you are going to turn the oven on, it had better be for more than one lonely beet. So when the oven is on to make a casserole, I put a tray full of beets on the other rack and feel smugly methodical. Then, later in the week, when there is no time for a hot meal, I have a dish full of beets that are ready to be sliced and **tossed** with whatever else is in the refrigerator. The smugness continues.

Shopping at farmers' markets, I realized that there is a world of beets beyond the pickled ones that adorned my grandmother's relish tray. There is terrific variety resting atop the burlap-covered tables—golden, torpedo shaped, candy striped, and blood red.

The darker the beet's color, the earthier and richer the flavor; the lighter the color, the sweeter and less complex the flavor. I find this to be true for almost all foods—from cherries to carrots—and that isn't a judgment on the quality of the plant but factors into how it will be paired.

How a beet's color will complement what else is on the plate is another decision driver. Golden beets blaze next to greens. Red beets look almost black against the white of goat cheese or sour cream. As a side note, I cook golden and red beets in the same pan so that the red juice stains the bottoms of the golden beets, turning them into a sunset for the plate. Store them separately, or else in a couple of days they will all be one shade of orangey red.

The market is also where I first saw what the greens of the plant looked like. I discovered that they were not only edible but delightful. Beet greens can be used any way that you would use kale or chard, though they are a touch more fibrous. They are also compostable if you just can't be bothered, which happens to the most committed vegetable eaters of us. The delight of those leaves, combined with my eternal guilt around waste, has forced me to pull those red-ribbed greens from the compost bin more than once. Thankfully the vegetable goddess, Demeter, invented smoothies, the most efficient of all the meals, ever.

HOW TO BUY

- Tops on means they were dug up within the week. The greens should be perky, and the skin should be free of deep blemishes.
- No tops probably means they have been stored for a while—beets do store well. Look for firm skin and no sponginess when squeezed.
- Similar size beets will cook at the same rate.

HOW TO STORE

- Remove tops and store separately. If left on, the beets will respire moisture more quickly.
- Store the roots in a paper bag in a plastic bag in the refrigerator or cellar. Plastic keeps moisture in; paper shields light and wicks excess moisture away to prevent mold.
- Avoid dramatic shifts in temperature, which will encourage sprouting.
- Beet root stores for months on end.
- Once the beets are cooked, store in the refrigerator in an airtight container for a few days.
- If the beets get slimy or start to look like they are dressed in vinaigrette, pitch them; they are starting to break down.

NOTES

- The lighter the flesh of the beet, the less earthy (more sugary sweet) the flavor. They do not contain more sugar but taste sweeter because the other flavors are not present.
- I cook large batches of beets at a time and keep the extras in the refrigerator for a quick meal.
- When beets are fully cooked, their skins should rub off easily. If you are having trouble freeing the skin from the root, try cooking them longer and see if that helps.
- I have had trouble peeling beets that are fully cooked after they have been in the root cellar for several months. After February, I always peel cooked beets with a knife.
- Beets can be eaten raw (or any stage between raw and fully cooked) but be warned that the oxalic acid in raw beets can irritate some people's throats. It makes me feel like I have to cough for a few hours.
- After eating beets, remember that you have eaten beets, and remind your guests. The color stains all things passing out of your body, not just your hands.

STEAM ROASTED

This is my preferred method for cooking beets because the little bit of water speeds the cooking time, and the flavor is concentrated because there is no excess liquid to wick the flavor away, unlike when boiled. Plus, this is the best method for cooking a lot of beets in one go with little active attention. Cook as many beets as you want, but don't stack them or they will cook unevenly.

beets w/smoked whitefish, sour cream, and dill

6 beets (2 lb | 910 g)

Olive oil

Salt and freshly ground
  black pepper

4 oz (115 g) smoked
  whitefish, flaked, pin
  bones removed

2 oz (55 g) sour cream

6 sprigs dill, stemmed,
  leaves left whole

¼ cup (35 g) sunflower
  seeds

Heat the oven to 350°F (180°C). Scrub the beets and <u>toss</u> with olive oil, salt, and pepper, then place them in a roasting pan in a single layer. Add a good <u>glug</u> of water—about ¼ cup (60 ml) or so—and cover with foil.

Cook until the beets yield easily when pierced with a small knife. If there is any resistance, give them more time. When the beets come out of the oven, let them cool a bit, then rub their skins off with a paper towel. If the skins don't slip off easily, peel with a knife.

Depending on the shape you prefer, slice the beets into wedges, ¼-inch (6-mm) rounds, or half-moons—a mandoline will make quick work of this, but watch your fingers! Dress the beets with a <u>glug</u> of olive oil, adding salt and pepper as desired.

On a serving platter, lay out half the ingredients, starting with the beets, then the whitefish, and dot with half the sour cream, the dill, the olive oil, and the sunflower seeds. Repeat the layers. Serve.

variations

w/orange pinwheels, pecans + feta

w/apples, cheddar + walnuts

w/parmesan, dried cherries + wheat berries

PURÉED

I'm often working to find new ways to incorporate vegetables into foods. Puréeing them until very smooth in a food processor, and then using that purée either in addition to (or as a replacement for) other sauces, is my favorite method. I then have an ingredient ready to be snatched from the refrigerator and transformed on a whim. It also plays with our expectations of what a vegetable can be—using a vegetable purée instead of mayo on a sandwich or to bind a pasta dish, for example.

beet-dressed pasta w/golden raisins and poppy seeds

Generally, I use a microwave to warm up my forgotten morning coffee and for little else. But there are other uses. The beets in this recipe will purée to a significantly smoother texture if they are warm. If you have prepared a load of beets earlier in the week and want to make this sauce, simply warm them up in the microwave with a splash of water. Alternatively, if you are cooking loads of beets, it's smart to make the purée when they are warm out of the oven. It will store in the refrigerator for a week or in the freezer for a good long time.

This pasta salad also works as a cold salad, but often needs an extra pinch of salt, since the flavors will be muted when cold.

¼ cup (35 g) golden raisins

Juice of ½ lemon (0.75 fl oz | 22 ml)

2 steam-roasted beets (1 lb | 455 g)

¼ cup (60 ml) olive oil

Salt and freshly ground black pepper

Cream (optional)

1 lb (455 g) small pasta, bow ties, orecchiette, or penne

1 Tbsp (10 g) poppy seeds

Soak the golden raisins in ½ cup (120 ml) hot water with a squeeze of lemon for 10 minutes or until they are plump. Strain the raisins, saving the water.

In a food processor, purée the beets with the olive oil, raisin water, and a good pinch of salt and pepper until very smooth. If you like dairy, toss in a glug of cream.

Boil the pasta in well-salted water and drain.

Toss the pasta with the beet purée (to warm and coat), soaked raisins, and poppy seeds. Transfer to serving platter or individual bowls. Drizzle with additional olive oil.

variations

risotto (page 42) w/apples, squash + parmesan

couscous (page 46) w/dukkah (page 63) + feta

beet hummus for veggie dipping

BEET PURÉE

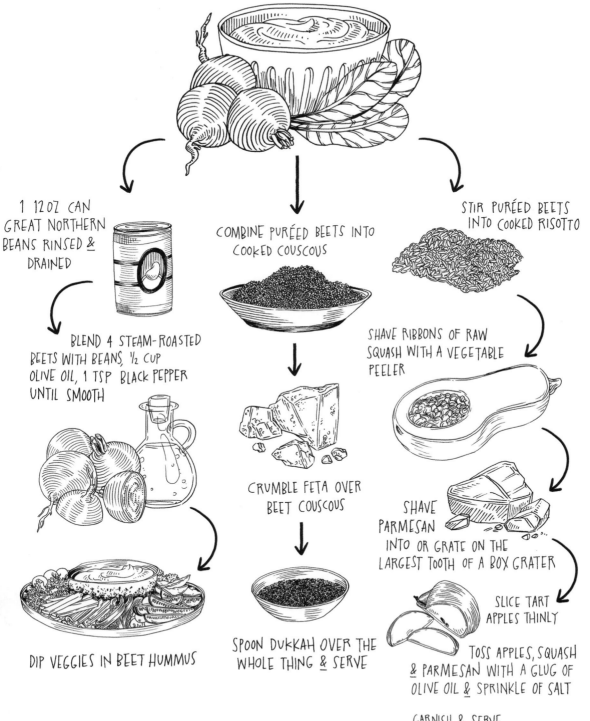

1 12 OZ CAN GREAT NORTHERN BEANS RINSED & DRAINED

BLEND 4 STEAM-ROASTED BEETS WITH BEANS, ½ CUP OLIVE OIL, 1 TSP BLACK PEPPER UNTIL SMOOTH

DIP VEGGIES IN BEET HUMMUS

COMBINE PURÉED BEETS INTO COOKED COUSCOUS

CRUMBLE FETA OVER BEET COUSCOUS

SPOON DUKKAH OVER THE WHOLE THING & SERVE

STIR PURÉED BEETS INTO COOKED RISOTTO

SHAVE RIBBONS OF RAW SQUASH WITH A VEGETABLE PEELER

SHAVE PARMESAN INTO OR GRATE ON THE LARGEST TOOTH OF A BOX GRATER

SLICE TART APPLES THINLY

TOSS APPLES, SQUASH & PARMESAN WITH A GLUG OF OLIVE OIL & SPRINKLE OF SALT

GARNISH & SERVE

broccoli

I woke up and the house smelled of bacon.

Lying in my childhood bed, I suddenly felt a rush of comfort. Mom was making breakfast. The house smelled like food again. Again. Pause. Intake of breath. Suddenly like cold wind rushing in through an open window. Not Mom; Mom's dead.

She died April 5. What's the date? Early August. It has been four months.

She's still dead. This won't change. Remember when you kept thinking you heard her come in through the back door, home from work, how it used to be? Four months. This isn't going to change.

But, wait, no, it definitely smells like bacon in here. Someone is cooking. Dad?

I remember my dad cooking only a handful of times. I was thinking of this as I made my way downstairs to the kitchen. The glass doors were closed, a signal he was trying to not wake me with the noise. I swung them open, and Dad looked up.

"Good morning. There's coffee," thrown over his shoulder as he continued cutting what appeared to be forty pounds of onions. I scanned the countertops, which were full in a way I had never seen them before. Wide-eyed, I poured myself a cup of coffee.

Quietly, "What's going on, Dad?"

"Well, Abra, I decided I need to start cooking for myself. You've been doing a lot of it, but you need to go back to school in a few weeks. I found these cast irons in the basement. Your mother never liked using cast iron, but I like them and so I thought I could start to use them. The internet said that to cure a cast-iron pan you need to cook a pound of bacon and then use the fat to seal the metal. So I'm doing that, but then, that's a lot of bacon . . . so I remembered that there was a broccoli salad that we used to make that had bacon in it. I remember always liking that one. I found the recipe; nice to see her handwriting. And now I'm getting pretty good at dicing these onions."

And that was that. My father is perfectly logical and completely nonsensical at the exact same time.

He was trying to heal. The love of his life, the woman who introduced him to his career, who helped him raise three women, who traveled with him, who cooked 95 percent of our meals, who loved him, had vanished. She died in an accident on a Saturday morning. We were all trying to make sense of the loss and what the hell comes next. None of us were sure that there was anything next, anything beyond crippling grief.

I had no words. I set up a cutting board next to him and started trimming broccoli florets. We were both crying—forty pounds of onions and the biggest loss we'd ever faced.

The grief isn't gone. It never will be. Somehow it still feels disloyal—to have continued to live and not be so sad every day. We had to try. We had to start doing the things that you do in normal life—normal life before you realize that it is possible to die. Before you learn the lesson that absolutely everything is fragile and can break irreparably in a moment when you're not looking.

The way we started trying to heal was through food. Cooking was the hallmark both of the loss and of the recovery. Food is culture. It bound us together before, and maybe it could bind our wounds now. My dad looked back to the broccoli salad he knew and thought maybe he could use it to rebuild his future. There were new lessons each time on how to move forward, and most days we found something to eat.

There were other, practical lessons learned that morning.

Fat from a pound of bacon is, in fact, a good way to cure a cast-iron pan.

Not every recipe should be scaled up just because you have a lot of one ingredient.

Broccoli salad does not freeze well.

HOW TO BUY

- Look for dense, tightly packed heads, aka crowns.
- Avoid broccoli with obvious signs of yellowing, which indicate age.
- The florets should be closed and not have opened into flowers—which means the plant is bolting, making the stems woody and slightly more bitter.
- If you can get the greens that surround the crowns, all the better. The greens can be used as you would kale or kohlrabi leaves.

HOW TO STORE

- Separate the leaves from the crowns, as the greens will respire more quickly.
- Store the crowns in a paper bag in a plastic bag (either sealed or left slightly open). The paper will keep the broccoli moist without pooling moisture, which can lead to rot.
- Store the greens as you would kale or chard.

NOTES

- Broccoli is a brassica and so prefers cool weather—look for broccoli in the spring and fall.
- Broccoli stems are often overlooked and can be used in addition to the florets.
- If the stems are tough, peel away the fibrous skin with a vegetable peeler.

RAW

Raw broccoli can be simply bite-size pieces of broccoli. I also like shaving the broccoli into thin, cross-section broccoli trees. To shave broccoli, simply cut the crown in half, place the cut-side down, and slice as thinly as possible. In the end, it doesn't matter the shape of the broccoli as long as it is pleasant to chew.

broccoli salad w/warm bacon vinaigrette, sunflower seeds, and dried cherries

This is a version of a classic Midwestern summer buffet salad with a warm bacon dressing in place of the mayo. It can be made in advance but always serve room temperature or the bacon fat will congeal a bit. If you prefer mayo or don't eat bacon, substitute mayonnaise or vinaigrette for the bacon fat and extra olive oil.

½ lb (230 g) bacon, cut into ¼-in (6-mm) strips

One 4-oz (115-g) shallot or small red onion, cut into thin slices

¼ cup (60 ml) apple cider vinegar

½ tsp (3 g) salt

½ tsp (3 g) freshly ground black pepper

2 Tbsp (30 ml) olive oil

2 crowns (2 lbs | 8 cups | 910 g) broccoli, shaved thinly or cut into florets, stalks peeled and cut into half-moons

1 cup (140 g) dried cherries, either sweet or sour

½ cup (70 g) sunflower seeds, toasted (page 24)

Place the bacon in a cold frying pan and then cook over medium heat, until the bacon is crispy, rendering the bacon fat.

In a bowl, combine the shallot, vinegar, salt, and pepper and let sit for 5 to 10 minutes. Strain the bacon fat into the shallot-vinegar mixture, reserving the crispy pieces. Add the olive oil to the mixture and whisk to combine.

Toss the broccoli, bacon bits, cherries, and sunflower seeds with the bacon vinaigrette and a pinch of salt.

variations

w/tomato + anchovy vinaigrette

½ cup (120 ml) anchovy vinaigrette (page 59)

2 heads (2 lb | 8 cups | 910 g) broccoli, shaved into ribbons

4 (1 lb | 455 g) plump, heavy tomatoes of various colors, cut into large chunks

½ cup (70 g) sunflower seeds, toasted (page 24)

Combine the anchovy vinaigrette with the broccoli and tomatoes. Toss to combine. Taste and adjust the seasoning, top with the sunflower seeds, and serve.

w/cauliflower, lemon vinaigrette + garlic bread crumbs

1 head (1 lb | 4 cups | 455 g) broccoli, shaved into ribbons

1 head (1 lb | 4 cups | 455 g) cauliflower, shaved into ribbons

½ cup (120 ml) lemon vinaigrette (page 58)

Salt and freshly ground black pepper

4 eggs, hard-boiled (page 22)

½ bunch parsley (1.2 oz | ¾ cup | 34 g), stemmed, leaves left whole

¼ cup (35 g) garlic bread crumbs (page 48)

Dress the broccoli and cauliflower with the lemon vinaigrette and a big pinch of salt and pepper. Grate the egg on the widest teeth of a box grater. Combine the broccoli with the egg and parsley and top with the bread crumbs.

crudité salad w/ranch dressing

4 cups (weight varies) any and all veggies you like, shaved or cut into various textures: broccoli (duh), carrots, radishes, cherry tomatoes, roasted potatoes, cauliflower, salad, turnips, bell peppers, mushrooms, summer squash, rutabaga, and so on

½ bunch parsley (1.2 oz | ¾ cup | 34 g), roughly chopped

½ bunch cilantro (1.2 oz | ¾ cup | 34 g), roughly chopped

1 cup (240 ml) ranch dressing (page 60)

Combine all ingredients and serve.

OVEN ROASTED

The beauty of oven-roasted broccoli is that the florets get frilly and crispy and caramelized, while the stems are tender. Don't get nervous; let them brown.

broccoli w/melty cheese and chili oil

This is the adult version of broccoli covered in cheese sauce. As with roasting all vegetables, get the oven hot enough, allow space between the vegetables so they roast, not steam, and cook till just beyond where you are comfortable to get that burnished, crackly outside. Be warned: this recipe is intended as a side dish for four people, but #realtalk it has served just one more than once.

2 crowns (2 lb | 8 cups | 910 g) broccoli, cut into large florets

Neutral oil

½ tsp (2 g) chili flakes

Salt

3 oz (85 g) Swiss cheese and/or Cheddar of any sharpness, grated on the largest holes of a box grater

Heat the oven to 425°F (220°C).

Toss the broccoli with a big glug of neutral oil, the chili flakes, and a big pinch of salt. Spread out on a baking sheet and roast until golden brown and crispy, about 20 minutes.

Remove the broccoli from the oven and sprinkle with the cheese. Return to the oven until the cheese is melted; serve immediately.

variations

w/warm bacon vinaigrette + cheddar

2 crowns (2 lb | 8 cups | 910 g) broccoli, cut into florets

½ cup (120 ml) warm bacon vinaigrette (page 59)

1 small (2 oz | 55 g) onion or shallot, cut into <u>thin slices</u>

2 oz (55 g) Cheddar, grated

Roast the broccoli. <u>Toss</u> with the bacon vinaigrette, onion, and Cheddar. Return to the oven until the Cheddar is melted. Serve immediately.

w/wheat berries, blue cheese + dried cranberries

2 crowns (2 lb | 8 cups | 910 g) broccoli, cut into florets

2 oz (55 g) blue cheese

2 cups (360 g) cooked wheat berries (page 43)

½ cup (70 g) dried cranberries

2 Tbsp (30 ml) balsamic vinegar

1 Tbsp (15 ml) apple cider vinegar

¼ cup (60 ml) olive oil

Roast the broccoli. Crumble the blue cheese. Combine all ingredients together, <u>toss</u>, taste, and serve.

roasted broccoli w/lemon-caper mayo + sunflower seeds

2 crowns (2 lb | 8 cups | 910 g) broccoli, cut into florets

½ cup (120 ml) lemon-caper mayo (page 61)

¼ cup (35 g) sunflower seeds, toasted (page 24)

Roast the broccoli. Remove from the oven and spoon the lemon–caper mayo over the broccoli, sprinkle with the sunflower seeds, and serve.

QUICK STEAMED

This idea came to me when I really, really couldn't be bothered to wait for an entire pot of water to come to a boil, so I put as little in the bottom of the pot to steam as I felt practically possible (about 1 inch [2.5 cm]). The next time, I couldn't find the steamer basket anywhere and so I thought, well, how about just even less water in a frying pan with the lid on. Worked like a charm.

The basic technique is to prep the florets of the broccoli and then in a large frying pan (with a lid) heat ½ cup (120 ml) of water until you see small bubbles. Add the broccoli and a pinch of salt, cover with the lid, and leave on the heat for about 4 minutes. Check the broccoli—but not too often or you'll let out all the steam (there isn't that much water in there to start). The water should be all but evaporated and the broccoli bright green and tender.

The stems can also be steamed this way but need to be cut smaller than the florets because they are denser and will take longer to cook. You can also steam the stems separately and then refresh the water to do the florets. Or leave the stems raw to add a textural difference to the whole thing.

bright green broccoli w/seared whitefish and lemon butter

2 crowns broccoli (2 lb | 8 cups | 910 g) broccoli

4 Tbsp (55 g) butter, softened

2 lemons (1½ fl oz | 45 ml), zest and juice

2 oz (55 g) Parmesan, grated

½ bunch parsley (1.2 oz | ¾ cup | 34 g), roughly chopped

½ tsp (3 g) salt

½ tsp (3 g) freshly ground black pepper

Neutral oil, for frying

4 whitefish fillets (6 oz | 170 g each)

½ cup (120 ml) water

½ cup (60 g) walnuts, toasted (page 24)

Heat the oven to 400°F (200°C).

Cut the broccoli into florets by removing from the stalk and cutting the crown into bite-size pieces.

Combine the butter, lemon zest, Parmesan, parsley, salt, and pepper and mix until well combined.

Heat a glug of oil in a frying pan over medium-high heat until just about to smoke.

Meanwhile, pat the skin of the whitefish dry and season with salt. Fry skin-side down, pressing the fillets into the pan.

Reduce the heat to medium and allow the fish to cook until the fillets will slide in the pan when gently nudged with a metal spatula (ensuring that the skin is cooked through, crispy, and released from the pan). Transfer the fish to the oven and bake until the flesh is opaque white and the texture of a clenched bicep when pressed with a finger, about 7 minutes). Or sear (see page 24).

In a clean, lidded frying pan, heat the water until you see small bubbles, then add the broccoli and a big pinch of salt. Cover with the lid and allow the broccoli to steam until bright green, about 5 minutes. Remove from the heat and add the lemon juice.

Remove the fish from the oven.

Serve the fish skin-side up, topped with a big glob of the lemon butter. Place the broccoli next to the fish. Crunch the walnuts in your hands and scatter them over the broccoli.

variations

w/baked potato + tuna mayo

1 large russet potato (10 oz | 280 g) per person

Salt and freshly ground black pepper

½ head (½ lb | 1 cup | 230 g) broccoli per person, quick steamed

¼ cup (60 g) tuna mayo (page 61) per person

Bake the potato until fully cooked, cut along the top, and squeeze the flesh to fluff it up. Season liberally with salt and pepper. Top with the quick-steamed broccoli and tuna mayo and serve.

w/carrots, peas + lemon vinaigrette

2 carrots (6 oz | 170 g) per person, cut into wedges or ½-inch (12-mm) pieces

½ head (½ lb | 1 cup | 230 g) broccoli per person

½ cup (60 g) peas per person

1 lemon (1½ fl oz | 45 ml), zest and juice

¼ cup (60 ml) olive oil

Salt

½ bunch parsley (1.2 oz | ¾ cup | 34 g), leaves left whole (optional)

Heat the oven to 400°F (200°C). Roast the carrots until tender, 30 to 45 minutes, and remove from the oven. Steam the broccoli, adding the peas for the last 3 minutes. Mix the lemon zest and juice with the olive oil and a big pinch of salt. Toss the hot veggies immediately with the lemon vinaigrette and parsley leaves (if using). Serve warm or at room temperature.

w/chili oil, crispy chickpeas + cilantro

½ head (½ lb | 1 cup | 230 g) broccoli florets per person

¼ cup (40 g) crispy chickpeas (page 45)

3 Tbsp (45 ml) chili oil (page 55)

½ bunch cilantro (1.2 oz | ¾ cup | 34 g) (optional), stemmed, leaves left whole

Steam the broccoli and toss with the chickpeas, chili oil, and cilantro (if using).

cabbage

In interviews chefs are usually asked which vegetable is their favorite, and almost without fail they respond, "Oh, that's like asking which child is your favorite. I just can't choose."

Nope. Cabbage is my favorite, hands down. I hope that if I have children it will be harder to decide, but not with vegetables. Don't mistake me, I love all vegetables and relish their idiosyncrasies, but it is cabbage I come home to.

She is a reliable and hard-working friend. As in people, these crucial but not fancy attributes are rarely as highly praised as showier traits. Tomatoes are darlings, it's true, but they are around for only a handful of weeks, and when it gets cold or rainy, they are as lively as a wet blanket.

Not you, cabbage. You are at the ready straight from the field or after months of storage. You come in many colors and shapes, ranging from the tight-headed scarlet red to the loose and frilly Napa. You feel refreshing as a salad and can take a good deal of heat in the kitchen. You are healthy and stand up to a "healthy" amount of ranch dressing. Dressed with vinegar and a pinch of salt, you leave drips of purple essence at the bottom of the bowl. I eschew spoon for finger to lap up the last. While you have a reputation for coarseness, I know that you are sweet and mild. You can be the star or the support.

Cabbage, don't tell your vegetable sisters, but I've always loved you the best.

HOW TO BUY

- Look for tightly packed heads. The outside leaves may be loose, but the head should feel dense and rigid when squeezed.
- Avoid any heads with any obvious gashes or cracks.
- Avoid any with obvious downy mildew (a dusty gray powder) or signs of aphids on the lower leaves.
- If the heads have any of this damage, consider asking about a discount, because there is still good food there but you will lose some yield.

HOW TO STORE

- Store in the refrigerator in a plastic bag without excess water. The plastic protects the leaves from being wind whipped by the fans moving the refrigerated air.
- If there are very wilty leaves on the outside, simply peel them away, revealing crisp leaves inside.
- Same goes for storing cut cabbage. The smaller the cut, the faster the leaves will dry out, so use it up within the week.
- Unfortunately, unlike lettuce, cabbage leaves don't seem to perk back up when soaked in cool water, so if you have wilted cabbage leaves, consider cooking them.

NOTES

- Cabbage is a brassica that usually turns up at farmers' markets in the fall, as it takes a long time for the heads to form.
- Red cabbage will bleed its color a bit; if you want to keep it bright purple, add a splash of vinegar, which will increase the acidity and the color.
- Boiled cabbage's sulfuric aroma is the smell most evocative of bad dining halls. Minimize the brassica farty smell by cooking quickly and with high heat.

RAW

It seems like the simplest thing in the world to <u>shave</u> some red cabbage into your salad. The original salad-in-a-bag had little flecks of purple along with the cut romaine and iceberg lettuce. It is rarer to see a salad entirely of cabbage. I prize these salads because they are quick, can be dressed ahead of time, are good for parties or feeding a lot of people inexpensively, and they always feel surprising.

shaved cabbage salad w/chili oil, cilantro, and charred melon

I tend toward cantaloupe for this dish. Charring the pieces in an exceedingly hot frying pan caramelizes the sugar and lends a bitter quality to contrast the internal sweetness. I cook only one side to ensure good color; also, when I've flipped them the pieces over-cook and fall apart.

This process is also great for pineapple or underripe mangoes and is equally successful done on the grill. If using the juiciest melons of summer, cut them into larger pieces to maintain some structure.

I generally eat this dish as a side, but it could be a full meal especially if combined with some chickpeas, stewy black beans, or a grilled piece of fish.

½ melon (1 lb | 455 g) melon, cut into ½-inch (12-mm) cubes	½ head red cabbage (1½ lb | 3 cups | 680 g), shaved thinly, avoiding the core	2 limes (1 fl oz | 30 ml), zest and juice
Neutral oil	1 bunch cilantro (1.2 oz | ½ cup | 34 g), stems and leaves, roughly chopped	¼ cup (60 ml) chili oil (page 55)
		2 Tbsp (30 ml) olive oil
		½ tsp (3 g) salt

Heat a frying pan (preferably cast iron) until it's screaming hot. Add just enough melon cubes to cover the pan but with space between, as with roasting vegetables. Char in batches if necessary. Don't stir; let the melon brown and char; there will be smoke, and that's OK.

Add a glug of neutral oil to loosen any pieces sticking to the pan and continue to fry the melon until it's got a golden crust on the pan side (you're charring just one side) and has loosened from the pan, about 7 minutes. Remove from the heat.

Combine all the ingredients except the melon and toss to coat evenly. Taste and adjust the seasoning as desired. Scatter the melon over the top and serve.

variations

w/apples, ham + mustard vinaigrette

½ head (1½ lb | 3 cups | 680 g) red cabbage, <u>shaved</u> thinly, avoiding the core

2 tart cooking apples (1 lb | 455 g) (Greenings, Granny Smith, Mutsu), cut into ¼-inch- (6-mm-) thick slices

4 oz (115 g) <u>shaved</u> ham, roughly chopped

½ cup (120 ml) mustard vinaigrette (page 58)

½ <u>bunch</u> parsley (1.2 oz | ¾ cup | 34 g), roughly chopped

¼ tsp (2 g) salt

w/lemon vinaigrette, parsley, dukkah + ricotta

½ head (1½ lb | 3 cups | 680 g) red cabbage, <u>shaved</u> thinly, avoiding the core

1 <u>bunch</u> parsley (2.4 oz | 1½ cups | 68 g), roughly chopped

½ cup (120 ml) lemon vinaigrette (page 58)

Salt

4 oz (115 g) ricotta

½ cup (60 g) dukkah (page 63)

w/radishes, tuna mayo, cilantro + sunflower seeds

½ head (1½ lb | 3 cups | 680 g) red cabbage, <u>shaved</u> thinly, avoiding the core

1 <u>bunch</u> radishes (1 lb | 455 g), <u>shaved</u> thinly

1 <u>bunch</u> cilantro (½ cup | 34 g), roughly chopped

1 cup (240 g) tuna mayo (page 61)

¼ cup (35 g) sunflower seeds

ROASTED/GRILLED

Cabbage takes well to all forms of high-heat cooking. In summer I cut the cabbage into wedges and grill them to create frilly, singed leaves and a tender steamed core. In the winter, I'll sear those same wedges in a very hot frying pan or pan roast <u>shaved</u> leaves. For big parties I'll oven roast the cut greens in a ripping hot oven because you can cook three to four cabbages in one go. The link between all of these is high-heat searing and caramelizing the leaves without zapping the structure of the greens. If done at a low heat or in a crowded pan, the cabbage will steam, not caramelize, creating a smell like the most classic of cafeterias.

seared duck breast w/brown sugar–vinegar cabbage, roasted potatoes, and herb salad

The richness of duck elevates the commonness of cabbage to fancy dinner status. That said, this dish would be perfectly at home with chicken, pork chops, or seared salmon. Note that if you don't have the rendered duck fat in the pan, simply pan roast it with olive oil. Also note that if the skin softens while finishing the cabbage salad, simply kiss it in a hot pan or recrisp under the broiler.

This brown sugar–vinegar sauce lives on my counter, close to the stove, ready to turn up the volume on anything I'm cooking that day. I love this dish because it combines a variety of textures and simultaneously blends rich, comforting flavors with a bright, acidic, herby lightness. I tend to use red cabbage for the color, but any variety will work.

2 lb (910 g or 2 to 3 potatoes per person) Yukon gold or red-skinned potatoes, cut into wedges	4 (6 to 8 oz | 170 to 230 g) duck breasts	½ bunch parsley (2.4 oz | 1½ cups | 68 g), roughly chopped
Olive oil	1 head (3 lb | 6 cups | 1.4 kg) (red cabbage, cut into ribbons	10 sprigs chives, minced (optional)
Salt and freshly ground black pepper	½ cup (120 ml) brown sugar–vinegar sauce (page 61)	1 sprig rosemary, minced (optional)

Heat the oven to 425°F (220°C).

Dress the potatoes with a glug of olive oil, a big pinch of salt, and several grinds of black pepper. Transfer to a baking sheet and roast until crispy on the outside and tender on the inside, about 35 minutes. Reserve, rewarming if necessary for the final steps.

Meanwhile, score the skin of the duck breast into either diamonds or slices, trying to avoid cutting the flesh, and season liberally with salt and pepper.

In a large, cold frying pan, place the duck breasts skin-side down and turn on a medium heat. As the heat builds in the frying pan, the fat will render through the cuts in the skin and crisp. Let it go longer than you might think you should. Cook until the skin is brown and crispy, and the meat medium rare, about 15 minutes. Flip the breasts for 4 minutes to cook in the fat. Remove the duck breasts from the pan and let rest for 7 to 10 minutes.

Increase the heat under the frying pan to high and add the cabbage with a pinch of salt to roast in the rendered duck fat. Allow to sizzle and lightly brown, about 7 minutes. Remove from the heat, add the brown sugar–vinegar sauce, and toss to coat well.

Toss the warm potatoes with the dressed cabbage and the parsley, chives, and rosemary (if using).

Place the duck breasts on a serving platter next to the potato-cabbage salad, and serve.

variations

w/sausages, apples, mustard + cheddar

Heat the oven to 400°F (200°C) and brown 6 large 4-oz (115-g) sausages like bratwursts or Toulouse in a sauté pan. Transfer to a baking sheet and put in the oven to cook through, about 15 minutes. Roast 1 head of <u>shaved</u> cabbage in the sausage drippings until crispy edged, about 7 minutes. Dress the cabbage with ¼ cup (60 g) whole-grain or Dijon mustard and ¼ cup (60 ml) olive oil and <u>toss</u> with 2 cored and sliced apples. Serve the sausages next to the cabbage-apple salad and garnish with Cheddar cut into <u>ribbons</u> with a vegetable peeler.

w/pears, pecans + goat cheese

Heat a grill to high. Cut ½ head of cabbage into 6 wedges. Drizzle the wedges with olive oil and sprinkle with salt and grill on both cut sides until charred. Combine 3 sliced pears, 1 <u>bunch</u> of chopped parsley, and ½ cup (2 oz | 55 g) pecans with a <u>glug</u> of oil, 2 Tbsp (30 ml) apple cider vinegar, a pinch of salt, and several grinds of black pepper. Top the cabbage wedges with the pear mixture and dot with 4 oz (115 g) fresh goat cheese.

w/sunflower seeds + salsa verde

Heat a grill to high. Cut 1 head of cabbage into 6 wedges. Drizzle the wedges with oil and sprinkle with salt. Grill on both cut sides until the leaves are lightly charred. Remove from the grill, top with 1 cup (240 ml) salsa verde (page 57) over the wedges, and sprinkle with toasted sunflower seeds (page 24).

carrots

Farming taught me how much freaking work goes into food production, and that wasting food is truly a waste—of money, time, and resources. Take for example mirepoix, the carrot, celery, onion foundational trinity of classic cooking. Post-farming, I realized that it takes a minimum of 75 days to grow a carrot—80 days for celery; 108 days for onions—and that's best-case scenario. Not to mention that those day counts don't include the labor hours to start, transplant, weed, cultivate, clean, and store the crops. I suddenly knew the cost of these foods, not only to our customers but to ourselves.

We waste an astonishing 40 percent of food grown in the United States. That translates to 63 million tons of food valued at $218 billion. ReFED estimates that an average person wastes 400 pounds of food costing $1200 per year. By wasting this food, we are wasting 20 percent of our drinkable water supply, adding synthetic fertilizer, herbicides and pesticides to our ecosystem, and contributing to climate change through off-gassing as it decomposes in landfills. That waste happens in the field, in stores, and in homes.

Thankfully, curbing food waste is a low hanging fruit in making our food system more sustainable. You can take simple steps to avoid food waste in your home: reduce vegetable scraps, buy only what you need, buy imperfect foods, be skeptical of dates on packaging, eat your leftovers, donate your excess, and compost. Cook it, store it, share it; just don't waste it. See www.savethefood.com.

HOW TO BUY

- Look for carrots with firm, rigid roots.
- Squishy roots are fine for cooking, but won't store as long and are not good raw.
- Carrots with their tops have been harvested more recently than those without—an indication of time elapsed since being in the ground, but not necessarily of flavor or quality.
- If buying carrots without their tops, avoid ones with little green sprouts on top. This indicates that the carrots were cold and then warm, so the carrot is trying to send up a new stem and can yield a woody core.
- Avoid carrots with obvious pocks in the skin or flesh, which indicates that the carrots froze and the water in the cells burst, leaving holes in their wake. The flesh of formerly frozen carrots tends to be mushy, but can be used in stocks and such.
- Carrots sold before frost will be less sweet than those sold in the fall after frost.

HOW TO STORE

- Store in a cool dark place like a basement or root cellar. Short of that, store in the refrigerator in a paper bag within a plastic bag, which will help keep the roots hydrated, but not sitting in water. The plastic protects from the cold air movement of the refrigerator.
- If buying carrots with their greens, cut the greens and store separately because the greens will wick water away from the roots.

NOTES

- Peel carrots only if they are old and have unpalatably tough skins. Otherwise scrub them well, keeping the micronutrients in the skin and throwing away less of the root.
- Purple carrots will bleed their color into a soup or stock, so save those for salads unless you want bruise-colored stock.
- The darker the color of the carrot, the earthier the flavor. The lighter roots (white or yellow) will taste sweeter because they lack the polyphenols that taste earthy. They do not actually have more sugar.
- "Baby carrots" sold in bags at the supermarket are simply larger carrots that have had the outside flesh whittled away. True baby carrots look like small carrots, fine hairy roots and all.

RAW

As with all raw vegetables, the style of cut changes the texture of the ingredient. Any of these recipes can be made by shredding the carrot on the largest teeth of a box grater, shaving it with a vegetable peeler to make paper-thin <u>ribbons</u>, cutting into planks or half-moons, or leaving as large <u>batons</u> for the most crunch. The larger the cut, the longer the carrot will stay crisp after dressing— salt pulls moisture from vegetables, leaving the pieces limp, and the thicker the piece the slower the leaching of liquid. These salads are good <u>tossed</u> just before serving or on a buffet where the salad will be waiting around before being served.

carrot salad w/yogurt, pickled raisins, and pistachios

I like this dish to have some chew, so I cut the carrots into long <u>batons</u>. If you need to feed more people, <u>shave</u> the carrots with a vegetable peeler or grate for a fluffier dish. If you are using Greek yogurt, dot it over the finished salad; if using regular plain yogurt, drizzle it. For a vegan option use a nondairy yogurt or skip it.

1 cup (140 g) raisins

½ cup (120 ml) brown sugar–vinegar sauce (page 61) or ¼ cup (50 g) brown sugar and ¼ cup (60 ml) apple cider vinegar

1 <u>bunch</u> or 6 carrots (1½ lb | 680 g) of various colors, scrubbed and cut into long sticks or <u>batons</u>

¼ cup (60 ml) olive oil

Salt and freshly ground black pepper

½ cup (70 g) pistachios, toasted (page 24) and crushed or roughly chopped

1 <u>bunch</u> cilantro (1 oz | ½ cup | 30 g), roughly chopped, with stems if they are tender

½ cup (120 g) yogurt

Combine the raisins with the brown sugar–vinegar sauce and let sit for 10 minutes or so.

Dress the carrots with the olive oil, a big pinch of salt, and a grind of black pepper. Combine with the raisins and their soaking liquid, pistachios, and cilantro. Taste and adjust the seasoning, adding an additional splash of vinegar if too sweet. Transfer to a serving platter and drizzle or dot with the yogurt.

variations

w/salsa verde + ricotta

w/rosemary, honey, pecans + chili oil (page 55)

w/crispy chickpeas (page 45), lemon vinaigrette (page 58), parsley + smoked paprika

OVEN ROASTED

Roasting carrots concentrates the sugar in the root by evaporating the moisture and creating a crispy exterior skin with a soft marshmallowy texture inside. And speaking of marshmallows, if you let the carrots burn a bit, they taste remarkably like smoky-sweet burnt marshmallows. Leave the carrots in large pieces or even whole to give them enough time to roast thoroughly.

I rarely grill root vegetables, but in the summer, when turning on the oven in an already hot house feels like a mortal sin, wrapping the roots in foil and letting them roast on the grill will yield a similar result with a slightly smoky flavor.

carrots w/spicy apricot jam, mint, and almonds

This is a great way to use up the last ¼ cup (75 g) of jam often left in the refrigerator. I like apricot the best, but you can use raspberry, blueberry, cherry, or strawberry. Roast the carrots first, then dress and rebrown the carrots with the jam so the jam doesn't burn beyond the point of pleasantness. Note: If your jam is particularly sweet, add a squeeze of lemon over the whole thing to tart it up.

10 to 12 carrots (3 lb | 1.4 kg), scrubbed and cut into large chunks or left whole

Neutral oil

Salt

½ cup (70 g) almonds

¼ cup (75 g) apricot jam

¼ cup (60 ml) chili oil (page 55)

10 sprigs mint and/or cilantro, leaves picked off and torn roughly

Heat the oven to 425°F (220°C).

Toss the carrots with a glug of neutral oil and big pinch of salt.

Spread on a baking sheet, leaving some space between the carrots so they don't steam, and roast in the oven until fully cooked, about 35 minutes.

When the carrots are golden brown, crispy, and tender, spread the almonds on the baking sheet and return to the oven to toast until fragrant, about 5 minutes.

Whisk together the jam and chili oil.

Toss the carrots with the jam mixture and return to the oven to crisp, for 5 to 7 minutes.

Transfer the carrots to a serving platter and scatter with the mint and almonds.

variations

w/cherry tomatoes, parsley + tuna mayo

10 to 12 carrots (3 lb | 1.4 kg), scrubbed and cut into long batons	1 qt (1 lb | 450 g) cherry tomatoes, halved	1 cup (240 g) tuna mayo (page 61)
	½ bunch parsley (1.2 oz | 32 g), roughly chopped	

Heat the oven to 400°F (200°C) and roast the carrots. Toss with the cherry tomatoes and parsley. Transfer to a serving platter and drizzle with the tuna mayo.

w/basil oil + sunflower seeds

10 to 12 carrots (3 lb | 1.4 kg) of various colors, scrubbed and cut into long batons	¼ cup (60 ml) basil oil (page 56)	½ cup (120 g) sunflower seeds

Roast the carrots and transfer to a serving platter. Drizzle with the basil oil, and sprinkle with the sunflower seeds.

w/goat cheese, dill + garlic bread crumbs

10 to 12 carrots (3 lb | 1.4 kg) of various colors, scrubbed and cut into long batons	4 oz (115 g) fresh goat cheese	½ cup (70 g) garlic bread crumbs (page 48)
	5 sprigs dill, roughly chopped	

Roast the carrots and transfer to a serving platter. Dot with goat cheese and dill, and sprinkle with bread crumbs.

cauliflower

There are always dishes in my sink. I find it annoying yet strangely comforting—the byproduct of cooking at home regularly. Either Erik or I will clean the kitchen in the morning as the other one makes the coffee. As soon as all of the dishes from last night are drying on the counter, the coffee cups go into the basin. As soon as those are soaped up and drying, the plates from lunch stack up in the sink. It never ceases until we go out for dinner and break the cycle.

The same is true of the food in our kitchen. It feels like there is always some dredge of yesterday's meal that needs to be worked into this morning's breakfast. I made a bunch of squash purée and had a container full of it left over, so I combined it with this morning's grits and now have two containers of squashy, cheesy grits in the refrigerator. Maybe I'll make grit cakes for dinner tonight . . .

I used to be embarrassed by this style of cooking—it isn't particularly cheffy. Once a coworker told me that I thought and cooked like a home economics teacher. I smiled until I realized it was not a compliment.

A year or so later my friend Lauren tucked a copy of Tamar Adler's book, *An Everlasting Meal*, into my work locker with a note saying, "This cooking reminds me of you and your food. Hope you enjoy it." I dove into the book and quietly nodded my head along with every articulation of how the leftovers from last night's dinner inform this morning's breakfast, how the liquid used to boil the beans could also be a foundation for a stew, and how scraps of bread were never to be discarded. It wasn't just me. This lady had a book and wrote for the newspaper! Maybe there was no need to be sheepish about repurposing leftovers.

Recently I had a particularly Tamar-like week. I bought two heads of cauliflower on Friday—one white, one purple. I had been craving it, because cauliflower is a favorite, and you don't often see purple ones at the store.

The first night, I took the brain-like crowns and cut them into quarters, wrapping six of them in a storage bag and stashing them in the refrigerator. I **shaved** the two left on the cutting board into thin pieces that looked like purple-and-white cross sections of cartoon trees. **Tossed** with dates, chili oil, and parsley, the cauliflower made a multicolored salad, perfect alongside some chicken thighs. I wished we had some green olives.

Naturally there was some left over, so for Saturday lunch I picked the chicken from the bone and **tossed** it with the last of the cauliflower salad for sandwiches.

Sunday it was chillier, and we wanted something warm and to make ahead for the week; a big batch of purée from the last of the white cauliflower. (PSA: purée made of purple cauliflower is best suited for your Halloween party, as it has a ghoulish tinge.) We made a dinner of the last of the roasted-then-frozen cherry tomatoes from who knows when and **ribbons** of chard cut three days ago atop a big bowl of cauliflower purée. The rest of the purée was thinned with two quarts of stock from the freezer and converted to soup.

Tomorrow we'll eat that for dinner with some bread, from which we will inevitably have the ends left over and will need to make something from that. A happy need that I no longer feel embarrassed about, thanks to Lauren and Tamar's validation. It's OK to want someone else to say, "Yay!" now and again.

HOW TO BUY

- Look for tight heads free of browning or black bruises.
- If you can get cauliflower with leaves still attached, use them as you would kale or kohlrabi leaves.
- The white, yellow, and purple varieties taste mostly the same. I buy various colors for their looks and because they are probably more nutritious because of the micronutrients that lend the color.

HOW TO STORE

- Store in the refrigerator in a plastic bag free of excess moisture.
- Lots of water in the bag will promote rot and spread any blackening that has already occurred.
- If you do lose some to browning, simply cut it away and use what still looks good. There is no danger there.

NOTES

- Cauliflower tends to turn up in farmers' markets in the fall; as it is a brassica, it doesn't care for hot weather, yet it takes too long to mature into a head to be suitable for spring harvest.
- Romanesco, the green psychedelic-looking cauliflower, can be used exactly the same way.
- Cauliflower is packed with vitamins and minerals. Just because it is white doesn't mean it's fatty.

RAW

There is no right or wrong way to cut a vegetable as long as it feels good in your mouth. Here you could cut the cauliflower into florets, <u>shave</u> into thin cross sections with a knife or mandoline, or grate to make a tabbouleh-like texture. I'm partial to shaving cauliflower so you can see the shape of the cauliflower and to keep a nice wafer-like texture, but it is simply a matter of preference. If you don't want to use the whole head of cauliflower, use as much as you like; just reduce the other ingredients in proportion.

shaved cauliflower salad w/smoked whitefish mayo, lemon, radicchio, and herbs

I regularly use smoked fish, as it's a large part of the food culture in the Northern Midwest, but it is not always available in every grocery store. Always feel free to substitute canned tuna. I also use roasted fish (often as a leftover from last night's dinner) as a replacement. You won't get the smoky flavor, but that's OK.

If you can't find radicchio, use arugula or any other green you like. It won't have the same bitterness or pretty purple color, but that's fine. Same if you don't feel like making mayo; use a cup of store-bought, and blend in the fish and lemon in the same way. If you don't have sunflower seeds, use garlic bread crumbs (page 48) or any other nut you like, chopped finely.

Swap herbs in and out as you like. I also like this recipe with mint, but then I leave out the dill. The key is to use their fresh hits of flavor to lighten the richness of the mayo and the creamy one-note-ness of the cauliflower.

Finally, this salad is plenty hearty to be a meal on its own but plays well with others as a side dish.

1 egg

½ tsp (3 g) salt, plus more for seasoning

2 lemons (3 fl oz | 90 ml), zested and juiced separately

10 fl oz (300 ml) neutral oil

4 oz (115 g) smoked whitefish, deboned and flaked

1 small (4 oz | ½ cup | 115 g) red onion or shallot, cut into thin slices

Freshly ground black pepper

1 head (2 lb | 8 cups | 910 g) cauliflower, cored, cut into quarters, cut into thin slices

1 head (½ lb | 230 g) radicchio, cut into quarters and cored leaving the leaves as big petals

½ bunch parsley (1.2 oz | ¾ cup | 34 g), stemmed, leaves left whole

5 sprigs dill, stemmed, leaves left whole (optional)

½ cup (70 g) sunflower seeds, toasted (page 24)

In a food processor, whiz the egg, ½ tsp salt, and the zest and juice of 1 lemon. Slowly drizzle in the oil to make mayo. Add the white-fish to the mayo and blend until mostly smooth.

Combine the onion with the zest and juice of the second lemon, a big pinch of salt, and several grinds of pepper.

Toss the cauliflower, radicchio, parsley, and dill with the onion-lemon mixture and a pinch of salt.

Drizzle with the whitefish mayo and top with the sunflower seeds.

variations

w/kale, tomato, sherry vinaigrette + garlic bread crumbs

1 bunch kale (½ lb | 4 cups | 230 g), midribs stripped, torn into bite-size pieces

½ cup (120 ml) sherry vinaigrette (page 58)

1 head (2 lb | 8 cups | 910 g) cauliflower, shaved

1 quart (1 lb | 455 g) cherry tomatoes, halved

Salt and freshly ground black pepper

¼ cup (35 g) garlic bread crumbs (page 48)

Massage the kale (page 251) and then dress with the sherry vinaigrette, toss with the cauliflower and tomatoes and a big pinch of salt and pepper, and top with the bread crumbs.

w/dates, chili oil + parsley

1 cup (145 g) pitted, sliced dates

½ cup (70 g) green olives, sliced (optional)

2 lemons (3 fl oz | 90 ml), zest and juice

1 small (4 oz | ½ cup | 115 g) red onion, cut into thin slices

¼ cup (60 ml) olive oil

1 head (2 lb | 8 cups | 910 g) cauliflower, shaved

1 bunch parsley (2.4 oz | 1½ cups | 68 g), stemmed, leaves kept whole

Salt

¼ cup (60 ml) chili oil (page 55)

Combine the dates and olives with the lemon zest and juice, onion, and olive oil. Toss with the cauliflower, parsley, and a pinch of salt, and drizzle with the chili oil.

w/curry yogurt + almonds

¼ cup (60 ml) neutral oil

2 Tbsp (12 g) curry powder

1 cup (240 g) yogurt

1 head (2 lb | 8 cups | 910 g) cauliflower, shaved

Salt

1 bunch cilantro (1 oz | ½ cup | 30 g), roughly chopped

5 sprigs mint, roughly chopped

1 cup (140 g) almonds, roughly chopped

Heat the oil in a frying pan until just about smoking. Remove from the heat, add the curry powder, and let bloom until fragrant, swirling in the oil to cook evenly. When it's done sizzling, stir it into the yogurt. Dress the cauliflower with the yogurt and a big pinch of salt, and top with the herbs and almonds.

OVEN ROASTED

Keep the pieces of cauliflower larger to get a crunchy "exoskeleton" without the whole piece getting cooked to mush. The larger the piece, the longer the cooking time, though the crunchier the outside will be. As with all roasted vegetables, give them plenty of space on the baking sheet so that the moisture doesn't steam the neighboring pieces as it evaporates away while cooking. If your oven has a convection function, it will help wick the moisture away and make the outside crispier.

cauliflower w/roasted tomatoes, parsley, and bread crumbs

The roasted tomatoes provide the only acidity in this recipe. If you have perfect sweet, tart tomatoes, feel free to leave them raw, but roasting them will evaporate the extra moisture and concentrate their acidity. Plus, you can make your oven do double duty while the cauliflower cooks. The olives add an extra layer of salt and brightness, but if you don't have them, don't sweat it.

1 head (2 lb | 8 cups | 910 g) cauliflower, cored and cut into florets

Olive oil

Salt and freshly ground black pepper

2 qt (1.2 kg) cherry tomatoes or 10 plum tomatoes, halved or quartered if large

½ bunch parsley (1.2 oz | ¾ cup | 34 g), roughly chopped, or ¼ cup (60 ml) parsley oil (page 56)

½ cup (70 g) pitted olives, roughly chopped (optional)

½ cup (70 g) garlic bread crumbs (page 48)

Heat the oven to 425°F (220°C).

Toss the cauliflower with a <u>glug</u> of olive oil and sprinkle with the salt and pepper. Spread on a foil-lined baking sheet; don't over heap the cauliflower. Roast until the cauliflower is golden brown, crispy on the outside, and tender when poked with a knife, about 25 minutes.

Either leave the cherry tomatoes raw or <u>toss</u> them with a <u>glug</u> of olive oil and pinch of salt and roast in the oven, stirring regularly, until the liquid is reduced and syrupy, 15 to 25 minutes.

Toss the cauliflower with the tomatoes, parsley (or oil), and olives. Top with the garlic bread crumbs and serve.

variations

w/yogurt, dried cherries + pecans

1 head (2 lb | 8 cups | 910 g) cauliflower, cut into florets

½ cup (120 g) plain yogurt (preferably Greek)

½ cup (70 g) dried cherries

½ cup (2½ oz | 70 g) pecans

½ tsp (3 g) black pepper (as coarsely ground as you can get)

Big pinch of salt

Heat the oven to 400°F (200°C). Roast the cauliflower, <u>toss</u> together with the remaining ingredients, and serve.

w/massaged kale, lemon vinaigrette + parmesan

2 lemons (3 fl oz | 45 ml), zest and juice

½ cup (120 ml) olive oil

4 garlic cloves (0.8 oz | 28 g), minced

1 head (2 lb | 8 cups | 910 g) cauliflower, cut and roasted

1 bunch kale (½ lb | 4 cups | 230 g) (any variety), midribs stripped, torn into bite-size pieces

Salt

4 oz (115 g) Parmesan, grated or shaved into ribbons

Massage the kale (page 251). Combine the lemon zest and juice, olive oil, and garlic. Combine the roasted cauliflower, kale, and lemon dressing with a big pinch of salt, top with Parmesan, and serve.

w/apples, walnuts, raisins + pickled raisins

½ cup (120 ml) apple cider vinegar

1 Tbsp (20 g) honey

⅓ cup (45 g) raisins (golden or regular)

½ cup (120 ml) olive oil

Salt

1 head (2 lb | 8 cups | 910 g) cauliflower, cut and roasted

2 apples (1 lb | 455 g) (preferably tart, like Greening, Mutsu, or Granny Smith), cut into ¼-inch (6-mm) slices

½ cup (60 g) walnuts, toasted (page 24)

Warm the vinegar over low heat until it steams. Remove from the heat and dissolve the honey in the vinegar, then pour over the raisins and let sit for 10 minutes. Stir in the olive oil and a big pinch of salt. Combine the cauliflower and apples, and dress them with the warm raisin dressing. Top with the walnuts, crunching them up a bit as you sprinkle them on.

PURÉED

<u>Chunk</u> the cauliflower to make this recipe. It will all be blended so it doesn't have to be pretty, but remember that the smaller the pieces, the faster it will cook. This is also a perfect recipe to make in advance for a dinner party or a fast midweek meal. Just allow it to cool and then refrigerate; simply reheat on the stovetop or in the oven when you're ready to eat. And purées freeze well, setting you up for a super-fast meal the next time around. This base recipe does have a good deal of cream, but don't replace it with milk; the proteins will split with the long simmer and never become silky·smooth.

cauliflower purée topped w/seared pork cutlet

You can blend this purée in a food processor or blender or with an immersion blender. The smoothness will vary slightly but all methods give a good result. Pork cutlets are traditionally pieces of uncured leg or loin meat pounded thin and cooked like minute steaks in a pan. Ask your butcher for this cut or substitute a chicken breast pounded thin.

Olive oil or butter

1 large onion (½ lb | 1 cup | 230 g), cut into <u>thin slices</u>

2 tsp (12 g) salt

1 cup (240 ml) white wine

1 head (2 lb | 8 cups | 910 g) cauliflower, cut into <u>chunks</u>

2 cups (480 ml) cream

Neutral oil

4 boneless pork cutlets (4 to 6 oz | 115 to 170 g)

¼ cup (35 g) all-purpose flour

Salt and freshly ground black pepper

¼ cup (60 ml) apple cider (dry or sweet) or white wine

1 bag (4 oz | 115 g) arugula

Heat a **glug** of olive oil or a knob of butter in a large sauté pan over medium-low heat. Add the onion and salt, and <u>sweat</u> until tender, about 7 minutes. When soft but not browned, add the white wine. Reduce until almost dry, about 3 minutes, then add the cauliflower <u>chunks</u>.

Add the cream and bring to a simmer, then turn down the heat to avoid a boilover. Cook until the cauliflower is tender, about 20 minutes. Remove from the heat and blend (in batches unless you have a jumbo food processor) until very smooth.

Just before serving, heat a frying pan over medium-high heat with a big <u>glug</u> of neutral oil. Pat the pork dry, dredge in flour, and season with salt and pepper. Panfry the pork on both sides, allowing the cooking side to become golden brown before flipping. To test for doneness, the meat will be firm like a clenched bicep, 3 to 4 minutes per side (cutlets tend to cook quickly because they are thin).

Remove the pork from the pan and <u>deglaze</u> the pan with the apple cider.

Dress the arugula lightly with a <u>glug</u> of olive oil and a pinch of salt. Spoon the purée onto a plate or serving platter, top with the pork cutlets and then the deglazing liquid, and heap the arugula on top.

variations

w/salmon, brown butter + orange zest

Make the same purée, but brown 4 oz (115 g) butter before adding the onions and use 1½ cup (360 ml) cream. Add the zest of 2 oranges when puréeing. Sear one 6-oz (170-g) salmon fillet per person, skin-side down (page 24), and serve with a green salad or dressed spinach.

w/raclette, chives, chard + roasted tomato

Add 4 oz (115 g) raclette (or Swiss cheese) when puréeing the cauliflower. Cut 1 <u>bunch</u> of chard (½ lb | 3 cups | 230 g) into <u>ribbons</u> and dress with a <u>glug</u> of olive oil and ½ cup (120 g) roasted, chopped tomatoes (page 435). Top with 1 <u>bunch</u> of fresh chives, minced.

CAULIFLOWER SOUP W/FRIED SAGE + PECANS

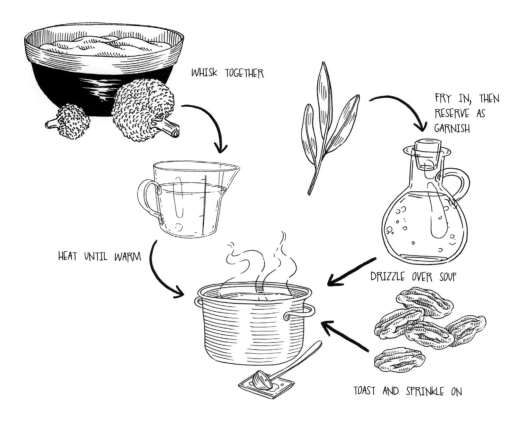

WHISK TOGETHER

FRY IN, THEN RESERVE AS GARNISH

HEAT UNTIL WARM

DRIZZLE OVER SOUP

TOAST AND SPRINKLE ON

celery and celery root

Whenever I think of celery, I hear the voice of Paul Child. He is quoted as saying, "It was Julia all along," in reference to how it took him some time to realize that he loved Julia Child, the woman who had been right in front of him for so long.

I had the same shock of the obvious with celery. I can think of no other vegetable that gets less fanfare; in part, I imagine, because it is so omnipresent in classic cooking. It is one-third of mirepoix, a base of flavors for stocks and sauces. It selflessly plays a supporting role.

Another reason is that the store celery available is often pretty nondescript, its main selling points being its crunch and mild astringency. It is humble and plays well with others.

Farmers' market celery is a horse of a different color—and an almost untamable bucking bronco at that. I have yet to eat a local celery that isn't so stringy, tough, and mouth-numbingly tannic that I can't even chew, let alone enjoy, a mouthful.

What will tame that stallion before harvest is blanching, a technique that shields the inner stalks from the sun, limiting the amount of chlorophyll the cells produce and yielding a more mild, delicate flavor.

Yet each fall, I buy local celery and try. This year I finally found two saving graces—the leaves and some time alone in the oven. The tender foliage gives me the celery flavor I want without the fibrous chew. The stalks can be coaxed into submission with a long, slow cooking time. These techniques renewed my interest in celery as an ingredient in its own right. This fixation now has me buying grocery store celery when locally produced isn't available—though the more mild-mannered, conventional celery needs an additional hit of seasoning, spice, and/or acid to bring it into the spotlight. It also needs a firmer scrub, because conventionally grown celery has some of the highest pesticide retention of all vegetables. Large organic farm celery is a nice middle option—not stringy, no synthetic pesticides.

Like beets and chard, celery and celeriac (celery root) were originally the same plant. Then farmers selected their seed to highlight different characteristics—in celery, long tender stalks and little root; in celeriac, scraggly, even tougher leaves but a big, beautiful, creamy root ball. Whereas stalk celery is assertive, celeriac is mild and crisp, and somehow perfumed with the scent of soil.

Like stalk celery, celeriac can be eaten both raw and cooked. The most classic raw preparation is celeriac rémoulade—grated celery root with a jazzed-up mayo. It is the most refreshing form of coleslaw I've ever had.

Cooked celery root makes people ask, "What is this?" It has the texture of a potato, though less starchy, and the earthiness of a parsnip but without the sweetness. Because it is low in both starch and carbohydrates, it makes a lovely purée and, by extension, soup. You can mash and mash and never worry about rendering it gluey.

To get at the root ball, simply **tip and tail** the ball—the roots tend to have a good amount of sand in their knobby clutches—and with a knife cut away the bumpy exterior. These trimmings are packed with celery flavor, for which the best use is in making stocks. Chuck them into any pot of bone or veggie broth.

When your guests delight in the crisp, astringent stalk or the mild, creamy root and ask, "What is this?" you can coo, "It was celery all along."

HOW TO BUY

- Look for celery stalks that are rigid and not bendy.
- The darker the green, the deeper and more tannic the flavor will be.
- If there are large strings visible on the stalks, be prepared to remove them before eating.
- Look for celery root that is firm when squeezed. It shouldn't be soft or have any obvious signs of rot.
- Dirt will still cling to the roots; that's OK, you'll cut it away.
- If the celery root has its stalks still attached, be prepared to cut those away, as they will soften the root more quickly. Those stalks are good for stocks and soup bases but too intense for me to eat.

HOW TO STORE

- Store both celery and celery root in clean, dry plastic bags in the refrigerator.
- Keep excess water off the roots and stalks to avoid rot.
- Celery root can be stored in cool damp areas like a basement or root cellar, but avoid any big swings in temperature; this will prompt the root to send up a new stalk, making the roots softer and less palatable.

NOTES

- Celery root will oxidize quickly after being cut, so either cut just before being used or store in acidulated water to keep the root from browning unpleasantly.
- The baby leaves in the center of the celery crown are deliciously tender and tasty, so don't discard them.

RAW CELERY ROOT

Raw celery root blends traditional celery astringency with a squeaky, creamy texture. It is refreshing and cuts through rich dressings, pairing well with meats and fish.

celery root salad w/lentils and bagna cauda

When someone asks, "What is your style of food?" I always wish I could make them a bowl of this dish. It is deeply flavorful and balanced: the salty, garlicky bagna cauda with the light, creamy tang of the celery root.

Neutral oil

1 large onion (½ lb | 1 cup | 230 g), cut into thin slices

Salt and freshly ground black pepper

½ cup (120 ml) white wine

2 cups (400 g) black or green lentils

4 cups (1 L) water

2 medium (2 to 3 lb | 3 cups | 910 g to 1.4 kg) celery roots, ends trimmed, peeled, cut into matchsticks

2 lemons (3 fl oz | 90 ml), zest and juice

½ bunch (1.2 oz | ¾ cup | 34 g) parsley, stemmed, leaves kept whole

1 cup (240 ml) bagna cauda (page 60)

Heat a glug of oil in a saucepan and sweat the onion with a big pinch of salt and pepper, about 5 minutes. Add the white wine and cook until evaporated. Add the lentils and toast for about 1 minute. Add the water, bring to a boil, reduce to a simmer, and cook until the lentils are cooked through and the water is evaporated, about 25 minutes.

Dress the celery root with the lemon zest and juice.

When the lentils are cooked, toss them with the celery root, parsley, and bagna cauda until well combined. Taste and adjust the seasoning.

Serve warm or at room temperature. If it gets cold and congealed, simply reheat gently in the oven or a saucepan.

variations

w/kale, apples, walnuts + lemon vinaigrette

2 celery roots (2 to 3 lb | 3 cups | 910 g to 1.4 kg), ends trimmed, peeled, cut into <u>matchsticks</u>

1 <u>bunch</u> kale (½ lb | 4 cups | 230 g), <u>midribs</u> <u>stripped</u>, cut into <u>ribbons</u>, and massaged (page 251)

2 tart apples (1 lb | 455 g) Greening, Mutsu, or Granny Smith, cut into thin half-moons

1 cup (120 g) walnuts, toasted (page 24), roughly chopped or crumbled

½ cup (120 ml) lemon vinaigrette (page 58)

Salt and freshly ground black pepper

w/dried cherries, arugula + garlic bread crumbs

2 celery roots (2 to 3 lb | 3 cups | 910 g to 1.4 kg), ends trimmed, peeled, cut into <u>matchsticks</u>

1 cup (140 g) dried cherries

1 bag (4 oz | 115 g) arugula

½ cup (70 g) garlic bread crumbs (page 48)

<u>Glug</u> of olive oil

Salt

w/tuna mayo + wild rice

2 celery roots (2 to 3 lb | 3 cups | 910 g to 1.4 kg), ends trimmed, peeled, cut into <u>matchsticks</u>

2 cups (360 g) wild rice, cooked (page 43)

½ <u>bunch</u> parsley (1.2 oz | ¾ cup | 34 g), roughly chopped, or a 4-oz (115-g) bag of hearty greens

Salt

Olive oil

½ cup (120 g) tuna mayo (page 61)

PURÉED

I have never made this purée without someone asking incredulously, "What is this?" This purée is sweet and creamy but still tastes brightly of celery. It also hits one of my key marks of a good recipe: calling for only a handful of ingredients. In the first recipe and first variation, the purée is left plain; in the second and third variations, adding the other flavors to the purée makes it present very differently. Like all purées in this book, it freezes well, so feel free to make a big batch and save some for other quick meals, including thinning the purée with water or stock to make a very fast soup or schmearing on toast for sandwiches.

celery root purée topped w/seared chicken thigh and green salad

This dish is all about texture: silky smooth purée, crispy-skinned chicken thighs, bright crunchy salad greens.

Neutral oil or butter

1 onion (½ lb | 1 cup | 230 g), cut into thin slices

½ tsp (3 g) salt

½ cup (120 ml) white wine or stock

2 to 3 (2 to 3 lb | 910 g to 1.4 kg) celery roots, ends trimmed, peeled, cut into chunks

1 cup (240 ml) cream

4 chicken thighs (6 to 8 oz | 170 to 230 g each), at room temperature

Salt and freshly ground black pepper

1 bag (4 oz | 115 g) salad greens

¼ cup (60 ml) apple cider vinegar

½ cup (120 ml) olive oil

Heat a glug of neutral oil or knob of butter in a saucepan over medium-low heat and sweat the onions with the salt until tender, about 7 minutes. Add the white wine and cook until evaporated, about 3 minutes.

Add the celery root and cream, bring to a boil, and reduce to a simmer. Cover with a cartouche and cook until the celery root is fork-tender, about 20 minutes. Remove from the heat and blend in a food processor until smooth. Taste and adjust the seasoning.

Pat the skin of the chicken dry and season liberally with salt and pepper.

Heat a glug of neutral oil in a large frying pan over high heat and sear the skin-side of the thighs until golden brown and crispy, 8 to 10 minutes (page 24). Flip and cook the other side until the chicken is cooked through, 7 to 10 minutes.

Toss the greens with vinegar, olive oil, and salt and pepper.

Divvy the purée among 4 dinner plates, top each with a chicken thigh, and garnish with green salad.

variations

w/grilled portobello mushrooms + herb oil

Top the purée with grilled mushrooms, then drizzle with basil oil or parsley oil (page 56).

w/mustard, cheddar + sausage

Add ¼ cup (60 g) whole-grain or Dijon mustard and ½ cup (40 g) grated Cheddar to the purée and serve with roasted sausages.

w/dill, lemon + seared salmon

Add 5 sprigs dill and the zest and juice of 1 lemon to the celeriac purée, and serve with crispy-skinned salmon (page 24) and greens.

RAW

Like I said in the introduction, most stalk celery is pretty meh, but when paired with an acidic bite and a good dose of seasoning, it can be a revelation. If you have the intense local celery, the leaves alone can replace the celery stalk in these recipes, which will make it even more surprising.

celery stalk salad w/grapes, apples, goat cheese, and pecans

This flavor combination is straight Waldorf salad territory but with goat cheese rather than mayo. Use any color grapes but choose the most flavorful ones you can get your hands on. Serve this on its own or as a side with something like roast chicken or seared fish. The variations that follow can also be served solo or as second fiddle. I particularly like the blue cheese version with beef, and the lemon one with lamb.

This is also one of the rare times I suggest an amount of salt beyond a big pinch or two. To make this salad really sing, it needs the extra lift of salt and pepper. Naturally dial it in as you see fit. If you are sensitive to salt, start with half as much and add the rest as you like it.

1 head (8 oz | 4 cups | 230 g) celery, root end and stalk tips removed, leaves reserved, stalks cut in diagonal slices

1 lb (455 g) grapes, halved

1 tart apple (½ lb | 230 g), preferably Greening, Mutsu, or Granny Smith, cut into ¼-inch (6-mm) slices

½ cup (120 ml) olive oil

¼ cup (60 ml) apple cider vinegar

1 cup (120 g) pecans, toasted (page 24)

¼ tsp (2 g) salt

½ tsp (3 g) freshly ground black pepper

4 oz (115 g) fresh goat cheese

Combine all the ingredients except the goat cheese (include the celery leaves) and <u>toss</u>. Taste, adjusting the seasoning as desired. Transfer to a serving platter and dot with the goat cheese.

variations

w/blue cheese + walnuts

1 head (8 oz | 4 cups | 230 g) celery

½ cup (60 g) walnuts, toasted (page 24)

¾ cup (180 ml) apple cider vinaigrette (page 58)

¼ tsp (2 g) salt

¼ tsp (2 g) freshly ground black pepper

4 oz (115 g) blue cheese

w/lemon, capers + thyme

1 head (8 oz | 4 cups | 230 g) celery

2 lemons (3 fl oz | 90 ml), zest and juice

2 Tbsp (18 g) capers

5 sprigs thyme, leaves stripped

½ cup (120 ml) olive oil

¼ tsp (2 g) salt

¼ tsp (1 g) chili flakes (optional)

w/dill, chickpeas + yogurt

1 head (8 oz | 4 cups | 230 g) celery

One 12-oz can (340 g) chickpeas, drained and rinsed

5 sprigs dill, roughly chopped

¼ cup (60 g) yogurt

¼ cup (60 ml) olive oil

1 lemon (1½ fl oz | 45 ml), zest and juice

¼ tsp (2 g) salt

W/TOMATOES + BACON

W/ORANGE, GOAT
CHEESE + PAPRIKA

W/GARLIC, LEMON,
THYME + CAPERS

BRAISED

Like slow-cooked fennel, braised celery feels both refreshingly new and comfortingly old-fashioned. It should be melty and bathed in the cooking liquid's flavorful sauce, a product of the combination of wine and butter. If you are using the very intense local celery stalks, you may want to peel the outside with a vegetable peeler. If you have cooked it to the point where everything else is soft except the strings, you can also peel them out of the stalk after it has cooked and cooled, but that can be a hassle.

braised stalk celery

This recipe is delicious in its simplicity—one of those magical dishes when the end is more than the sum of its parts. The only fussy bit is deciding how much celery to use. The recipe is written for one head of celery because most grocery store celery is very big and a quarter head per person is plenty. If it is small, use two; if long, cut it as needed to make it fit in the pan. I like to leave the core intact for ease of serving after it is cooked, but it isn't critical.

What goes with that? Because the celery ends up very soft and silky, I like to pair this with something crunchy—either roasted chicken thighs; a fillet of crispy-skinned, seared salmon; grilled skirt steak; or garlicky white beans and a salad of spinach with dukkah (page 63) or sunflower seeds.

1 head (8 oz | 230 g) celery, root end and stalk tips removed

¼ cup (60 ml) olive oil

¼ cup (60 ml) white wine or apple cider

1 cup (240 ml) chicken stock, fish stock, or water

2 oz (55 g) butter

1 tsp (6 g) each salt and freshly ground black pepper

5 sprigs thyme and/or 3 bay leaves

Heat the oven to 325°F (165°C).

Cut the celery head in half lengthwise, removing any battered outer stalks but retaining the root end that holds the stalks together.

In a baking dish, lay the celery-head halves cut-side up. Pour the oil, wine, and stock into the bottom of the dish.

Dot the butter over the top, sprinkle with the salt and pepper, and scatter the herbs over the lot. Cover with foil and bake until fork-tender, about 45 minutes.

Remove from the oven, discard the herbs, and serve the celery with the liquid spooned over the top.

variations

w/tomatoes + bacon

Add 1 pint (300 g) halved cherry tomatoes, 2 onions cut into wedges, and 4 oz (115 g) bacon cut into ½-inch (12-mm) chunks.

w/garlic, lemon, thyme + capers

Add 3 garlic cloves, zest (left in long peels), the juice of 2 lemons, 5 sprigs thyme, and 1 Tbsp (9 g) capers.

w/orange, goat cheese + paprika

Add 1 Tbsp (7 g) smoked paprika and zest and juice of 2 oranges; dot with 4 oz (115 g) goat cheese before serving.

corn

At the start of my sophomore year in college, I brought a friend to my family home. It was early fall, when tomatoes and corn are at their best. We stopped by for lunch, and my mom made BLTs, green salad, and corn on the cob. As the bacon was frying she asked me to get six ears of corn and three tomato "slicers." My friend assumed she was talking about from the refrigerator and scanned the shelves.

"Oh, no. From the garden," I said. A blank stare was his response.

He was from Chicago (actually Deerfield, a northern suburb of Chicago, but he always just said "Chicago"). Despite the locale, I'm pretty sure he had outside space where he grew up, but they clearly hadn't had a garden.

We went out the back door, down the hill, and to the end of the yard to our vegetable patch with its slightly crooked rows. We snapped the corn from the stalks while finishing our conversation about Toni Morrison's *Beloved*—reading from our shared class. We talked about cadence and relationships of triangulation as we pinched the heavy, irregularly shaped Brandywine tomatoes from the vine and headed back to the house.

On the brick patio, I stopped and started shucking the ears, peeling back the light green husks and revealing the cool white corn silk inside. There were a couple of corn worms at the base of two of the cobs. My friend nearly jumped out of his skin.

I tried to reassure him, almost apologetically. "We'll just cut that part off. Such a small patch isn't worth spraying, so there are bugs."

We walked into the house and deposited the produce on the counter. I moved to plunge the lettuce greens into the cool water filling the sink. My friend, standing next to me, whispered with a laugh, "I never knew you were sooo country, farm girl," employing the hee-haw accent so often adopted when depicting rural residents.

I was again confronted with the feeling that my country upbringing did not fully prepare me for the world I was beginning to know in college. I often struggled with feeling naïve or uncultured by my lack of experience. These feelings were extra confusing, because my family was well-traveled and prioritized education. In the face of my fellow students, I felt my identity slipping from well-rounded to hopelessly ignorant. Suddenly having a garden represented my backwardness instead of all the lessons learned in the yard—biology, botany, earth science, and self-reliance. I felt shame. I unconsciously slumped.

My mom's back stiffened. She looked at him over her glasses with a raised eyebrow and spoke with her voice ringing like a bell: "You sling 'farm girl' like it's an insult. Well, from what I've seen, there are all sorts of ways to be raised and get an education. Don't mistake where that learning happens with the depth or the quality of the knowledge gained. Because in addition to all the books we've read and all the science that nature teaches, we 'farm girls' also always know how to feed ourselves—and others, if they're lucky. Additionally, not one of us speaks like that. Now, I suggest you go wash your hands. Lunch is ready."

As she spoke, my back straightened up again.

You see, my mom was tough as hell. Her parents had told her that daughters (unlike sons) weren't worth educating, so she put herself through school and became a nurse. A coworker watched her and said, "You need more." She went back to school to become a Certified Registered Nurse of Anesthesia. In a time when women were still referred to as "girls" in the workplace, she managed herself and her patients without a doc around. She took care of hers long before she met my father.

Dad saw her during surgery while he was in medical school. She married him after much persuasion. She pushed him to go into anesthesia and helped support him as he finished his schooling. Six months into his residency, he needed to move back to Michigan to support his parents and their ailing farm. She, of course, moved with him. They were a unit, they were equal, and she'd always wanted to have goats.

He farmed his parents' land while working as a medical administrator. She practiced anesthesia and pitched in with him when she got home. She pioneered driving a tractor in a tube top because she hated tan lines and had no reservations about being foxy. She calculated dosages and acre yields in her head, and when my dad looked at her and said, "Jo, we've moved back here with no money and no land of our own, and I'm a doctor who farms for a living," she smiled and said, "Let's have a baby."

They had three girls.

As the farm stabilized, he went back to Chicago (Chicago, Chicago) to finish his anesthesia residency. She held down the home front, made dinner, and taught us to get ourselves up and ready for school because she was gone long before we needed to be. She worked three hundred days of being on call and picked up extra shifts in the ER to be sure the bills got paid. We all went to Chicago every other weekend because letters and phone calls were never going to replace being together.

Dad finished school. He moved back home and started his practice in Holland, Michigan. They had medical privileges at each other's hospitals to be able to go and help as needed. His practice, her role at her hospital, and their daughters grew.

Now they had more time together—back to dating, with no kids around to ruin the mood. Saturdays were filled with weekend things—no longer just more work. Both practices were stable. They had raised women who knew their worth. They could take the afternoon and tend a garden if they wanted.

She wasn't about to allow someone she saw as a soft-handed punk from somewhere devoid of deer and fields imply that being "country" had any sort of podunk, uneducated implications.

Not in her kitchen.

Not in front of her girl or her man.

Not now and not ever.

HOW TO BUY

- A farming friend once told me that she never even starts eating sweet corn until September when it is the sweetest. I tend to agree—and also, the delayed treat of corn staves off my diving into the fall crops before all the summer foods are done. She also said once, "Why do people want Brussels sprouts in September when there is corn, and we're going to be eating Brussels until February?" Point taken.
- You want fresh-looking greens and tassels on unhusked corn.
- Peel back the husk to find bright plump kernels.

HOW TO STORE

- The longer corn is stored, the more of its sugar will convert to starch, so eating quickly is best.
- If you need to store, keep in a paper bag either on the counter or in the refrigerator.

NOTES

- If you see a wormhole on either the top or the bottom of the ear, there is most likely a corn worm inside. They don't do too much damage (probably ate a few of the kernels) and are a good sign that the corn isn't sprayed.
- When sweet corn is out of season, substitute frozen corn for the fresh. It is tastier and less processed than canned corn, and performs just as well as straight from the cob.
- Undeveloped kernels are a sign of poor pollination. All the kernels that are developed are just fine.
- If substituting frozen corn for fresh kernels, assume each ear equals about 4 oz (115 g) frozen kernels.

GRILLED CORN WITH
PARMESAN BUTTER
& CHILI

WITH ROASTED GARLIC
PURÉE & PARSLEY

WITH LEMON BUTTER,
DUKKAH (PAGE 63)
& MINT

WITH MAYO, PARMESAN,
CHILI FLAKES, CILANTRO
& LIME

GRILLED

grilled corn on the cob w/parmesan butter

Chomping corn from the cob is one of summertime's most tactile pleasures. Using regular table butter is just fine, but replacing it with a quick compound butter makes corn on the cob seem like more of a dinner party dish. Plus, the flavor of the three different fats together feels unexpected, as does the heat from the chili flakes and the cool of the parsley. The method for toasting the chili flakes is tried and true for me (an unabashed multitasker known for burning spices by forgetting them in the pan).

½ cup (120 ml) neutral oil

½ tsp (2 g) chili flakes

4 oz (115 g) butter, at room temperature

½ tsp (3 g) salt

2 oz (55 g) Parmesan, grated

½ bunch parsley (1.2 oz | ¾ cup | 34 g), leaves only, chopped

6 ears corn, shucked

Heat the neutral oil in a frying pan until it begins to smoke. Add the chili flakes and remove from the heat. Let steep in the oil for 10 minutes.

In a stand mixer or a bowl, combine the butter, salt, chili oil, Parmesan, and parsley. Paddle until well combined. Taste and add salt as needed.

Lay a sheet of plastic wrap or parchment on the counter and spoon on the butter in a strip. Gently roll into a round log, tightening with each pass, and chill until firm (this butter can be frozen for later use).

When you're ready to grill, heat a grill at medium to high heat. Cut the butter into coins.

Grill the corn until the kernels are golden brown and slightly charred. Top with the butter rounds and serve immediately.

variations

w/mayo (page 61), parmesan, chili flakes, cilantro + lime

w/lemon butter, dukkah (page 63) + mint

w/roasted garlic purée + parsley

ROASTED

You can roast corn either in a pan on the stovetop or in the oven. The stovetop method, described in the recipe, requires more active attention. To roast in the oven, <u>toss</u> the kernels with a <u>glug</u> of neutral or olive oil and a big pinch of salt, and spread evenly on a baking sheet. Roast anywhere from 350°F to 425°F (180°C to 220°C), stirring every 7 to 10 minutes because the corn near the edges will darken more quickly. Both yield corn candy: golden kernels with crispy browned edges.

corn kernel salad w/soybeans, cherry tomatoes, and basil

The best way to cut kernels from the cob is to take a bowl much larger than you think you'll need (trust me on this), hold the stem end of the corn like a handle, and cut the kernels away from you into the bowl. You need a large bowl to catch the juice that will inevitably splatter.

Neutral oil

4 ears sweet corn (½ cup | 70 g per ear), shucked, kernels cut off

Salt and freshly ground black pepper

1 small (2 oz | ¼ cup | 55 g) red onion or shallot or any onion you have including scallion, sliced

3 garlic cloves (0.6 oz | 17 g), minced

1 cup (240 ml) white wine

8 oz (230 g) soybeans, preferably fresh or frozen (don't use dried)

1 pint (16 oz | 455 g) cherry tomatoes, halved

2 Tbsp (30 g) butter (feel free to use Parmesan butter)

3 sprigs basil

Dollops of sour cream

Heat a glug of neutral oil in a large frying pan over high heat until shimmering. Add the corn and pinches of salt and pepper. Allow to brown without stirring, about 7 minutes—stir too much and it won't caramelize. When lightly browned, give a good flip or stir to cook the other side, about 7 minutes. Transfer the corn to a bowl.

Add another glug of oil to the pan and sweat the onion and garlic until tender, about 7 minutes. Add the wine and reduce by half.

Add the soybeans and allow to steam in the residual wine until the beans are bright green (they are hard to overcook!) and the wine is fully reduced, about 5 minutes. Add the tomatoes to the soybeans. Add the butter and let it melt and make everything glossy. Combine with the corn; taste and adjust the seasoning.

Tear the basil leaves over the whole lot and garnish with the sour cream. Serve warm or at room temperature.

variations

w/roasted eggplant, mint + feta

1 eggplant (1 lb | 455 g), roasted (page 187)	4 oz (115 g) feta, crumbled	8 mint sprigs, leaves torn

Toss together the corn and eggplant. Garnish with the feta and torn mint leaves. A drizzle of chili oil (page 55) would not be out of place on this salad.

w/shaved zucchini, dill + sour cream

2 medium zucchini, shaved (page 385)	8 sprigs dill, chopped	Salt
	Olive oil	¼ cup (60 g) sour cream

Toss the roasted corn with the shaved zucchini, chopped dill, a glug of olive oil, and a pinch of salt until coated. Taste and adjust the seasoning. Garnish by dotting the sour cream over the whole salad.

w/roasted mushrooms, marjoram + fromage blanc

½ lb (230 g) mushrooms, roasted (page 24)	5 sprigs marjoram or oregano, leaves picked	¼ cup (60 g) fromage blanc or ricotta

Combine the roasted corn with the roasted mushrooms and marjoram leaves. Toss to coat. Adjust seasoning and transfer to a serving platter. Garnish all over with dots of the fromage blanc.

CORN SOUP W/CHILI OIL,
SOUR CREAM + CILANTRO

W/ARUGULA +
ROASTED MUSHROOMS

W/GRILLED PEPPERS, BASIL + YOGURT

PURÉED

Unlike all the other purées in this book, the corn purée won't get as silky smooth because of the structure of the corn kernels. The soup variation will get very smooth if blended in a burr blender for long enough, because the extra liquid facilitates the movement in the blender—something I can't get to happen in the food processor.

cream-less corn w/sautéed greens and seared salmon

Creamed corn conjures images of cafeterias and frozen TV dinners. But freshly cut corn, blended with a touch of butter to engage the natural starch in the kernels, is as surprising as it is satisfying. Making a quick broth with the cobs ensures that every last drop of flavor and starch is pulled from them.

6 ears sweet corn (½ cup | 70 g per ear), shucked, kernels cut off, cob liquid reserved

Neutral oil

2 sprigs thyme

1 medium red onion or shallot (4 oz | ½ cup | 115 g), cut into thin slices

Salt

4 Tbsp (55 g) butter

Freshly ground black pepper

6 fillets of salmon (6-oz | 170-g), skin on

2 or 3 bunches kale (1 lb | 8 cups | 455 g) or any hearty greens you have (chard, cabbage, beet greens, or a mix), cut into ribbons

2 garlic cloves (0.4 oz | 14 g), minced

¼ cup (60 ml) white wine

¼ tsp (1 g) chili flakes

In a medium pot, place the cobs and just enough water to cover and bring to a simmer for 10 minutes. Remove the cobs from the liquid, giving them one final scrape with the back of a knife.

Bring the liquid to a boil and reduce to 2 cups (480 ml).

In a new pot (or transfer the boiled liquid to a bowl and reuse the pot if you like), heat a glug of neutral oil over high heat until shimmering, and fry the thyme, about 1 minute. Reduce the heat to medium and <u>sweat</u> the onion with a big pinch of salt, about 5 minutes.

Remove the thyme sprigs and add the corn kernels and the 2 cups (480 ml) cob broth. Bring to a boil, then remove from the heat.

Use an immersion blender or food processor to whiz the corn until well blended, knowing there will be some chunks left. Add the butter, a pinch of salt, and pepper. Taste and adjust the seasoning.

In a large frying pan, heat a glug of oil until smoking. Season the salmon fillets with salt and pepper. Pat the skin-side dry and sear until medium (page 24). Remove from the pan, transfer to a plate, and let rest.

Wipe the frying pan clean and heat another glug of neutral oil over high heat until smoking. Add the greens and lightly fry. Add the garlic, a pinch of salt, the wine, and the chili flakes and let cook until the liquid is reduced.

Spoon the corn onto dinner plates. Add a big forkful of greens to each and top with the salmon, skin-side up.

variations

w/arugula + roasted mushrooms

1 bag (4oz | 115 g) arugula

Olive oil

Salt and freshly ground
black pepper

½ lb (230 g) mushrooms,
roasted (page 24)

Spoon the corn into four bowls or plates. Dress the arugula with a
glug of olive oil and pinch of salt and pepper. Spoon the roasted
mushrooms (warm or room temperature) over the portions of
creamed corn and top with the dressed arugula.

w/grilled peppers, basil + yogurt

2 peppers, grilled and cut
into ribbons (page 327)

¼ cup (60 g) yogurt

8 sprigs basil, leaves torn

Spoon the corn into four bowls or plates. Top with the (warm or
room-temperature) peppers. Dot or drizzle the yogurt over the
whole thing. Garnish with the torn basil leaves. (A healthy spoonful
of dukkah [page 63] over this is delicious, too.)

corn soup w/chili oil, sour cream + cilantro

Thin 3 cups (720 ml) corn purée with 2 cups (480 ml) water or
chicken stock and 1 tsp (6 g) salt. Bring to a boil, taste, and serve
with a dollop of sour cream, drizzle of chili oil (page 55), and
sprinkle of cilantro over the top.

cucumbers

My earliest memories of cucumbers are of sitting in the back of
a five-ton wagon being pulled behind a combine tractor, with
pickling cucumbers flowing off a conveyor belt into the wagon.
The vines and leaves separated and rolled into the field rows. My
sisters and I had the job of sitting in the wagon and sorting the
cucumbers as they fell, throwing out any that were broken or
the wrong size or shape.

This is one of those jobs that felt very important—I was the
final quality check before the wagon (one of a three-wagon-long
chain) was driven to the pickle processing plant for delivery. It is
also one of those jobs that, as I look back on it, I truly have no idea
if it was actually helpful or a way to keep us occupied as the real
work took place.

I suppose it doesn't really matter if the jobs weren't truly
helpful; I felt a part of the farm. By sorting the pickles that fell
as a waterfall into the wagon, hoeing the spiky nightshade from
between the plants, and delivering a half-gallon jug of cold water
with big cubes of ice still in it via bright red three-wheeler, I was
an active member of the family farm.

My dad grew up on his family's pickle farm—his mother
a school teacher and his father farming full time—but never
intended to be a farmer. He was the first member of his family
to go to college and then to medical school. He moved to

San Francisco to complete a three-year anesthesia residency before starting to practice. Six months into that residency, the family farm started to falter, and he moved back to help. Dad has never described this to me as family loyalty alone. His parents had invested in him, splitting the revenue of the farm three ways, with his third going toward his education. He couldn't have become a doctor without the farm, and it was time to give back.

He spent ten years as a medical administrator during the day and farming at night. I was insulated from the stress that this situation must have caused. All I knew was that we ate dinner at ten o'clock at night because we ate as a family and that was when Dad came home.

Oddly enough, we didn't eat cucumbers that much. Except that my mom would always make a lightly pickled version to keep in the refrigerator. She would slice up about ten cucumbers and one red onion, cover the whole thing with water, and add several pinches of salt and **glugs** of vinegar. We would pull the cucumbers from the Tupperware when we wanted a snack and then just slice in more cucumber when it got low. In my memory we would refill the same tub for months on end, though in practice it was probably refreshed every week or so. There are no proportions; it should just taste slightly salty and slightly vinegary.

There are four general types of cucumbers: English, American, pickling, and lemon. The English, the classic salad cucumber, grows as one long even fruit with very moist flesh and small seeds. Their skin is thin (insert joke here), and so they are often packaged wrapped in plastic to protect the flesh from bruising during transport.

American cucumbers are coarser and have a thicker skin (insert joke here) and more torpedo-like fruit. In general, the seeds are bigger, and the skin is prickly. Choose medium-size ones; very small ones lack flavor, very large ones will have tough skin and unpalatably big seeds. I now like this variety best for my mom's refrigerator salad because the skin holds the slices together nicely and it doesn't get soft if left in the water for more than a week at a time.

Pickling cucumbers, which we grew, are smaller, with drier flesh, and a small seed cavity, making them better for preservation because there is less water in the cells to dilute the brine and allow for rot. These are harder to find in the grocery store but usually show up at the farmers' market for home canners. I like this variety best for **blistering** cucumbers, because the drier flesh means that you can get a good sear and not just a weird soggy vegetable. Beyond pickling cucumbers, look for Persian cucumbers that are an older variety showing up lately. They are also smaller and really great for preserving or searing.

Lemon cucumbers are one of those new/old vegetables that has been grown for ages but fell out of favor as the industry mechanized. It has been revitalized by small growers who can explain what it is to customers at the market. Lemon cucumbers are round and yellow—looking, you guessed it, like a lemon. They have a moderately tough-textured skin with a slight tang in the bite. You can use them anywhere you'd use another cucumber.

For our family, pickle farming is not central to our identity anymore. As we have moved away or moved on, it remains our foundation but is about as relevant to our everyday life as the pickle ornament on our Christmas tree every year. The farm is still running, though it looks very different. Meals are still the way we connect as a family. I still bring my dad ice-cold water when he's working outside, though delivered by car because three-wheelers are incredibly unsafe and not allowed on the roads.

HOW TO BUY

- Look for rigid skin without wrinkles, which indicate age and broken cells under the skin.
- Most cucumbers have a pale underside where the sun hasn't developed the chlorophyll in the cells.
- Avoid cucumbers with obvious yellowing (unless it is a lemon cucumber), which can indicate age and rot.

HOW TO STORE

- Store in a cool dark place or the refrigerator. They will last longer in the refrigerator but don't have to be in there if you don't have space.
- If they have been chilled in a refrigerator, then keep them there. Quick changes in temperature stress the cells and cause them to break down more quickly.
- If storing in the refrigerator, store in a plastic bag to keep the skins firm and tight.

NOTES

- If you find cucumber skins unpalatable, peel in strips creating a beach ball effect. You will minimize the amount of tough skin but keep some texture and flavor of the skin intact.
- Cucumbers hold a ton of water in their cells. Avoid salting the cucumbers much before serving, as the water will leach from the cells and make the whole dish watery and the texture of the cucumber more rubbery.
- If preserving cucumbers, salting in advance will help ensure that the acid and salt preserve the cucumber by removing excess water.
- Cucumber and melons are in the same family, and if you grow them near each other, the cucumbers will prevent the melon from ripening. (Plants are so weird and cool.)
- Some find cucumbers bitter. There is an old technique for removing the bitterness by slicing the flower end (non-stem side) and rubbing the cut sides together, creating a foam as the liquid in the skin is drawn out. I haven't found this to make a bit of difference, but it is kind of fun and worth a shot if you taste bitterness in cucumbers.

RAW

It is no surprise that cucumbers are tasty raw. What can be surprising is how cutting them into different shapes changes their texture and therefore their role in a dish. Consider cutting cucumbers into large planks to make them more of a star. Cut them into half-moons, matching the size of the other ingredients, to put them on equal footing. Slice them paper thin and heap them together as a side dish.

cucumber salad w/cherry tomatoes, parsley oil, and cottage cheese

The cooling feel of cucumbers pairs incredibly well with any sort of dairy, especially on a hot day. That crisp quasi-blandness is a great foil for very spicy or acidic elements in a dish. Here the cherry tomatoes and parsley oil add the acid and astringency to lift the cucumber flavor. In the variations, the chili oil, lemon, and curry yogurt contrast with the silky, cold flesh, but truly the sky's the limit on how to complement and challenge the steadfast characteristics of the cucumber. Similarly, not everyone loves cottage cheese as much as I do. Swap it for torn pieces of fresh mozzarella or Greek yogurt, or skip dairy all together.

3 cucumbers (8 oz | 3 cups | 230 g), any variety or a mix

1 pint cherry tomatoes (16 oz | 455 g), halved; use 1 cup roasted (page 435) if the fresh aren't tasty

Olive oil

½ tsp (3 g) salt

½ tsp (3 g) black pepper

1 cup (230 g) cottage cheese

¼ cup (60 ml) parsley oil (page 56), or use the leaves of ½ bunch fresh parsley (1.2 oz | ¾ cup | 34 g) and ¼ cup (60 ml) oil if you prefer

Cut a little piece off the end of each cucumber and taste. If the skin is thick, peel the cucumber or half peel it in alternating stripes like a beach ball. Cut the cucumber into rounds, planks, or a large dice, removing the seeds if they are distractingly large.

Just before serving, toss the cucumbers with the tomatoes and a big glug of olive oil and the salt and pepper. (If your tomatoes are not super flavorful, salt them in advance to bump up the flavor of the tomatoes as the salt leaches water from the flesh, then add the cucumbers, oil, and pepper just before serving.) Taste and adjust the seasoning.

Spoon the cottage cheese onto a platter and top with the cucumber salad. Drizzle with the parsley oil and serve.

variations

w/chili oil, melon, feta + mint

3 cucumbers (8 oz | 3 cups | 230 g), any variety or a mix

½ melon (1 lb | 455 g) (I like cantaloupe best), sliced into <u>chunks</u>

4 oz (115 g) feta, crumbled

6 sprigs mint

¼ cup (60 ml) chili oil (page 55)

Olive oil

Salt and freshly ground black pepper

w/red onion, lemon vinaigrette + parsley

3 cucumbers (8 oz | 3 cups | 230 g), any variety or a mix

1 medium (4 oz | ½ cup | 115 g) red onion, <u>shaved</u>

1 <u>bunch</u> parsley (2.4 oz | 1½ cups | 68 g), stemmed, leaves kept whole

½ cup (120 ml) lemon vinaigrette (page 58)

w/carrots, summer squash, crispy chickpeas + curry yogurt

¼ cup (60 ml) neutral oil

1 Tbsp (6 g) curry powder

½ cup (120 g) yogurt

3 cucumbers (8 oz | 3 cups | 230 g)

3 carrots (9 oz | 255 g), <u>shaved</u> into <u>ribbons</u>

2 medium (16 oz | 455 g) summer squash, thinly <u>shaved</u>

2 cups (350 g) crispy chickpeas (page 45)

½ <u>bunch</u> cilantro (1 oz | ½ cup | 30 g), stemmed, leaves left whole

Salt

Heat the oil in a large frying pan until shimmering. Remove from the heat, add the curry powder, and allow it to <u>bloom</u> off the heat, about 5 minutes. Whisk the curry oil into the yogurt. <u>Toss</u> the cucumbers with the carrots, squash, chickpeas, cilantro, and a pinch of salt. Taste and adjust the seasoning.

BLISTERED

In cooking school, we made buttered cucumbers, which are the most disgusting thing I've ever eaten (in my humble opinion). By peeling and cooking the cucumbers, the characteristic crunch was rendered at best slippery, at worst mushy. I swore off ever cooking a cucumber. Then my friend Tim Mazurek (of the lovely food blog *Lottie + Doof*) wrote about charring cucumbers, and I was newly intrigued. I tried it and was in love. The key is to get a ragingly hot frying pan, to blot as much of the liquid as possible from the cut side of the cucumber to ensure a good sear, and to cut the cucumber large enough to keep the internal structure of the vegetable in place even after being cooked. For doneness, I look for a dark, almost burnt crust, and a slight softness to the cucumber structure. Leave the skins on the cucumbers when <u>blistering</u>, as they will act as insurance to keep the cucumber together even after cooked. The slightly burnt flavor of the charred skin combined with the warm temperature epitomizes how changing one little thing can make a vegetable feel new and fresh, reinvigorating its role on your table.

It is best to source a drier-flesh cucumber for this, but you can certainly cook any cucumber you have on hand. Just be sure to really blot the skin dry and don't be scared that it might pop as the water hits the hot oil.

cucumber w/cumin yogurt and parsley

I tend to use Greek yogurt for this because I like the thick texture. If using traditional yogurt, it will be easier to drizzle. Pick your poison. If your onion is making you tear up while cutting, give it a soak in cold water to wick away some of the bite. Then drain and carry on as you would.

3 unpeeled cucumbers (8 oz | 230 g), cut into thick irregular chunks

¼ cup (60 ml) olive oil, plus more for frying

2 tsp (6 g) cumin seed

1 cup (240 g) yogurt

½ tsp (3 g) salt, plus more for seasoning

1 small red onion or shallot (2 oz | ¼ cup | 55 g), thinly shaved

1 bunch parsley (2.4 oz | 1½ cups | 68 g), stemmed, leaves whole or roughly chopped

Lay out the cucumbers on paper towels, dabbing moisture away from the cut sides.

Heat the oil in a large frying pan until shimmering. Remove from the heat, add the cumin seed, and allow to bloom, about 3 minutes. When fragrant, scrape the cumin oil into the yogurt, add the salt, and stir to combine.

Heat the frying pan with an additional glug of oil until smoking. Sear the cucumbers (in batches if necessary) without crowding the pan, allowing enough space for the steam to evaporate. Hold your nerve and let the skin blister and burn slightly (watch out for splatter). Flip to sear the other cut sides.

Remove from the pan and sprinkle with salt.

Toss the cucumber with the onion and parsley. Taste and adjust the seasoning.

Dot with the cumin yogurt and serve.

variations

w/peaches, mint + chili oil

3 unpeeled cucumbers (8 oz | 230 g), cut into thick irregular <u>chunks</u>

2 Tbsp (30 ml) chili oil (page 55)

2 peaches (1 lb | 455 g), sliced

6 sprigs mint, leaves torn off

Salt

Blister the cucumbers, <u>toss</u> together with chili oil, peaches, mint, and a pinch of salt. Taste, adjust, and serve.

w/buttermilk, tomato + herb salad

3 unpeeled cucumbers (8 oz | 230 g), cut into thick, irregular <u>chunks</u>

1 pint (1 lb | 455 g) cherry tomatoes, halved

¾ cup (180 ml) buttermilk

Salt and freshly ground black pepper

2 cups (80 g) picked fresh herbs: any/all of parsley, mint, cilantro, tarragon, dill, chervil, chives, borage, lemon balm

Blister the cucumbers and <u>toss</u> with the tomatoes, buttermilk, a big pinch of salt, and several grinds of black pepper. Taste, adjust the seasoning, and transfer to a serving platter. Garnish with handfuls of the herb salad.

w/red onion, vinegar + dill

1 medium (4 oz | ½ cup | 115 g) red onion, cut into <u>thin slices</u>

¼ cup (60 ml) apple cider vinegar

2 Tbsp (30 g) sugar

1 tsp (6 g) salt

3 unpeeled cucumbers (8 oz | 230 g), cut into thick, irregular <u>chunks</u>

5 sprigs dill, roughly chopped

Combine the onion with the vinegar, sugar, and salt. <u>Blister</u> the cucumbers and <u>toss</u> with the onion mixture. Garnish with the dill and serve.

eggplant

It's hot as blazes outside, and the eggplants are just coming in. The lake finally feels warm. There's a veil of sweat on my back throughout the day. I'm cooking dinner in a dress because, after a swim, I can't with pants. The eggplants are ready. Transformed from a yellow-flecked, purple flower to glossy-skinned, heavy-fleshed rounds. Different varieties showing different shapes and colors—ranging from the deep purple euphemism to stark white globes to obelisks streaked ivory and violet down the length.

I'll never understand people who complain about the heat. It gets truly hot for only a few weeks a year. Soak it up. Nights slept without clothes under a sheet alone with a fan blowing straight at the bed. Hot kitchens made even hotter with a turn of the oven knob. Or maybe yet, get the grill going and hold my hips while I stand next to the flames. Everything else on the table is a toss of a salad. Easy. The wine is ice cold and has droplets on the glass. So too does the back of my neck.

This is the time for eggplant. They originated in India. They thrive in the Mediterranean. We get them for only a few weeks. Their silken texture and beguiling, tannic skin melt on the tongue as the sun fades, throwing its own shades of purple across the sky.

Summer is fast and hot and goes long into the night.

HOW TO BUY

- Eggplant come in all colors and shapes, from deep purple to white to orange. Consider buying a mixture or one you haven't tried before.
- The flavor is mostly the same from variety to variety.
- Look for tight, even, glossy skin. Shriveled skin indicates water evaporation since harvest—meaning it has been off the vine for a while.
- Avoid plants with large bruises or brown spots unless you can buy at a discount. The rest of the fruit will be fine, but you'll lose some yield by cutting out the bad spots.
- The larger the eggplant, the more likely the seeds will be large, too. I usually go for medium size.
- The flesh should feel heavy in your hand.

HOW TO STORE

- Keep eggplant in a cool dark place but do not refrigerate—below 45 degrees, eggplant cells start to break and deteriorate, causing little pits below the skin.
- Wash just before using, because the skin's natural waxiness protects the flesh from losing moisture during storage.
- Cut eggplant will last a day or two in the refrigerator before cooking but will oxidize and has a tendency to taste more bitter. Ideally, cut the fruit just before cooking.

NOTES

- Much is made of eggplant's bitterness. Most varieties have been bred to have smaller seeds, minimizing the bitterness.
- Degorging is the process of salting eggplant ahead of time to leach out the excess liquid. I find it makes the texture rubbery, the extra prep time of letting it sit inhibits me from cooking the eggplant, and I like it plenty as is.
- If you decide to salt ahead, be sure to blot all that excess liquid away from the surface when oven roasting, or it will never crisp.
- Eggplants can absorb a good deal of fat, so be liberal with your **glugs**.
- Eggplant is all about texture (unctuous flesh, crispy skin), but its mild inherent flavor relies on punchier ingredients to lift the dish.
- For doneness, look for flesh that is golden brown and inviting to eat. If it isn't, cook it longer, knowing it is basically impossible to overcook eggplant.

BRAISED

Stewed eggplant lacks the textural difference between the skin and flesh, but what it lacks in contrast it gains in velvety mouth-feel. I find it comforting not only in flavor and texture but also in versatility. These recipes are tasty straight from the oven, at room temperature, or as a cold snack from the refrigerator.

stewy eggplant and tomato coddled eggs

If you don't have jars or ramekins, simply poach or boil the eggs (pages 22 and 23) and serve over a big spoonful of the eggplant stew.

The variations are other ways to use the stew, because baking it in the jars is only one of a million ways to eat it up with abandon. Make it in large batches because it takes only a bit more time, it freezes well, and it's a great way to use up the glut of eggplant and tomatoes in the early fall.

1 cup (240 ml) olive oil

1 Tbsp (15 g) salt

½ tsp (2 g) chili flakes (optional)

3 onions (1½ lb | 3 cups | 680 g), cut into thin slices

10 garlic cloves (2 oz | 55 g), minced

5 eggplants (5 lb | 2.3 kg), cut into large chunks

5 slicer tomatoes (2½ lb | 1.2 kg), cut into large chunks

1 cup (240 ml) white or red wine

¼ bunch cilantro (0.25 oz | 7 g), stemmed, leaves left whole

¼ bunch parsley (0.5 oz | ⅓ cup | 15 g), stemmed, leaves left whole

5 sprigs basil, stemmed, leaves left whole

5 sprigs mint, stemmed, leaves left whole

1 loaf crusty bread

4 eggs

Heat the oven to 325°F (165°C). Have ready six 4-oz (60-ml) jelly jars or ramekins.

Heat the olive oil in a large pot or Dutch oven over medium heat. Fry the salt and chili flakes until fragrant, 1 minute. Add the onion and garlic, reduce the heat to medium-low, and sweat until slightly soft, 7 to 10 minutes. Add the eggplant and tomatoes, and toss to combine. Add the wine, bring to a boil, cover, and transfer to the oven. Cook until the eggplant is tender, the tomatoes have given up their liquid, and the whole thing is thick and stewy and tasty, about 40 minutes.

Toss the herbs together to combine. Slice the bread into thick pieces and toast.

When the stew is done, fill the jars halfway and top each with an egg. Place on a baking sheet and bake until the egg white is cooked through, about 8 minutes. Remove from the oven, sprinkle with salt, garnish with the herbs, and serve with the toast on the side for dunking and spooning the eggplant from the jars.

variations

w/seared salmon + kale

1 side of salmon or 4 fillets (24 oz | 680 g total)	Neutral oil Salt 4 cups (1 L) eggplant stew	1 bunch kale (½ lb | 4 cups | 230 g), midribs stripped, cut into ribbons

Sear the salmon (page 24). Combine the eggplant stew with the kale. Top the salmon with the eggplant salad, and serve.

w/wild rice + spinach

2 cups (500 ml) eggplant stew	2 cups (330 g) cooked wild rice (page 43) ½ bag (2 oz | 55 g) spinach	Salt and freshly ground black pepper

Toss all the ingredients together, season with salt and pepper, and serve.

w/grilled chicken thigh + arugula

4 chicken thighs (6 oz | 170 g each) 1 bag (4 oz | 115 g) arugula 5 sprigs basil, stemmed, leaves torn	5 sprigs mint, stemmed, leaves torn Olive oil Salt	2 cups (500 ml) eggplant stew, at room temperature

Grill the chicken. Combine the arugula and herbs and dress with a glug of olive oil and sprinkle of salt. Put the chicken on a serving platter, and serve with the eggplant stew and dressed salad.

OVEN ROASTED

Cooking eggplant in pieces yields crispy skin and tender, creamy flesh. The simplest way to roast is to cut it into pieces—either <u>chunks</u> or rounds—<u>toss</u> with oil, salt, and any other seasonings, and spread out evenly on a foil-lined baking sheet. The unimpeachable Deb Perelman, of *Smitten Kitchen*, recommends greasing the baking sheet to keep the eggplant from sticking, and I have benefited tremendously from this tip.

The other tip that has changed my relationship with eggplant came from my eighty-five-year-old former landlady, Julia. She brushes eggplant with mayo and then presses it into bread crumbs before oven roasting. It is the best version of the traditional-but-messy three-step process of flour, egg, and bread crumbs.

Use either of these methods when oven roasting; just remember to leave space on the baking sheet to allow the steam to evaporate as the eggplant cooks.

crispy eggplant w/fresh mozzarella, tomatoes, pickled raisins, and mint

Make this with hot eggplant or eggplant that has been roasted and cooled. Room-temperature eggplant has the same allure as takeout food the morning after. It is slightly greasy and incredibly satisfying. Plus, a room-temperature dish means that you don't have to be in the kitchen right up to the moment that the food is served.

1 large or 2 medium (1½ lb | 680 g) eggplant, cut into large <u>chunks</u>

½ cup (120 ml) olive oil

½ tsp (3 g) salt

1 cup (140 g) golden raisins

½ cup (120 ml) brown sugar–vinegar sauce (page 61)

2 balls (16 oz | 455 g) fresh mozzarella

¼ cup (60 ml) cream

Zest of 1 lemon (1 Tbsp | 3 g)

½ tsp (3 g) freshly ground black pepper

2 slicer tomatoes (1 lb | 455 g), as ripe as possible, cored and cut into large irregular <u>chunks</u>

5 sprigs mint, leaves torn into pieces

¼ cup (35 g) garlic bread crumbs (page 48)

Heat the oven to 400°F (200°C).

Toss the eggplant with the olive oil and salt. Put on a greased, foil-lined baking sheet and roast until golden brown and tender, about 25 minutes.

Combine the raisins with the brown sugar–vinegar sauce and let marinate.

Tear the mozzarella into irregular <u>chunks</u> and dress with the cream, lemon zest, and pepper.

Toss the roasted eggplant together with the tomatoes and mint. Top with the dressed mozzarella, raisins, and bread crumbs and serve.

variations

"ratatouille"—all the flavors of ratatouille but layered up as a salad

1 eggplant (1 lb | 455 g), cut into a large <u>dice</u> or <u>chunks</u>

1 sweet pepper (7 oz | 200 g), cut into ½-inch- (12-mm-) thick strips

1 small (2 oz | ¼ cup | 55 g) red onion, cut into <u>thin slices</u>

2 garlic cloves (0.4 oz | 14 g), minced

2 slicer tomatoes (1 lb | 455 g), cut into irregular <u>chunks</u>, or ½ cup (120 g) roasted cherry tomatoes (page 435)

1 medium (8 oz | 230 g) summer squash, <u>shaved</u> into thin rounds

5 sprigs basil, leaves torn, or ¼ cup (60 ml) basil oil (page 56)

Oven roast the eggplant, pepper, and onion together and immediately stir in the garlic (the hot vegetables will cook it slightly). Toss the eggplant mixture, tomatoes, and squash together with the torn basil and serve.

pickled eggplant w/hazelnuts + parsley

2 eggplants (2 lb | 910 g)	½ bunch parsley (2.4 oz | 1½ cups | 68 g), stemmed, leaves left whole	½ cup (60 g) hazelnuts, toasted (page 24) and roughly chopped
½ cup (120 ml) brown sugar–vinegar sauce (page 61)		

Oven roast the eggplant and immediately dress with the brown sugar–vinegar sauce. Toss the eggplant with the parsley and sprinkle with the hazelnuts.

w/prosciutto, parmesan + lentils

1 eggplant (1 lb | 455 g)	1 lemon (1.5 fl oz | 45 ml), zest and juice	2 oz (55 g) Parmesan, shaved into ribbons with a vegetable peeler
1 cup (200 g) cooked lentils (page 41)	2 oz (55 g) prosciutto or thinly shaved ham or salami	

Oven roast the eggplant and toss with the lentils, lemon zest, and juice. Mingle the prosciutto with the eggplant mixture and garnish with the Parmesan ribbons.

PURÉED

This technique stems from my desire to make grills a more efficient cooking method—that is, using the indirect and residual heat from a grill to cook as much stuff as possible. You can also use an open rack in an oven, though the eggplant will lack the smoky quality imparted by a grill. You can also use a gas burner to char the skin of the eggplant, but be prepared for some smoke in your house and some drips on your stove. No matter where you are roasting your eggplant, be sure to prick little holes all over to allow the steam from interior flesh to escape. If it can't escape via this planned route (the breaks in the skin) it will escape via an unplanned route (exploding the side of the vegetable).

smoky eggplant pasta w/pounded walnut relish, mozzarella, and basil

This recipe purées the eggplant to give it an even texture and maximize the smoke flavor by using the skin. If you don't want to use the skin, which is unpalatable unless blended into oblivion, I also like to scoop the eggplant flesh from the skin and roughly chop it. When you lift the flesh away, some of the smoke flavor is retained, as is the irreplaceable texture of slow-cooked eggplant.

1 large or 2 medium (1½ lb | 680 g) eggplant

1 cup (120 g) walnuts

2 lemons (3 fl oz | 90 ml), juice and zest

½ bunch parsley (1.2 oz | ¾ cup | 34 g), roughly chopped

2 tsp (12 g) salt

½ cup (120 ml) olive oil

¼ tsp (1 g) chili flakes

16 oz (455 g) long pasta noodles: spaghetti, bucatini, linguine

2 balls (1 lb | 455 g) fresh mozzarella

5 sprigs basil, stemmed, leaves torn into pieces

Start the grill or heat the oven to 400°F (200°C).

Prick the eggplant all over and roast or grill until the flesh is fully collapsed and soft, about 35 minutes (if grilling, the skin will be dark and charred; that's OK).

Meanwhile, toast the walnuts until fragrant (page 24), about 7 minutes. Remove from the oven and transfer to a zip locking bag. Bash with the back of a frying pan until coarsely chopped.

Combine the walnuts with the lemon juice, zest, parsley, and a big pinch of salt, and set aside.

Remove the eggplant from the heat and let cool.

When cool, remove the stem of the eggplant and roughly chop the eggplant and skin. Transfer to a food processor and blend with the olive oil, chili flakes, and salt until very smooth.

Bring a large pot of heavily salted water to a boil. Boil the pasta and drain, reserving ½ cup (120 ml) of the cooking liquid.

Toss the pasta with the eggplant purée and water to make a coating sauce. Taste and adjust the seasoning.

Transfer the pasta to serving dishes. Tear the mozzarella into pieces and scatter over the pasta. Garnish with the walnut mixture and basil leaves, and serve.

variations

on toast w/feta + mint

Slice bread thickly and toast, schmear with eggplant purée, crumble a bit of feta over the top, and garnish with torn mint leaves.

w/summer vegetables

Cut up any assortment of vegetables and serve with a bowl of eggplant purée drizzled with olive and basil oil (page 56).

stuffed peppers w/rice + eggplant

1 bell pepper (7 oz | 200 g) per person

½ cup (120 ml) eggplant purée per person

¾ cup (180 g) cooked rice (page 41) per person

2 Tbsp (30 ml) basil oil (page 56) per person

Remove the top of the bell pepper. Combine the rice and purée, stuff the pepper, and grill, roast, or broil until the pepper is cooked and the filling warm. Remove from the heat, drizzle with the basil oil, and serve.

fennel

For years there has been a movement toward eating whole animals—respecting the animal enough to eat all parts (organs, bones, and secondary cuts) with as much gusto as the prime pieces. There is less urgency around whole plant consumption because vegetable production is less energy-intensive than animal protein, and carrots don't have the same emotional capabilities that cows and pigs do.

That said, there is good reason to prioritize eating all parts of vegetables. One, it is more economical. Getting two or three meals out of a plant instead of one, you're saving money, energy, and time. Two, the flavors are different throughout the plant, and by consuming all of it, you get to taste those subtle differences. Three, we waste a tremendous amount of food in our food system. By demanding (and using) all parts of the plant, consumers have the power to mitigate that waste and divert it from landfills, easing the volume of greenhouse gasses entering the atmosphere—just by eating dinner.

Fennel epitomizes plants that are edible in their entirety. It wasn't until I saw fennel in the garden that I realized how much plant exists around the bulb sold alone at the store. That bulb grows along the ground with a thick tap root in the soil. At the top of each "petal" wrapped around the core is a hollow stalk jutting two feet into the air. Each stalk is crowned with little leaves, fronds, almost indistinguishable from dill.

I prize the bulb for its squeaky texture and mild anise flavor. The stalks, when thin and tender, can be used in any way the bulb is, though the flavor is a bit stronger and the texture more fibrous. When the stalks are too stringy to enjoy raw, they lend their licorice flavor to stocks and soups and make a great base for fish-poaching liquid. The pin-shaped leaves are the most intensely flavored in the way that all herbs taste magically concentrated. I save the fronds to garnish a cooked plate of fennel and at the very least toss them into my green salad to dazzle with little pops of flavor in each bite.

At Zingerman's Deli in Ann Arbor, Michigan, we witnessed Italian fennel pollen mania the first time we got it into the shop. It was golden and downy, tasting like a love child between anise and chamomile. It could be sprinkled on anything—freshly cooked pasta, toast with butter in the morning, yogurt with honey and pistachios. I have never been able to collect it from my own plants in quantity but still buy a jar every time I pass through that town. In place of the pollen alone, I love pulling the flowers from the stalks, picking the buds, and adding them to herb salads or to garnish big platters of roasted and raw vegetables. Edible flowers often seem like a pointless decoration in a dish, but when they serve a purpose and further a flavor, it feels like fairytale hedonism to eat them.

After the plant flowers, it sets seed—propagation is the primary goal, after all. Fennel seeds are readily available now in grocery stores. They taste the most like licorice and have a deep sweetness—presumably sugar that is meant to feed the plant during germination. The seeds can be ground, left whole, fried, or candied and added to many a dish for a bright hit of herby anise.

These fennel recipes are written for the bulb alone, because that is what is most often available in my grocery store. If you find fennel with its stalks and fronds still attached, slice it thinly, close your eyes, and taste it to envision where it can be added to your meal. There is more food there than you might have realized.

HOW TO BUY

- Look for fennel heads that are tight and plump.
- Some bruising is inevitable, but if the outside petals are very damaged, be sure that there is enough fennel on the bulb to eat if you peel away the mucky ones.
- If the fronds are attached, they should be bright and rigid.
- Fennel grows as two different shapes: flat and round.
- The flat female, with its propensity to bolt and go to seed, tends to be smaller in size and stronger in flavor, and it requires more time to soften when cooking.
- The round male, giving off the pollen to pollinate the female plants, are crisper, less fibrous, and more likely to be found in grocery stores.
- Fennel found at the farmers' market is dramatically different in size from grocery store fennel. I generally assume one person will eat one small fennel or one-half to one-quarter of a large one.

HOW TO STORE

- If you have the bulb and the fronds, separate them and store separately in a plastic bag. Use the stalks and fronds first, as they will wilt more quickly.
- Fennel oxidizes quickly, so store raw cut pieces in **acidulated water**, which will also make them curl a bit.

NOTES

- The bruised outer petals are still good to add flavor to stocks and soups.
- The stalks are a good base for poaching fish or chicken (page 23), as they impart a delicate anise flavor and prop up the protein, making it easier to lift from the liquid.
- I prefer fennel fronds chopped even roughly because if left whole they have a texture similar to fish bones, which I find unpleasant.

RAW

As with other raw vegetables, the trick lies in the knife work.
I generally cut the fennel in half, leaving the core intact, place
the cut-side down, and slice thinly from right to left all the way
across. Alternatively, for super thin shaving, cut in half, leaving
the core intact, and run it along a mandoline. You can also cut
any which way and any thickness, and the result will be edible
if not picture perfect.

shaved fennel salad w/apricots, chili oil, parsley, mint, and lamb chops

There is enough acidity in this salad to prevent the browning. If you want to prep this in advance, cut the fennel and store in the acidulated water, drain, and toss with the rest of the ingredients. I generally allow for three lamb chops per person but do more or less based on your guests. Replace the dried apricots with fresh if they are ripe and fragrant.

12 lamb chops (3 oz | 85 g each)

Salt and freshly ground black pepper

1 cup (190 g) dried apricots, cut into thin slices

1 shallot or small (2 oz | ¼ cup | 55 g) red onion, cut into thin slices

¼ cup (60 ml) any vinegar except balsamic, or freshly squeezed lemon juice

2 small heads (1 lb | 455 g total) fennel

¼ cup (60 ml) chili oil (page 55)

½ bunch parsley (1.2 oz | ¾ cup | 34 g), stemmed, leaves kept whole

10 sprigs mint, stemmed, leaves kept whole

Season the lamb chops with salt and pepper and bring to room temperature.

Toss the apricots, shallot, and vinegar together with a big pinch of salt to soak for a few minutes.

Cut the fennel in half from top to bottom and then shave thinly, leaving the core in place if it is tender or if you want to hold the fennel petals together. Add with the chili oil to the apricot mixture.

Pat the chops dry, season again with salt and pepper and grill or sear the chops (page 23) over high heat to medium-rare, 5 to 7 minutes per side, and let rest for 5 to 10 minutes after cooking. Top the chops with the fennel salad and the herbs and serve.

variations

w/apples, brown butter vinaigrette (page 59), arugula + salmon

w/lemon vinaigrette (page 58), parmesan, parsley + seared chicken thighs

w/sherry vinaigrette (page 58), parsley, orange + ricotta

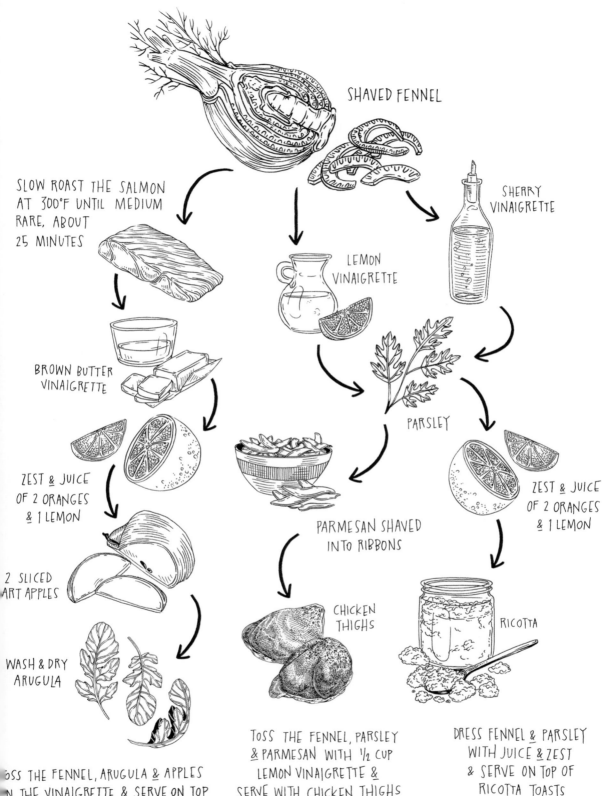

SHAVED FENNEL

SLOW ROAST THE SALMON AT 300°F UNTIL MEDIUM RARE, ABOUT 25 MINUTES

SHERRY VINAIGRETTE

LEMON VINAIGRETTE

BROWN BUTTER VINAIGRETTE

PARSLEY

ZEST & JUICE OF 2 ORANGES & 1 LEMON

ZEST & JUICE OF 2 ORANGES & 1 LEMON

PARMESAN SHAVED INTO RIBBONS

2 SLICED TART APPLES

CHICKEN THIGHS

RICOTTA

WASH & DRY ARUGULA

TOSS THE FENNEL, ARUGULA & APPLES IN THE VINAIGRETTE & SERVE ON TOP OF THE SALMON

TOSS THE FENNEL, PARSLEY & PARMESAN WITH ½ CUP LEMON VINAIGRETTE & SERVE WITH CHICKEN THIGHS

DRESS FENNEL & PARSLEY WITH JUICE & ZEST & SERVE ON TOP OF RICOTTA TOASTS

BRAISED

This method is one of my favorite ways to handle a lot of fennel. It requires very little active time and yields silky smooth fennel that can be served warm, cold, or room temperature. It can be the star of the dish or play second fiddle. It also will soften even bolted fennel (fennel that is trying to go to seed and sending up flower shoots, making the core very tough and unpalatable when raw). Following is the method and then some ideas about what you can pair with the final result.

Traditionally, I sear fennel (cut-side down) until it is golden brown and then braise it. That said, you can also grill it first or leave it completely raw before braising. Think about what flavor you want in the end: raw will be sweet and taste exclusively of fennel; searing it will add a caramelized nuttiness to the flavor; grilling it will add a smoky-sweet flavor. I tend to make this in a frying pan or Dutch oven, making it a one-pot dish. If the lid doesn't fit tightly, just be sure to check that the braise hasn't dried out in the cooking time. If it is getting dry, add a splash more water or stock.

The long stalks can also be braised along with the bulb. Simply remove the fronds, as they get really wimpy when cooked for so long. They can be saved and used as a fresh garnish to contrast the stewy fennel. Allow to cool and then add to the fronds with a squeeze of lemon to jazz up the cooked fennel and tie the whole thing together. I also encourage you to start with this basic recipe and then vary it as you like—add orange, add chiles, use sweet apple cider in place of the wine/lemon, try it with beer, and on and on.

braised fennel

This dish does well made in large batches, but it is, paradoxically, one of my favorite meals to be eaten alone—either out of the cast-iron pan in which it was cooked or a shallow bowl laden with the cooking liquid. Thick crusty bread, grilled until crunchy and flecked with char, rounds out the meal. It pairs beautifully with a glass of ice-cold white wine, a magazine, and a paper towel for a napkin.

2 to 6 heads (1 lb | 455 g total) fennel

1 onion (8 oz | 1 cup | 230 g), cut into thin slices or into chunks

3 garlic cloves (0.6 oz | 17 g), left whole or roughly chopped

Zest of 1 lemon (1½ oz | 45 g), stripped with a vegetable peeler

1 cup (240 ml) white wine or hard cider

Salt

½ tsp (3 g) chili flakes (optional)

2 cups (480 ml) chicken stock or water

4 Tbsp (2 oz | 55 g) butter

Heat the oven to 350°F (180°C).

Trim the fennel, removing any bruised outer leaves and any wild stalks or fronds. Cut the bulbs in half or leave whole if they are small (remember, the larger the vegetable, the longer the cooking time), keeping the core intact. Wash well, removing the dirt from inside the petals, and allow to dry.

In a large Dutch oven or frying pan over medium-high heat, sear or grill the fennel, cut-side down, until dark and caramely. Add the onion, garlic, lemon zest, wine, 3 big pinches of salt, and chili flakes (if using). Bring to a boil and reduce the wine by half. Add the stock and butter and bring to a boil.

Remove from the heat, cover tightly with aluminum foil, and bake until the fennel is tender when pierced with a knife; check after 30 minutes and periodically after that.

Serve warm, or let cool in the liquid and serve when you're ready.

variations

w/white beans + chard

4 garlic cloves (0.8 oz | 28 g), minced

½ cup (120 ml) olive oil, plus more for dressing

Salt

One 19-oz (539-g) can white beans (or cooked from 1 cup [160 g] dry beans), drained and rinsed

2 bunches chard (½ lb | 4 cups | 230 g), cut into ribbons

Braised fennel (see master recipe)

½ cup (60 g) pecans or other nuts

Sweat the garlic in the oil with a big pinch of salt. Add the beans and stir to combine. Dress the chard with a glug of oil and pinch of salt. Serve the beans topped with the fennel and the chard salad. Sprinkle with the pecans.

w/lake trout, parsley + sunflower seeds

4 lake trout fillets (6 oz | 170 g each)

Salt and freshly ground black pepper

Braised fennel (see master recipe)

1 bunch parsley (2.4 oz | 1½ cups | 68 g), stemmed, leaves kept whole

½ cup (70 g) sunflower seeds, roughly chopped

1 lemon (1½ fl oz | 45 ml), zest and juice

Olive oil

Season the trout liberally with salt and pepper and poach or sear (pages 23 and 24). While still warm, place on serving plates with the fennel on the side. Combine the parsley and sunflower seeds with the lemon zest and juice and a glug of olive oil. Spoon the parsley mixture over the trout and fennel.

w/eggs, garlic bread crumbs + lemon vinaigrette

1 or 2 hard-boiled eggs per person (page 22)

½ to 1 braised fennel head per person, sliced into wedges

¼ cup (35 g) garlic bread crumbs (page 48)

¼ cup (60 ml) lemon vinaigrette (page 58)

Herbs (optional)

Peel and quarter the eggs and combine with the fennel, bread crumbs, herbs, and vinaigrette.

garlic

To grow garlic, you'll have to start in the fall.

Buy organic or unsprayed hardneck garlic—softneck and elephant garlic can both be grown similarly but are not as fool-proof in my experience. Get it home and break up the cloves, leaving the papery skins on. If you buy garlic from a farmers' market, you're almost guaranteed to have garlic that will germinate.

Go to your patch of dirt and poke into the ground to form holes about 1 inch (2.5 cm) wide and 6 inches (15 cm) deep. Much deeper than that and the garlic sprout won't make it to the surface. Much wider and the clove can flip over when dropped. The traditional tool for this is called a dibbler—literally a pointy stick about 1 inch (2.5 cm) wide and 6 inches (15 cm) long, designed to dig the hole for garlic.

Drop or push a single clove into each hole, ensuring that the "foot" of the clove–the flat end that originally secured the base to the central core—is facing down. The pointy part of the clove should point up. Add some compost to fill in the hole, top with straw, and wait.

Wait through the winter, through the drifts of snow. Wait until the bracing wind of earliest spring. The green shoots will poke through the ground and through the straw. Before most other greenery is out, the garlic will begin to stand tall.

This is green garlic. The stalk is still tender (edible and slice-able) and not yet hardened to support the rest of the plant. It tastes like garlic, yes, but also a bit like the smell of the just-cut grass of the summer that is on its way. The way that a leek is like an onion but also an entity in its own right, so too is green garlic.

Green garlic is on the scene for a couple of weeks. As it ages and the five leaves branch out, the stalk will get too woody to cut, strengthening to support the flower, the garlic scape. Garlic is an allium, and the alliums (domesticated lilies) propagate in two ways: either by flowers setting seed and that seed rooting in the ground, or by dividing the root structure. The garlic scape is the first attempt. If left on the plant, it will bloom and look a bit like the purple chive flowers (same family) and create dozens of mini garlic cloves.

This is why farmers remove the scapes from the plants, to encourage the garlic to try to propagate through its base. The plant will redirect its focus toward the root structure as it tries to survive, pushing energy into the head of garlic cloves formed by that initial clove, making it bigger and stronger, more likely to survive the next winter.

The other reason why we cut the scapes is that they taste like garlic and can be used anywhere a clove of garlic is called for. The scape still has the grassy greenness and, like green garlic, tastes of garlic but not exactly.

After the scape harvest, toward the end of July (at least where I grow them), pull the entire garlic plant from the ground—a magic wand with a head of garlic at its end. This is technically uncured garlic. Uncured because the papery skin is still wet and tightly bound. I find that these cloves are sticky and pungent like garlic but the flavor dissipates quickly when heat is applied. As luck would have it, this is also the time of year when tomatoes, zucchini, and corn are plentiful. A clove of garlic rubbed on toast and topped with a salad of summer veg is divinity incarnate.

Allow the garlic wands to dry out in a cool place with good airflow. Well-cured garlic will last through the winter. But don't forget to set aside as many single cloves as you'd like to have heads of garlic next summer to plant again in the fall.

HOW TO BUY

- Green garlic hits the markets in mid-spring, usually around the beginning of May.
- Garlic scapes come on in the middle of June.
- Garlic is harvested in my area, and sold uncured, in the middle of July.
- Cured garlic is generally available early September.
- Look for tight, compact heads that are free of bruising or rot.
- Green garlic should have long, even stems that are slightly bendy. If they are very rigid they will be too woody to use the whole stem.
- Garlic scapes should have an even coloring and no wrinkly skin. The looser the skin, the longer since they've been picked, and the milder the flavor.

HOW TO STORE

- Cured heads can be stored in a cool, dark place like any storage onion or potato.
- Green garlic and garlic scapes should be kept refrigerated, as they are uncured and will dry out and have a greater likelihood of rotting.

NOTES

- Garlic is edible in all of its life stages.
- All of the recipes here are written for garlic cloves because they are universally available.
- As a rule of thumb, clove garlic is the strongest, followed by scapes, and then green garlic.
- I use this general ratio for converting scapes and green garlic into a recipe:
  - 3 garlic cloves = 5 garlic scapes = 2 stalks of green garlic (less because they are longer).
  - These are rough approximations, so please taste as you go.

RAW

Chewing on a raw garlic clove or scape can be a bit much for people, because a little goes a long way. In these recipes, the garlic will mellow in the vinegars of the sauce or be spread so thinly (as on toast) that it will add only depth of flavor and not steal the show in an overly aggressive manner.

grilled pork chops w/garlic and kale relish

Like other condiments in this book, this relish can be made in large batches and frozen. I make it in very large batches when garlic scapes are most abundant. The sky's the limit to what you can spoon it over: soups, roasted roots, pasta, eggs in the morning, etc.

Should you not have a food processor, an immersion blender will work just as well. The kale stems are often tender enough to be blended into the relish, ensuring that you aren't wasting any of the food you've paid for.

1 <u>bunch</u> kale (½ lb | 4 cups | 230 g), sliced into <u>ribbons</u> with the stems included

1 <u>bunch</u> parsley (2.4 oz | 1½ cups | 68 g), roughly chopped

5 (1 oz | 30 g) garlic cloves, roughly chopped

1 Tbsp (10 g) sunflower seeds, toasted (page 24)

2 Tbsp (30 ml) red wine vinegar, plus more as needed

1 tsp (3 g) smoked paprika

½ tsp (3 g) salt, plus more for seasoning

¼ cup (60 ml) olive oil

One or two 6- to 8-oz | (170- to 225-g) pork chops per person

Freshly ground black pepper

Combine all the ingredients but the olive oil, pork chops, and pepper in a food processor and whiz for a couple of pulses to roughly combine to the texture of salsa verde or pesto. Drizzle in the olive oil, taste, and add more salt or vinegar if needed.

Bring the pork chops to room temperature and, just before grilling, season liberally with salt and the pepper.

Heat a grill to high and grill the pork chops until cooked through, about 7 minutes per side depending on thickness (page 23).

Just before serving, slather heavy-handedly with the relish.

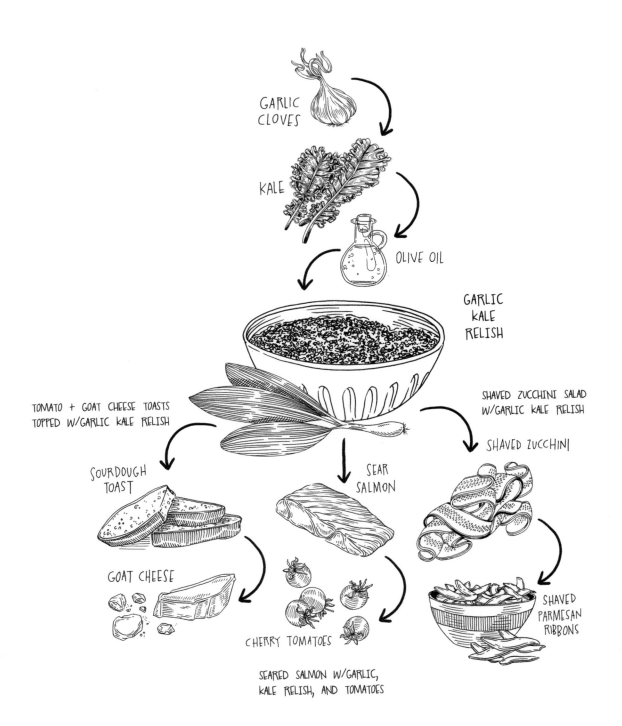

GARLIC CLOVES

KALE

OLIVE OIL

GARLIC KALE RELISH

TOMATO + GOAT CHEESE TOASTS TOPPED W/GARLIC KALE RELISH

SHAVED ZUCCHINI SALAD W/GARLIC KALE RELISH

SOURDOUGH TOAST

SEAR SALMON

SHAVED ZUCCHINI

GOAT CHEESE

CHERRY TOMATOES

SHAVED PARMESAN RIBBONS

SEARED SALMON W/GARLIC, KALE RELISH, AND TOMATOES

SAUTÉED

After working with garlic in all of its life stages, you will probably find that you prefer green garlic for some recipes and mature cloves for others. But in the end, garlic in any state can be used to lend a spicy pungency to a dish. Swapping out different stages of garlic is just trial and error.

For all of the following recipes, start with a knob of butter or a glug of oil and then slowly cook the garlic—with some salt and spices, if you like—until the garlic is tender and translucent. Then choose your own adventure—pasta sauce, the base for frittata, or risotto. Sautéed garlic is the base for just about anything.

garlic and spinach pasta

Making a pan sauce can be a bit of a trick, but the more you do it, the easier it will be. If your sauce breaks (the solids separate from the liquid), add a bit more butter to bring it back together. I always end up doubling the amount of garlic in any cookbook recipe I've ever made. This pasta has a real garlic punch. If you want a tamer dish, feel free to cut the amount of garlic in half.

This dish with green garlic is one of my favorite foods in the spring.

1 small (2 oz | ¼ cup | 55 g) onion, cut into thin slices

6 garlic cloves (1.2 oz | 34 g), slivered

Butter for frying

Salt

½ cup (120 ml) white wine or dry vermouth

1 cup (240 ml) chicken or vegetable stock or water

4 Tbsp (55 g) anchovy-caper butter (page 62), cut into cubes

1 cup (240 ml) cream

1 lb (455 g) long pasta, just finished cooking

1 bag spinach (4 oz | 115 g), chopped into strips

Raclette or Parmesan cheese

In a shallow frying pan, sweat the onion and garlic in a knob of the butter and a pinch of salt over low heat until soft, 5 to 7 minutes. Add the wine and reduce by half, about 3 minutes. Increase the heat and add the stock.

When the liquid comes to a boil, add the butter and cream and let reduce until slightly thickened, 3 to 5 minutes.

Drain the pasta and toss with the sauce and the spinach, allowing the heat of the pasta to wilt the spinach.

Serve with a satisfyingly hefty grating of cheese.

variations

pasta carbonara

1 lb (455 g) long pasta

½ lb (230 g) bacon, cut into ¼-inch (6-mm) strips

5 garlic cloves (1 oz | 30 g), minced

2 eggs

Bring a large pot of salted water to a boil. Render the bacon in a pan until crispy. Remove from the heat and add the garlic, letting it slowly cook in the hot bacon fat. Whisk the eggs until well blended. Cook the pasta and drain, reserving ½ cup (120 ml) of water. Whisk the pasta water into the eggs, whisking continuously. Add the pasta to the bacon mixture. Drizzle in the egg mixture, stirring, until it yields a creamy sauce.

frittata w/chard

6 eggs	3 garlic cloves (0.6 oz | 21 g), 2 stalks green garlic, or 5 garlic scapes, minced	1 bunch chard, midribs stripped and cut into thin slices, leaves sliced into ribbons
1 cup (240 ml) cream		
1 tsp (6 g) salt		
Neutral oil		

Heat the oven to 325°F (165°C). Whisk the eggs with the cream and salt. Heat a glug of neutral oil and sweat the garlic and the chard stems. Add the leaves and pour the egg over all, allowing it to set around the sides. Transfer to the oven and bake until set and slightly browning, about 25 minutes.

garlic risotto w/peas

10 garlic cloves (2 oz | 55 g), minced	½ cup (120 ml) olive oil	4 cups (720 g) cooked risotto (page 42)
	1 cup (120 g) peas	

Sweat the garlic in the olive oil, toss the peas in the garlic oil, and spoon out over the risotto.

CONFIT

The classic method for a true <u>confit</u> is to submerge the ingredient in its own fat and cook at a low temperature (traditionally 200°F or 95°C). Luckily, the technique is well suited to ingredients that don't have their own fat in which to stew. Garlic is one of those ingredients.

You can also <u>confit</u> whole heads of garlic, cut in half across the equator with the papery wrappers still on. Inevitably, I rue the ease of preparation when my hands are covered in garlic oil as I try to separate the cloves later on down the line. That said, it does present well, guests scooping out the cooked cloves to smear on their dinner bread. The perfumed oil should be swirled into any number of sauces and is the backbone of the garlic bread crumbs (page 48) that show up so often in this book.

Both green garlic and scapes also work when cooked this way. They will lose a bit of their grassiness, won't soften as succulently, and won't color as deeply caramely but are still delightfully good and a good way to preserve garlic in all of its life stages.

garlic confit

10 garlic cloves (or as many as you have) or 2 heads garlic, cut in half around the equator	2 big pinches of salt Neutral oil to cover the garlic by ¼ inch (6 mm)

Heat the oven to 150°F to 200°F (65°C to 95°C).

Peel the garlic cloves or leave the wrappers on if confiting the whole head.

Lay the garlic in the bottom of an ovenproof baking dish. Sprinkle with the salt. Top the garlic with the oil until the cloves are just submerged. Cover with a lid or foil to ensure a tight seal. Place in the oven and bake until the cloves are golden brown and soft to the touch, 45 to 60 minutes. Remove and let cool.

Store in the oil in your fridge for forever (or until you use it all up). The cloves should always be covered in the oil. If you use the oil before the cloves, transfer them to a smaller dish and freeze.

garlic marinated white beans w/celery and parsley salad

I prefer cooking dried beans for this dish because the beans will absorb more of the vinaigrette flavor if they are given time to cool in the liquid. If you abhor cooking beans, use canned, but warm them up a bit and then add the vinaigrette. The beans taste best when left to sit overnight in the vinaigrette but can be eaten right away.

8 oz (230 g) white beans (chickpeas also work well), soaked in water overnight

5 confit garlic cloves (1 oz | 30 g)

½ cup (120 ml) olive oil

½ cup (120 ml) sherry or red wine vinegar

2 tsp (12 g) salt

1 Tbsp (15 g) mustard (whole-grain or Dijon are my favorites)

1 bunch parsley (2.4 oz | 1½ cups | 68 g), roughly chopped

1 head (8 oz | 230 g) celery, cut into thin slices

Drain and rinse the soaked beans and boil in fresh water until tender but not falling apart, about 30 minutes.

Roughly chop the confit garlic and combine with the oil, vinegar, salt, and mustard.

Drain the cooked beans and immediately dress with the vinaigrette.

Combine the beans with the parsley and celery just before serving. Taste for salt, vinegar, or olive oil.

variations

chicken thighs w/confit garlic potatoes + a green salad

4 chicken thighs (6 oz | 170 g each)	5 confit garlic cloves (1 oz | 30 g)	1 bag (4 oz | 115 g) salad greens
1½ lb (680 g) fingerling or new potatoes	¼ cup (60 ml) garlic oil	¾ cup (180 ml) apple cider vinaigrette (page 58)
	Salt and freshly ground black pepper	

Pan roast the chicken thighs. Boil the potatoes, drain, and <u>toss</u> with the confit garlic and oil with a big pinch of salt and pepper. Dress the salad greens with the vinaigrette and season liberally with salt and pepper. Serve the chicken with the potatoes and greens.

garlicky tomato soup

2 oz (55 g) butter	Three 14.5-oz (428-ml) cans tomatoes, either whole, crushed, or <u>diced</u>	10 confit garlic cloves (2 oz | 55 g)
1 tsp (5 g) chili flakes		1 Tbsp (15 g) salt
5 sprigs thyme		1 cup (240 ml) cream
	2 cups (480 ml) water	

In a large soup pot, heat the butter until foamy and fry the chili flakes and thyme, about 1 minute. Add the tomatoes, water, garlic, and salt. Bring to a boil, reduce to a simmer, and cook until the tomatoes are soft, about 15 minutes. Remove from the heat and blend until silky smooth. Add the cream and taste and adjust the seasoning.

garlic confit w/mushrooms on toast

½ lb (230 g) mushrooms, any variety, sliced or halved	Salt and freshly ground black pepper	1 loaf sourdough bread
	10 confit garlic cloves (2 oz | 55 g)	¼ bag (1 oz | 30 g) arugula

Pan roast the mushrooms with a big pinch of salt and pepper (page 24) and <u>toss</u> with the garlic. Slice and toast the bread, top with the mushroom mixture and the arugula, and serve.

green beans

In *The Pastures of Heaven*, John Steinbeck told a story of a man wanting to woo a woman, so he remodeled his family's parlor room based on an image from a magazine. He crafted the room to match it just so. In the time this took, the woman married someone else, and the man locked the door to the parlor, letting it wither, picture perfect.

I struggle with the romanticism around gardening, cooking, and general lifestyle media. It isn't that the reality of what's being peddled isn't true; the room in the image is a real room. It's that these ideals often lack the context of what goes into the production, leaving the reader with feelings of inferiority for not having achieved the perfect meal, room, or sweater combination. Never laying bare the costs, or at least the compromises, of production.

Harvesting green beans epitomizes such romanticism-cum-fetishization. There is no more glorious an image than going out to the garden at 5 p.m. with a woven basket and a glass of chilled wine to collect part of that evening's meal. It is a pace with no urgency distracting from the light angling golden across the yard. My dog pouncing on the whiff of a rabbit and then tiring and finding shade under the deep green of the trellised pole beans from which I'm harvesting.

The truth is that picking beans hurts my back and my knees. I've never grown pole beans, because I'm discouraged by building the trellises. I rely on bush beans that grow into high masses with the beans invariably hidden under the leaves. I'm sweaty, never wearing a cotton sundress, but instead caked in dirt and sunscreen. I'm often awkwardly sitting on a bucket into which I'm dropping the beans and shifting to protect my lower back. (The bit about the dog is true.) The beans are not for dinner tonight, but if I don't keep picking them, the plants will stop producing.

A bean plant's only goal is to create seed to ensure the next generation. Green beans are the immature seed pod of the plant, which wants to swell the seeds inside and allow them to dry, protecting the seed through the winter only to be activated by warm, wet soil in the spring and start again. I always anthropomorphize the plants after I pluck their seed pod—be it a green bean or ready tomato—imagining them to say, "Fine. I'll ripen *another* one." (Italics mine.)

I want the plant to keep ripening for me. I want to pickle some beans, and I haven't eaten my fill of fresh ones yet. Home pickling is yet another recently fetishized activity that is entirely annoying, time consuming, and supremely satisfying. To be sure, I find this life romantic and feel grateful for the privilege to choose it. We've tried to make it lovely because that feels good; those tasks are also items on a to-do list that feels chaotically long.

Annie Dillard writes, "How we spend our days is, of course, how we spend our lives," and that feels like the antidote to Steinbeck's warning. Sometimes it is just so beautiful. Some days I feel like exploding because the light is just right. I do have a glass of wine. We just went lake swimming, washing away the dirt of the day, and now we'll make dinner together. It is glorious and freaking hard work and never done. It exists together.

HOW TO BUY

- Look for beans that are even in texture. Bulging beans generally mean the seeds inside are fully formed and the pods tough.
- Texture of beans is often most affected by the size. The more slender the bean, the smoother the texture. If you have particularly large beans, test them for toughness and, if tough, consider braising or long cooking to soften the fiber.
- Avoid beans that are wrinkled or dry.
- Beans come in myriad colors, from traditional green to yellow wax to deep purple to speckled between yellow and red. Dismiss the yellow ones only if it looks to be evidence of age as opposed to variety. No matter the color variety of beans, the taste will be very similar.
- Particularly skinny beans wilt easily; either soak them in cool water to rehydrate or cook them quickly.

HOW TO STORE

- Store in a plastic bag in the refrigerator to maintain the humidity and ensure that the beans don't get limp as the water respires from the cells.
- If freezing to preserve, give a quick blanch in boiling water and then allow to dry before freezing. The texture will be improved upon thawing.

NOTES

- Green beans are immature pods of the more common dried beans. At this stage green beans are treated as a vegetable rather than a legume or protein.
- Fresh (or shelling) beans are pods with mature bean seeds inside. The pods will be tough and should be discarded. The beans inside should be cooked as you would fava beans or peas.
- Dried beans are those shelling beans that have been dried for preservation. After this process the beans have the fullest amount of protein possible and are now considered a legume, not a vegetable.
- Purple beans will turn gray-green when cooked. To maintain the color, leave them raw and toss with either a hot vinaigrette or just-cooked green beans to take off the raw edge.
- The old wives' tale that picking beans with the dew still on them causes the unpicked beans to rust is accurate. The brown spots are a fungus that spreads more easily when handled wet. Pick beans in the afternoon to avoid spreading it.

PAN ROASTED

When pan roasting green beans, cook them as fast as possible to
<u>blister</u> the skin and keep their bright green color and crunch.

blistered green beans w/tomatoes, pounded walnuts, and raw summer squash

Pounding the walnuts while they're warm forces the oil from the flesh, making a softer yet textured garnish. You can chop them as well, but the nuts will have sharper edges. Plus, smashing them with a frying pan is fun, despite the fact that someone always makes an anger management joke.

1 cup (120 g) walnuts, toasted (page 24)

½ bunch parsley (1.2 fl oz | ¾ cup | 34 g), roughly chopped

1 lemon (1½ fl oz | 45 ml), zest and juice

¼ cup (60 ml) olive oil

½ tsp (3 g) salt

Neutral oil

1 lb (455 g) green beans, stems snapped off

1 pint (1 lb | 455 g) cherry tomatoes, halved

1 medium summer squash (8 oz | 230 g), shaved into paper-thin planks or rounds

Transfer the walnuts to a zip locking bag and bash with the back of a frying pan until the walnuts are in coarse pieces and have released some oil.

Combine the walnuts, parsley, lemon zest and juice, olive oil, and salt and stir to combine.

Heat a glug of neutral oil until smoking hot and add the green beans with a pinch of salt. Let the green beans blister, then toss to coat, flip, and blister all sides.

Remove from the heat and toss with the tomatoes and summer squash. Top with the walnut mixture and serve.

variations

w/raw fennel, orange, chili oil (page 55) + fromage blanc

w/beets, yogurt + sunflower seeds

w/lemon, garlic scapes + lemon parmesan butter (page 62)

GRILLED

Add green beans to the list of things that can be chucked onto the grill throughout the summer. The goal is to char the green beans while keeping the structure of the beans intact. To keep the green beans from slipping annoyingly through the grates, place a roasting or cooking rack on the grill running perpendicular to the grill grates, forming a mesh fine enough to catch the beans. Dress the beans with as little oil as possible to keep the grill from flaming up and blackening the beans. You can always add more oil or dressing to the beans after they are cooked. In case of lack of grill or excess bad weather, remember that a broiler is effectively an upside-down grill and works well too.

charred green beans w/crispy chickpeas and curry yogurt

This dish defines contrast—smoky grilled green beans, cool yogurt, spicy curry, crunchy chickpeas. I love it so much. Long beans and round chickpeas can be a bit unruly; feel free to cut the beans into smaller pieces or slightly smash the chickpeas before crisping if you like. Similarly, depending on the type of yogurt you're using, it might be thick or thin. If it is thin, drizzle; if thick, plop. If you are not a curry fan, I also like this recipe with paprika or cumin instead.

1 lb (455 g) green beans, roughly chopped

¼ cup (60 ml) neutral oil, plus more for cooking the beans

Salt

2 tsp (4 g) curry powder

¾ cup (180 g) yogurt

1 cup (120 g) crispy chickpeas (page 45)

1 bunch cilantro (1 oz | ½ cup | 30 g), roughly chopped

Toss the green beans with a glug of neutral oil and a big pinch of salt and grill.

Heat the ¼ cup oil over high heat and when hot, add the curry powder and let bloom.

Stir the curry oil into the yogurt.

Transfer the beans from the grill to a serving platter and drizzle with curry yogurt. Scatter with the crispy chickpeas and cilantro and serve.

variations

w/fresh tomatoes + tuna mayo

Grill 1 lb (455 g) green beans and put on a serving platter. Scatter with 1 pint (1 lb | 455 g) halved cherry tomatoes, drizzle with 1 cup (230 g) tuna mayo (page 61), and sprinkle with ¼ cup (35 g) sunflower seeds.

w/raw summer squash, parmesan + lemon vinaigrette

Grill 1 lb (455 g) green beans and 1 medium summer squash (½ lb | 230 g), shaved into thin slices or rounds. Toss with ½ bunch of roughly chopped parsley and ½ cup (120 ml) lemon vinaigrette (page 58). Garnish with 4 oz (115 g) Parmesan, cut into ribbons with a vegetable peeler.

w/black beans, peppers + roasted corn

Grill 1 lb (455 g) green beans, 1 sliced medium red onion, 2 sliced red bell peppers, and 3 ears sweet corn on the cob. Cut the kernels from the grilled corn and toss with the green beans, onions, peppers, one 12-oz (340-g) can black beans, drained and rinsed, 1 bunch of chopped cilantro, ¼ cup (60 ml) chili oil (page 55), and a big pinch of salt.

BRAISED

The opposite of the faster, hotter pan roast is the braise. Slow cooking green beans with a bit of liquid makes them silky soft and decidedly unsqueaky. Traditionally when braising meats, the heat should be low, to slowly break down the connective tissue. For vegetables, you can bump up the temp some; just always cover the baking dish to keep the environment moist. Because the slow cooking breaks down the cell structure in the green beans anyway, this is a great place to use frozen green beans if fresh aren't available.

green beans w/tomatoes, lentils, and onions

Olive oil

¼ tsp (1 g) chili flakes

1 medium (4 oz | ½ cup | 115 g) onion, cut into thin slices

3 garlic cloves (0.6 oz | 18 g), cut into thin slices

¾ tsp (4 g) salt

1 cup (240 ml) white wine

¾ cup (180 g) uncooked lentils

1 lb (455 g) green beans, stems snapped off

1 pint (1 lb | 455 g) cherry tomatoes, or ½ cup roasted cherry tomatoes (page 435)

2 cups (480 ml) chicken stock or water

2 oz (55 g) Parmesan

¼ cup (60 ml) basil oil (page 56), or 5 sprigs fresh basil

½ cup salsa verde (page 57) or pounded walnut relish (page 63) or lemon-caper mayo (page 61; optional)

Heat the oven to 350°F (180°C).

In a large Dutch oven, heat a glug of olive oil. When hot, briefly fry the chili flakes, about 30 seconds.

Add the onion, garlic, and salt and stir to combine.

Add the wine and reduce by half, about 5 minutes.

Add the lentils, green beans, tomatoes, and stock, bring to a boil, cover, and cook in the oven until the lentils are tender and the liquid is mostly absorbed, about 50 minutes.

Remove from the oven and grate the Parmesan over the whole thing.

Drizzle with the basil oil (or other toppings as desired) and serve.

variations

w/fennel, summer squash + lemon

Heat a **glug** of oil in a large Dutch oven and <u>sweat</u> a <u>thinly sliced</u> onion and 3 cloves of garlic, sliced. Add 1 lb (455 g) green beans, 2 heads of fennel cut into wedges, 2 cubed summer squash, the rind of a lemon, 2 sprigs oregano or thyme, and 1 cup (240 ml) chicken stock or water with two big pinches of salt and one of black pepper. Braise in the oven until the green beans and summer squash are cooked through and silky, about 30 minutes.

w/sweet corn, fromage blanc + chili oil

Heat a **glug** of oil in a large Dutch oven and <u>sweat</u> a <u>thinly sliced</u> onion and 3 cloves of garlic, sliced. Add 1 lb (455 g) green beans, kernels from 3 ears of corn, the cobs, ½ cup (120 ml) wine, and 1 cup (240 ml) chicken stock or water. Cover and braise in the oven until the green beans are cooked through, about 30 minutes. Remove the corn cobs (which will have imbued the broth with their creamy starch), dot with 4 oz (115 g) fromage blanc or other fresh cheese, drizzle with ¼ cup (60 ml) chili oil (page 55), and serve.

w/eggplant, tomatoes + chickpeas

Heat a **glug** of olive oil in a large Dutch oven and <u>sweat</u> 1 chopped onion and 2 cloves garlic with a big pinch of salt and black pepper. Add 1 lb (455 g) green beans, 1 sliced eggplant, 1 pint (1 lb | 455 g) tomatoes, one 12-oz (340-g) can drained and rinsed chickpeas, ½ cup (120 ml) white wine, and 1 cup (240 ml) chicken stock or water. Cover and braise in the oven until the eggplant is silky and cooked through, about 45 minutes. Drizzle with ¼ cup (60 ml) basil oil (page 56) and serve.

greens, delicate:

ARUGULA, LEAF LETTUCE, HEAD LETTUCE, SPINACH, BABY BOK CHOY

"You gotta get your ruffage," rings in my ears when I'm choking down a boring salad at the start of a meal. A plate of naked greens with the dressing on the side (never enough ranch; always too much vinaigrette), a lame yellowish red tomato, dried-out grated carrots, maybe a shred of purple cabbage holding out hope.

A bad salad pisses me off.

A green salad can be one of the most memorable parts of a meal. It can be the acidic precursor to the main event or the digestive reward after savoring several rich courses. I'm not dogmatic about when a salad is served (though I tend toward the end of the meal, to my father's dismay). I do firmly believe that it must be interesting. Not complicated but entertaining.

The idea of food as entertainment is simple. We exchange dollars and time to be delighted. That pleasure can come in the form of "being wowed"—seeing what that chef has come up with, how she has paired ingredients, techniques, and textures. That joy can be escapism—not needing to do the thing that we do each night. We can be charmed by food and use the experience as a foundation for new relationships or to cement old ones.

For food to be positively memorable it has to enchant to at least a small degree—potentially a tall order for a bag of lettuce. A perfect salad is enthralling, delightful, and never an obligation.

To achieve that excitement, I rely on variety. I want the salad to be colorful. A great salad mix will have bright and pale greens and ideally some red-leafed lettuces. Nothing makes me swoon like a salad garnished with a million different herbs and edible flowers, which is surprising because I mostly think that edible flowers are showy at best and gimmicky at worst. In a salad, they are decadence, lettuce gone romantic and mystical. Nasturtiums are classic, with their peppery heat and fiery yellow, red, and orange petals. Calendula petals taste vaguely of saffron and honey and the mysteries that lie within. Marigolds can be citrusy at best and at worst bland enough that at least they don't detract at all. But my favorites are violas. They range from great big silky petals to little, baby, wild violets. The purple against the green enlivens the dish. Lilacs are also edible, as are red buds in bloom. Beyond these, if you don't know for sure, just check with the internet.

I want my salad to have big hits of flavor. That can be achieved, again, with a variety of greens—the pepperiness of arugula against the more delicate butter lettuce and so on. But I also love adding picked herb leaves to a salad. The specific mix changes as the season carries on. In the spring I rely on what came up from last year's plantings or the herbs that love cool weather—chervil, tarragon, chive blossoms, mint. As it gets warmer—basil, parsley, cilantro, mint, anise hyssop, borage, lemon thyme. I almost never use the woody herbs like rosemary, oregano, sage, thyme, or lavender; they are powerful personalities that can easily dominate a salad. If you want to include these, I advise mincing them—so that your dinner guests aren't stuck gnawing on a whole rosemary sprig—or consider frying them in a bit of oil. This takes some of the volatility out of their leaves and adds a nice papery texture to the salad.

In addition to the wow factor of a million different flavors, I like an acidic salad. Traditionally vinaigrettes have an acid-to-fat ratio of 1:3. I generally go at least 1:2 or even 1:1. (Read: if you use ¼ cup [60 ml] vinegar, use ¼ to ½ cup [60 to 120 ml] oil.) The nice thing about this ratio, beyond the flavor, is that it often requires less vinaigrette to dress the leaves. But that also means that you need to be a bit careful with the first dressing. You can always add more vinaigrette after tasting. You can always add more greens to balance it out, too, but then you have a bigger salad and then need to invite more people over for dinner (because dressed salad does not keep), and it becomes a whole thing.

Finally, I want some extreme texture to a salad. My secret (not secret) weapon is garlicky bread crumbs. These add an undeniably pleasant crunch to a salad. You can make them in big batches, and if you make the bread crumbs with your random bread scraps by allowing them to dry and then grinding them either in a food processor or on a box grater, the crumbs will be fresher and cheaper than what you get in the classic cardboard cylinder from the store—all while getting double brownie points for not wasting the bread.

And when even the most perfect, enchanting salad starts to feel a bit expected, change the technique. Nothing is more entertaining than my uncle trying to dissuade me from putting the whole head of romaine for the Caesar salad on the grill right next to the steaks. "No really, it will be good—just wait and see." A teaser to the big reveal.

I delight in diners bracing themselves for something that sounds gross but is truly a tickling delight—enter Lettuce Soup.

We all need to be entertained now and again.

HOW TO BUY

- Look for salad greens that are not at all wilty.
- Avoid greens with significant browning on the ends.
- If buying head lettuce, look for heads with few damaged leaves on the outside.
- If buying greens that are very wet in the bag, give a whiff and be sure that the greens smell good and not swampy.

HOW TO STORE

- Excessive moisture and heat kills greens; be sure that the greens are dried before storing, and get them cool as fast as possible.
- Store in a plastic bag in the refrigerator.
- If the greens get wilty, soak in cool water until the leaves perk back up, then dry completely.
- If the greens won't perk, consider cooking them before you pitch them.
- If greens are wilty and smell like a dirty fish tank, it's probably best to throw them out, because it is damn near impossible to get that smell out.

NOTES

- Greens come in all sorts of colors and shapes; consider buying a variety.
- Classic lettuces will leach a milky liquid from the stem when cut. It is the plant trying to heal the abrasion. Just rinse it off and don't worry.

RAW

A simple green salad is one of my benchmarks for a truly great restaurant. Too often the salad station is the lowest rung on the kitchen ladder, yet that is where the most delicate vegetables are prepared. Thankfully, I trained at Vie Restaurant under the tutelage of Paul Virant, who always dressed the salads perfectly and knew when I did not. For a single person I always assume two healthy handfuls of lettuce and 1 Tbsp (15 ml) of vinaigrette. He taught me to place the dressing in the bowl and then lightly swoop the leaves through, always using your hand, because metal tongs will bruise. Taste each time and adjust as you go.

perfect salad

Feel free to reduce the amount of salad if you aren't feeding an army. I prefer to serve salads on a large platter rather than a deep bowl, ensuring that the herbs, flowers, and bread crumbs are evenly distributed both throughout the salad and among your guests.

1 bag salad (4 oz | 115 g) greens or 1 head (12 oz | 340 g) lettuce (preferably a mix)

1 bag (4 oz | 115 g) arugula

¼ cup (60 ml) favorite strong vinegar (sherry, apple cider, red wine—just not balsamic)

¼ cup (60 ml) olive oil

Salt and freshly ground black pepper

½ cup (35 g) garlic bread crumbs (page 48)

Any additions (edible flowers, microgreens, picked herbs)

Wash and dry all the greens. If using heads, give a rough chopping to the leaves to make them manageable but leaving them large.

Combine the vinegar, olive oil, and salt in a mason jar and shake to mix.

In a large bowl, combine the greens and dress lightly with the vinaigrette and several good grinds of black pepper. Taste and adjust the seasoning and amount of dressing.

Transfer the salad to a serving platter and sprinkle with the bread crumbs. Top with the additions and serve immediately.

Store the extra vinaigrette in the jar in the fridge or on the counter.

variations

w/roasted strawberries, pecans + goat cheese

Neutral oil

1 qt (1 lb | 455 g) strawberries

1 bag (4 oz | 115 g) mixed greens

½ cup (120 ml) red wine vinaigrette (page 58)

6 oz (170 g) goat cheese

1 cup (120 g) pecans

Freshly ground black pepper

Heat a frying pan until smoking and add a glug of neutral oil. Add the strawberries in a single layer and roast until they are dark and caramelized, and any juice is reduced. Dress the greens in the red wine vinaigrette. Spoon the strawberries over the greens, followed by dots of goat cheese, and finally the toasted pecans and lots of black pepper.

blt salad

6 oz (170 g) bacon, cut into small strips	1 head iceberg or romaine lettuce (12 oz | 340 g)	½ cup (120 ml) pickle liquid dressing (page 58)
1 pint (1 lb | 455 g) cherry tomatoes	Salt and freshly ground black pepper	

In a cold frying pan, set over medium heat, render the bacon until crisp. Remove the bacon, leaving the fat. Heat the frying pan till the fat starts to smoke. Add the cherry tomatoes and cook until the skin is blistered and the juice reduced, about 7 minutes. Cut the lettuce into wedges and season with salt and pepper. Drizzle with the pickle liquid dressing, spoon the roasted tomatoes over the wedges, and garnish with the bacon bits.

w/roasted mushrooms, soft-boiled egg + mustard vinaigrette (bread crumbs would also be great on this)

8 oz (230 g) mushrooms (any kind) cut into smaller pieces	1 egg per person	½ cup (120 ml) mustard vinaigrette (page 58)
	1 bag (4 oz | 115 g) mixed greens	

Roast the mushrooms in a hot pan until brown and crispy (page 24). Boil the eggs in their shells for 5 minutes (page 22). Dress the greens with the mustard vinaigrette, sprinkle with the mushrooms, and top with the soft-boiled egg.

LETTUCE SOUP

ROASTED CHICKEN THIGHS +
MARINATED PEAS

SEARED SALMON +
SHAVED RADISHES

BRAISED

Cooked lettuce makes everyone wrinkle their nose at first, myself included. I first saw braised lettuce on a Jacques Pépin cooking show in a hotel room before I knew who Jacques Pépin was. Every single step along the way I scrunched up my face even more— lettuce, butter, chicken stock, wine. I was wrong. The heat of the base converts the lettuce into silky little handkerchiefs.

braised lettuce

Like several of these base recipes, I pair this with proteins (like roast chicken or seared fish) and something crunchy to make a complete dinner. Though when home alone, I'm just as pleased to eat solely a pan of braised and buttery lettuce solo with a tumbler of white wine. I'll never be Elizabeth David, with her omelet, perfect words, and glass of sherry, but this brings me ever closer.

4 Tbsp (55 g) butter

1 onion (8 oz | 1 cup | 230 g), cut into <u>thin slices</u>

½ tsp (3 g) salt

½ cup (120 ml) white wine

1 cup (240 ml) chicken stock or water

1 head romaine (12 oz | 340 g) or the equivalent of any other type of lettuce, cut or torn into large pieces

Heat the butter in a frying pan until foamy. Add the onion and salt, and <u>sweat</u> about 4 minutes. Add the wine and reduce until almost dry, about 5 minutes. Add the stock and bring to a boil.

Put the lettuce in the stock until it wilts; add more butter if you want it to be richer. Serve warm or room temperature.

variations

w/roasted chicken thighs + marinated peas

Sear the chicken thighs in the frying pan first (page 24); remove and let finish cooking in a 350°F (180°C) oven while making the peas. Add 2 cups (240 g) peas to the chicken stock and cook for 5 minutes before adding the lettuce. Serve the thighs on top of the peas and lettuce.

w/seared salmon + shaved radishes

Sear the salmon in the frying pan first (page 24), then make the lettuce. Put the salmon on the lettuces, skin-side up, and top with the <u>shaved</u> radishes.

or make lettuce soup

Bring 1 quart (1 L) of water or chicken stock to a boil and add 1 lb (455 g) of peas and cook until the peas are bright green, about 5 minutes. Add the lettuces to the broth and cook for 2 minutes. Remove from the heat. Whiz in a blender until smooth. Add ¼ cup (60 ml) cream; taste and adjust the seasoning. Serve hot or cold—the color keeps, and it freezes well.

GRILLED

As when grilling ramps, I like to put the dense cores of lettuce over the hottest part of the fire, allowing the more delicate leaves to drape over a cooler zone. Remember, if you don't have or don't want to use a grill, a broiler or screaming hot cast-iron pan will add a good amount of singe to the greens; just be aware that it will smoke a bit.

charred whole romaine w/hard-boiled egg, anchovy vinaigrette, and garlic bread crumbs

Sturdy head lettuce can take some heat and benefits from the smoky char of the grill. Leaving the core intact makes the whole operation easier because stray leaves won't slide away and into the coals. You can grill hard, allowing the outside leaves to burn fully and steam the center. Or you can grill lightly, singeing the leaves but not cooking the crispness out of the center stems.

2 hard-boiled eggs (page 22), peeled

½ cup (120 ml) anchovy vinaigrette (page 59)

3 chives or scallions, minced (optional but really nice)

1 head romaine (12 oz | 340 g), cut into halves (if small) or quarters (if large) with core intact, rinsed and dried on paper towels

Olive oil

Salt

¼ cup (35 g) garlic bread crumbs (page 48)

Grate the eggs on the largest tooth side of a box grater and add to the vinaigrette along with the scallions. Lightly drizzle the dried lettuce with olive oil and sprinkle with salt. Grill until the outside leaves are charred and the core a bit tender.

Spoon the chunky vinaigrette over the grilled lettuce. Sprinkle with bread crumbs and serve.

variations

w/goat cheese, raw rhubarb + honey vinaigrette

¼ cup (80 g) honey

¼ cup (60 ml) cider vinegar

¼ cup (60 ml) olive oil, plus more for drizzling

Big pinch of salt

1 head romaine, cut into quarters with core intact, rinsed and dried on paper towels

Salt

4 oz (115 g) goat cheese

1 to 2 stalks (2 oz | 55 g) rhubarb, shaved and submerged in acidulated water

w/whitefish, summer squash + cherry tomatoes

1 pint cherry tomatoes (1 lb | 455 g), halved

½ summer squash per person (4 oz | 115 g), shaved

¼ cup (60 ml) red wine vinaigrette (page 58)

Salt and freshly ground black pepper

1 head romaine (12 oz | 340 g), cut into quarters with core intact, rinsed and dried on paper towels

Olive oil

Salt

6-oz (170-g) whitefish fillet per person

w/marinated white beans, mushrooms + radishes

½ lb (230 g) mushrooms (any variety), sliced in half or pieces

Salt and freshly ground black pepper

1 head romaine, cut into quarters with core intact, rinsed and dried on paper towels

¼ cup (60 ml) olive oil, plus more for grilling

One 15-oz (130-g) can or 2 cups (320 g) cooked great northern beans

¼ cup (60 ml) red wine or sherry vinegar

2 garlic cloves (0.4 oz | 14 g), minced

1 bunch radishes (1 lb | 455 g), shaved

Clean and roast the mushrooms (pages 23 and 24) until they are crispy, seasoning with salt and pepper.

Grill the romaine as in the master recipe and let cool, uncovered.

Heat the beans until warm, douse them in the olive oil, vinegar, garlic, and a big pinch of salt, and remove from the heat.

Roughly chop the romaine and combine with the beans and mushrooms. Taste, adjusting the olive oil and salt as desired. Top with the **shaved** radishes and serve warm or at room temperature.

greens, hearty:

CHARD, COLLARDS, KALE, RADICCHIO AND OTHER CHICORIES

In my first year of farming, an older couple walked by the stand, the woman saying to her man, "I wonder what that is," pointing to our bountiful kale and chard display. His response: "I don't know, but I don't like the looks of it."

Kale has gone from being the ugly duckling of the farmers' market to the regal and sought-after swan (and maybe, by the time you read this, on the general outs with everyone again, because we are a capricious bunch). I don't know if it is because of the bumper stickers, Beyoncé's sweatshirt, green smoothies, or because our zeitgeist has realized that greens are good. I don't really care.

The only downside is that kale now suffers from the same image problem as many old-school practical items that have taken a fashionable turn. To believe that this peasant's green is now suitable only for an $8-an-ounce juice bar is as misguided as thinking knee-high rain boots belong only at a music festival in the desert.

For me, kale's rise in popularity is a win for the reliable over the fickle. Kale has long been the green that would see you through the winter—there is a variety literally named Hunger Gap. Its leaves are frost hardy, and you can eat from the same plant for an entire year. It was so important to the Romans that February was known as Kalemonath, a sign of what was available and what they were grateful for. That's what I see when I look at a row of kale plants withstanding the spring frosts, darkening in the summer sun, and standing tall under the winter snow. And no juice bar will ever take that away from me.

I favor kale, and the other less paparazzi-ed hearty greens, because they are more forgiving. Tender salad greens may droop and get slimy after a few days in the refrigerator. If I suddenly have an opportunity to go out of town on a whim, the salad greens seem to wilt spitefully. The kale just waits patiently for me to come home and make dinner later in the week. It can be massaged into submission or dressed with a pungent vinaigrette hours before my dinner guests arrive. Whereas baby lettuces given such heavy-handed treatment will be found pouting in the bottom of the bowl.

Finally, hearty greens make me feel good both in the moment and after a few hours. I like food that I have to chew and that will make me full. Microgreens all but dissolve on my tongue, and while that can be ethereal, it's the dinner version of ghosting. When I eat a big bowl of kale with rice and lentils, the fact that I am still going several hours later is like getting a thank-you note after attending a particularly lovely party—simultaneously surprising and endearing.

HOW TO BUY

- Look for full, rigid leaves.
- Mild bug damage is common for organic kale and doesn't bother me.
- Beware of yellow or bruised leaves, both of which are signs of age and/or wet storage.

HOW TO STORE

- Store in a plastic bag in the refrigerator vegetable drawer or on the counter in a vase of water (like flowers). The plastic bag will keep the air in the refrigerator from wicking away the internal moisture; the vase of water replenishes that moisture as it is lost.
- Kale will get droopy as the moisture respires from the leaves. To revive, soak in cool water like lettuce. If cooking the kale, don't bother rehydrating, as you'll effectively be wilting it anyway.

NOTES

- Hearty greens of all sorts can be used interchangeably. Swap kale and chard for collards, beet greens, turnip greens, or kohlrabi greens.
- Similarly, any and all kale can be used for any and all kale recipes—play around and find the varieties that you like the best.
- I rely on three forms of preparation for hearty greens: raw, wilted, and oven roasted. The benefits of raw or massaged greens include a tender texture, quick turnaround time, and no loss of micronutrients from heat application. There are two ways to wilt greens: braising with fat and plenty of liquid and sautéing hot and fast with a bit of liquid. Braising yields greens that are silky and falling-apart tender. Sautéed greens keep their texture with an acidic tang. Oven roasting creates a crisp texture and can be done in advance, easing preparation for dinner parties or other gatherings.

RAW

The amount of time it takes to tenderize raw greens will vary depending on the age of the plant. The tougher the leaves, the longer it will take. Along the way, taste an individual leaf and once it is easily chewable, you're done.

massaged kale w/tomatoes, creamed mozzarella, and wild rice

This recipe calls for wild rice but substitute any cooked grain—especially any random grains that are in the back of your fridge. If you do use wild rice, you don't need to soak the grains overnight, but soaked rice will cook much more quickly and will "pop" when cooked, improving the texture, in my opinion. Unsoaked rice will take significantly longer than white rice to cook, so plan accordingly.

Olive oil

1 small onion (2 oz | ¼ cup | 55 g), cut into thin slices

2 garlic cloves (0.2 oz | 14 g), minced

Salt and freshly ground black pepper

¼ cup (60 ml) white wine

1 cup (180 g) wild rice, soaked overnight in 4 cups (1 L) water

1 bunch kale (½ lb | 4 cups | 230 g), midribs stripped, well dried and cut into ¼-inch (6-mm) ribbons

1 ball fresh mozzarella (8 oz | 230 g)

¼ cup (60 g) sour cream

1 lemon (1½ fl oz | 45 ml), zest and juice

1 pint cherry tomatoes (1 lb | 455 g), halved

Heat a glug of olive oil. Sweat the onion and garlic with the salt until translucent, about 5 minutes. Add the white wine and reduce by half. Add the wild rice and the soaking liquid and cook until tender, about 45 minutes.

In a mixing bowl, sprinkle the kale with a pinch of salt. Massage the kale until it is dark green, limp, and tender in mouthfeel.

Tear the mozzarella into rough <u>chunks</u>. Combine with the sour cream, lemon zest and juice, a good pinch of salt, and a couple of grinds of black pepper.

When the wild rice is cooked, drain any residual liquid and let cool.

<u>Toss</u> the tomatoes, kale, and wild rice together with a couple <u>glugs</u> of olive oil and a pinch of salt. Taste and adjust the seasoning. Dot with the creamed mozzarella and serve.

variations

chard, lemon vinaigrette (page 58), parmesan + lentils

radicchio, sherry vinegar, wheat berries, beets + goat cheese

kale, <u>shaved</u> summer squash, walnuts, smoked trout +
pickle liquid dressing (page 58)

W/GRITS + EGG

W/TOMATO SLABS + WHITE BEANS

W/SALMON + BUTTERED RICE

SAUTÉED

The French translation of "sauté" means to jump or bounce. In cooking terms, "sauté" is defined as cooking food in a small amount of fat over high heat. It is also the classic "cheffy" move of flipping food in a pan by jerking the pan forward and then backward. And it is so fun. You don't need to have mastered "the flip" to sauté successfully. Just remember high heat, a bit of fat, and a quick jump either with a stir of a spoon or the yank of a pan. And don't be discouraged by the term glug—a splash of oil. Enough to grease the pan, not so much that you are deep-frying the ingredients, roughly about 2 Tbsp (30 ml).

sautéed greens w/garlic and chili flakes

This is my favorite and most utilized method for cooking greens. Adding the garlic and chili flakes at the same time as the wine prevents those from burning, and they can steam in the reducing wine. The flavor is magically more than the sum of its parts. It is lightning fast. And pairs with just about anything else that you are making for breakfast, lunch, snack, or dinner.

Neutral oil

2 bunches chard or kale (1 lb | 8 cups | 455 g), midribs stripped out, cut into ribbons (add additional hearty greens like radicchio or cabbage)

½ cup (120 ml) white wine

Pinch of salt

Pinch of chili flakes

2 garlic cloves (0.4 oz | 14 g), cut into thin slices

Heat a large frying pan with a glug of neutral oil over high heat until smoking hot. Add the greens and let cook until lightly browned. Flip or stir the greens and add the white wine, salt, chili flakes, and garlic. Let the wine reduce until almost dry and serve immediately.

BRAISED

If you have greens that won't perk up in water, give them a wilt. This is also a great way to use up multiple types of greens that are cowering in the back of the refrigerator.

braised kale w/jowl bacon, onions, and parsley

Here the rich fat of the jowl bacon balances the saintly qualities of kale. Jowl bacon (also known as guanciale) is made the same way as regular bacon but uses the fatty cheeks of the pig in place of the fatty belly. I like it because it is a good use for an underappreciated part of the pig, but bacon, ham hocks, pancetta, or even anchovies will give you the same result. The beer provides acidity to lift the flavors of both the kale and the bacon. White wine, hard cider, or vinegar (but use half as much) are good substitutes.

¼ lb (115 g) jowl bacon, cut into bite-size chunks

1 onion (4 oz | ½ cup | 115 g), cut into thin slices

¼ tsp (1 g) chili flakes

3 sprigs thyme, tied into a bunch

2 bunches kale (1 lb | 8 cups | 455 g), midribs stripped out, cut into ribbons

½ cup (120 ml) beer, preferably a lager or brown ale

In a large frying pan, cook the bacon until the fat renders and the pieces are a bit crispy. Add the onion, chili flakes, and thyme and cook until golden brown. Add the kale and beer to the onion, cover, and let steam. After a couple of minutes, uncover and cook until the liquid is reduced, and the kale is tender. Taste and add salt or a splash of vinegar if needed.

variations

collards w/sausage + apples

4 oz (115 g) sausage

1 onion (4 oz | ½ cup | 115 g), cut into thin slices

Salt

2 bunches collards (1 lb | 8 cups | 455 g) or any other hearty greens, midribs stripped out, cut into ribbons

1 cup (240 ml) beer or white wine

2 tart apples (1 lb | 455 g), cut into half-moons

chard w/anchovies + white wine

Olive oil

4 anchovy fillets (0.5 oz | 15 g each)

1 onion (4 oz | ½ cup | 115 g), cut into thin slices

4 garlic cloves (0.8 oz | 28 g), minced

2 bunches chard (1 lb | 8 cups | 455 g), leaves stripped, stems cut into thin slices

Salt

½ cup (120 ml) white wine

kale w/parmesan, tomatoes + chili oil

1 onion (4 oz | ½ cup | 115 g), cut into thin slices

Salt

½ cup (120 ml) white wine

2 bunches kale (1 lb | 8 cups | 455 g), midribs stripped out, cut into ribbons

2 oz (55 g) Parmesan, shaved into ribbons

½ cup (120 g) roasted cherry tomatoes, halved

¼ cup (60 ml) chili oil (page 55)

OVEN ROASTED

As with all oven roasting, you should have the oven hotter than you might think and let the vegetables brown to get good and caramelized. The greens will darken as they cook. Don't be scared of brown leaves! Let the texture be your guide for doneness. You are looking for shatteringly crispy "chips." But beware: unlike oven-roasted root vegetables, greens cook much faster because they are so thin, so keep a sharp eye while simultaneously holding your nerve until they get brittle.

oven-roasted kale chips w/grated raclette

Kale chips have taken the nation by storm. In restaurants we deep-fry the greens until they are amazingly crispy. This can also be achieved in an oven, though with slightly less greasy decadence. The key to success is to be sure that the kale leaves do not overlap, or else they will steam and never crisp. Like all other kale recipes, a bit of fat and salt and acid balances the vegetable quality of the leaves. If you can't find raclette, substitute Parmesan or fontina.

2 bunches kale (1 lb | 8 cups | 455 g), midribs stripped out, leaves dried completely

Olive oil

Salt

2 oz (55 g) raclette, grated

Heat the oven to 425°F (220°C).

Toss the whole leaves with olive oil and lay out in a single layer on a sheet tray. You may need to do this in batches or on multiple pans to give them enough space to crisp, not steam. Sprinkle with salt. Roast until light and crispy, about 7 minutes.

Remove from the oven, immediately grate the cheese over them, and serve. The finer the grating of cheese, the more easily it will soften over the hot chips. To get them really melty, return them to the oven after grating and allow the remaining heat of the oven to just melt them.

variations

kale chips w/chili oil (page 55) + cheddar

kale chips w/soy sauce + maple syrup

kale chips w/dukkah (page 63)

kohlrabi

If you want to become a better cook, join a CSA.

Community Supported Agriculture (CSA) is a way for consumers to buy a stake in a specific farm's crops for the season. The basics of the program are as follows: consumers buy a share in the spring, giving the farm an infusion of cash when they need it most; the farm provides members with a portion of the farm's output each week for usually around twenty weeks. Lots of programs offer add-ons like eggs, flowers, fruit, meat, and grains, if not sourced from their farm, then from neighboring farms with similar growing practices.

The benefits are four-fold. One, you become a member of that farm and invested in the farm's successes and trials throughout the season. Even more than shopping at a farmers' market, CSAs offer you a way to be directly connected to food production. If there is a bounty of tomatoes, you, too, will be flush with tomatoes in the early fall. You, too, run the risk of no tomatoes if terrible hailstorms roll through and tear all of the tomatoes to tatters. The beauty of this investment is that the farm doesn't run the risk of going out of business because of not having those tomatoes; the community shares in the risks associated with agriculture.

Two, you will save money. This is the part of a CSA that I tend to not laud because I believe that we pay for the quality we want in our food, and that food is, in general, sold too cheaply. But it is true. For every CSA I've ever worked with, I paid up front for about $30 worth of weekly vegetables and easily averaged $40 of produce each week. Sometimes the shares are leaner in the spring, but by fall I've always made up the difference. It is a big check to write at the start of the year, but it has never not paid off. You also save money because the vegetables are often delivered in their whole form. Beets have edible greens that are often removed when shipped long distances because they don't keep as long as the roots. When you get the whole plant, you get two meals out of it instead of just one—a steal at twice the price.

Three, you will become healthier. When you're inundated with vegetables every week, the likelihood you'll eat more vegetables increases (let's hope), and a plant-based diet is good for us. Studies show that eating more vegetables and fruits decreases blood pressure and the likelihood of heart disease and diabetes. Increasing fiber intake promotes healthy digestion. I have **science feels** about this, and my evidence is only anecdotal, but when I eat more vegetables and fruits, I feel better. I think you will, too.

Four, you will become a better cook. Each week your portion of the farm's output will arrive on your kitchen counter. Sometimes you will get exactly what you would have bought from the store. Sometimes you won't. In the weeks when the share is not what you would have purchased, your skill set grows. What else can you do with chard? What the hell is a kohlrabi, and what do you do with that alien in your bag? No potatoes this week; let's substitute these sweet potatoes. Necessity is the mother of invention, and CSAs will provide you weeks of inventing new dinners and dishes, growing your comfort and skill set with an ever-wider range of ingredients. Plus, you might not be able to go back to carrots from a store that have been out of the ground for weeks. Great cooks are meticulous shoppers, and after twenty weeks of farm-fresh produce, it may be hard to settle for produce shipped from a world away.

Kohlrabi, for me, epitomizes all four of these CSA benefits.

One, kohlrabi is as easy to grow as kale and easier than broccoli, and it sells worse than both. By having a built-in captive audience, farmers can grow it and know that it will have a home. It is also a cold-weather crop, so by knowing it will be consumed, farmers have more diverse options for the cooler, shoulder parts of the season.

Two, both the leaves and the root balls are edible, providing multiple meals from one plant. Treat the leaves just as you would collards. The above-ground root—often referred to where I live as Midwestern jicama—is mild, juicy, and sweet. It has the texture of a radish but without the spice. The base also has a cell structure and starch that takes well to baking. It doesn't mash as smoothly as potatoes, but roasts and bakes in a casserole as fine as any spud and can be used almost interchangeably.

Three, kohlrabi is in the Brassicaceae (or Cruciferae) family and is packed with soluble fiber, vitamin C, vitamin B of several varieties, copper, and potassium. Unlike many vegetables, it is a source of carbohydrates, explaining its sweet flavor and making it easier for less-than-enthusiastic vegetable eaters to get on board.

Four, I have yet to meet anyone who goes to a market saying, *Oh, I just simply need to get some kohlrabi*, but I know several people who, after receiving it in their share, now seek out its cool, crunchy flesh and velvety leaves. CSAs created that demand. That demand is showing up at markets across the country, and now an almost-forgotten German standard is becoming as chic as the sleekest eggplant. You can be the sort of cook successfully wielding a strange-bird vegetable with confidence and happily answering the questions about that weirdo—*Oh, that, that's just some kohlrabi*.

To sum up: CSAs are rad! Consider buying into your local agricultural economy—it might just make you healthy, wealthy, and wise.

HOW TO BUY

- Look for an even, round shape and greens that are not overly wilty.
- Avoid kohlrabi with brown or black gashes in the skin.
- If the kohlrabi is super large, don't rule it out, but check with the grower or knowledgeable vendor to be sure it is a variety that is still tender when large.

HOW TO STORE

- Cut the greens from the roots and store in a plastic bag.
- Store the kohlrabi in the refrigerator in a plastic bag to protect the skin from evaporation.

NOTES

- When young, kohlrabi doesn't need to be peeled, but taste it to be sure you're happy with the texture.
- The purple variety doesn't taste of grape, no matter what your farmer tells you.
- I almost always peel the kohlrabi unless the skin is incredibly tender in the early spring. To do so, tip and tail the root ball, reserving the greens if there are any. Rest one cut side on the cutting board and, with a knife or vegetable peeler, slice away the outer skin, revealing the white flesh beneath.

BAKED

Baked kohlrabi has a silky texture that plays well against other mouthfeels—buttery potatoes, starchy celery root, the squeaky, green fibrousness of a kale salad. Any of these recipes can be made with potatoes if you're kohlrabi-less.

kohlrabi potato gratin

Gratins are beautiful in their simplicity and the magic of a dish being something more than the sum of its parts. The downside is that gratins can also border on very heavy and stodgy. Kohlrabi lifts the texture a bit, and because it has less starch in its cells, it will be less firm than a traditional gratin. If making this in advance (for parties or holidays), stop and cool the gratin after the roots are tender. Then when you're ready to serve it, top with the cheese and bake to warm and melt the cheese. If the cheese is melted the day before it never looks as good on day two.

Neutral oil or butter

3 kohlrabi (3 lb | 3 cups | 1.4 kg), peeled and sliced into ¼-inch (6-mm) rounds

2 lb (910 g) potatoes (I like Yukon or Carola gold), peeled or not, sliced into ¼-inch (6-mm) rounds

Salt and freshly ground black pepper

Thyme sprigs, stemmed, leaves picked off (optional)

1 cup (240 ml) cream

4 oz (115 g) hard cheese, ideally Swiss or Gruyère, grated

Heat the oven to 350°F (180°C) and grease a 9 by 9 inch (23 by 23 cm) baking dish or Dutch oven with a glug of oil or smear of butter.

Pick out 12 of the prettiest rounds of kohlrabi and potato for the top layer. Lay out one layer of potato, sprinkle with salt, pepper, and thyme. Layer the kohlrabi on top, season with salt and pepper. Continuing building the layers until out of vegetables, finishing with the pretty rounds. Drizzle the cream over the vegetables and cover with foil.

Bake until the potato and kohlrabi are tender when pierced with a knife, about 35 minutes. Remove the foil and top with the grated cheese. Return the dish to the oven until the cheese is melted, browned, and bubbly. Serve hot or warm.

variations

w/sweet potato, mustard + cream

Substitute sweet potatoes for the regular potatoes and add 2 Tbsp (30 g) Dijon or whole-grain mustard to the cream.

w/kale, celery root + bacon

Neutral oil or butter

½ lb (230 g) bacon, cut into ¼-inch (6-mm) <u>chunks</u>

1 onion (½ lb | 1 cup | 230 g), cut into <u>thin slices</u>

½ cup (120 ml) white wine or beer

2 celery roots (2 lb | 910 g), peeled and cut into ¼-inch (6-mm) rounds

2 kohlrabi (2 lb | 2 cups | 910 g), peeled and cut into ¼-inch (6-mm) rounds

1 <u>bunch</u> kale (½ lb | 4 cups | 230 g), <u>midribs stripped</u> out, cut into ribbons

1 cup (240 ml) cream

Heat the oven to 350°F (180°C) and grease a 9 by 9 inch (23 by 23 cm) baking dish with a <u>glug</u> of oil or smear of butter. Render the bacon in a frying pan over medium heat. Add the onion and <u>sweat</u> until soft. Add the wine and cook until evaporated. In the prepared dish, layer the celery root, kohlrabi, kale, and onion and bacon mixture. Continue layering and finish with either the celery root or kohlrabi. Pour the cream over it and bake until all is tender, about 35 minutes.

w/horseradish + dill

2 kohlrabi (2 lb | 2 cups | 910 g), peeled and sliced into ¼-inch (6-mm) rounds

2 lb (910 g) potatoes, peeled and sliced into ¼-inch (6-mm) rounds

¼ cup (60 g) grated horseradish (fresh or prepared)

1 cup (240 ml) cream

10 sprigs dill, minced

Follow the master recipe, adding the horseradish to the cream and sprinkling dill between the layers.

RAW

At the market we would always tell shoppers that kohlrabi is the Midwestern jicama. It is crunchy, juicy, and slightly sweet. Kohlrabi shares the Brassicaceae family characteristics of cabbage and broccoli stems and is perfect sliced raw in any sort of salad. I also like to cut them into planks or discs and use them to shovel dip into my mouth.

kohl-slaw w/apples, black lentils, sherry vinaigrette, and seared salmon

Black or green French lentils work best here. The salmon is not a must; this salad is lovely on its own or with a soft or hard egg on top, and also travels well for office lunches or picnics.

Neutral oil

1 cup (200 g) lentils

2 cups (480 ml) water

1 tsp (6 g) salt, plus more for the fish

¾ cup (180 ml) sherry vinaigrette (page 58)

4 pieces salmon (6 oz | 170 g each), skin on

2 tart apples (1 lb | 455 g) (such as Granny Smith, Greening, or Mutsu), cut into thin slices

2 kohlrabi (2 lb | 2 cups | 910 g) (leaves on or off), ends trimmed off, peeled and cut into matchsticks; if using the leaves, cut into thin ribbons

½ bunch parsley (1.2 oz | ¾ cup | 34 g), stemmed, leaves left whole

In a saucepan, heat a glug of neutral oil. When warm, add the lentils and toast them a bit, about 3 minutes.

Add the water and salt and bring to a boil, reduce to a simmer, cover, and cook uncovered until the lentils are tender, 20 to 35 minutes depending on the type.

When the lentils are cooked, drain any excess liquid, dress with the vinaigrette, and let cool.

Pat the salmon skins dry, season with salt, and sear (page 24).

<u>**Toss**</u> **together** the lentils, apple, kohlrabi, leaves if using, and parsley. Taste and adjust the seasoning.

Serve the salmon skin-side up with a generous spoonful of the salad on the side.

variations

w/anchovy vinaigrette + spinach

3 anchovies (0.35 oz | 12 g), roughly chopped

2 garlic cloves (0.2 oz | 14 g), roughly chopped

2 lemons (3 fl oz | 90 ml), zest and juice

½ cup (120 ml) olive oil

1 bag (4 oz | 115 g) spinach

2 kohlrabi (2 lb | 2 cups | 910 g), ends trimmed off, peeled and cut into <u>matchsticks</u>

¼ cup (35 g) garlic bread crumbs (page 48)

Blend the anchovy and garlic and combine with the lemon and olive oil. Dress the spinach in the vinaigrette, combine with the kohlrabi, and sprinkle with the bread crumbs.

chicken thighs w/delicata squash + brown butter vinaigrette

1 delicata squash (½ lb | 230 g), seeded and cut into half-moons (or substitute raw ribbons of butternut squash)

Neutral oil

4 to 6 chicken thighs (6 oz | 170 g each)

2 kohlrabi (2 lb | 2 cups | 910 g), ends trimmed off, peeled and cut into matchsticks

1 bunch kale (½ lb | 4 cups | 230 g) (midribs stripped out, leaves massaged with oil) or spinach or arugula

½ cup (120 ml) brown butter vinaigrette (page 59), warmed

Salt and freshly ground black pepper

Heat the oven to 400°F (200°C). Dress the squash with a glug of oil and roast until crispy. Sear the chicken thighs (page 24) and finish in the oven until cooked through, about 12 minutes. Toss the squash, kohlrabi, greens, and warmed vinaigrette with a big pinch of salt and black pepper. Spoon over the chicken thighs and serve.

w/radishes, asparagus + lemon vinaigrette

1 bunch radishes (1 lb | 455 g), shaved

1 bunch asparagus spears (1 lb | 455 g), shaved

2 kohlrabi (2 lb | 2 cups | 910 g), ends trimmed off, peeled and cut into matchsticks

½ bunch parsley (1.2 oz | ¾ cup | 34 g), stemmed, leaves left whole

5 sprigs mint, stemmed, leaves torn

1 bag (4 oz | 115 g) arugula

¾ cup (180 ml) lemon vinaigrette (page 58)

½ cup (120 ml) olive oil

Salt and freshly ground black pepper

Combine the vegetables and herbs with the vinaigrette and a big pinch of salt and pepper. Taste and adjust the seasoning, and serve.

leeks

I wish there was a term for the flavor of chlorophyll. "Greenness" circuitously describes it as grassy at best or vegetal at worst. Chlorophyll tastes of wet spring mornings or matcha tea. It is this green flavor that separates a leek from her cousins, garlic and onion.

Oddly enough, while I associate the taste of chlorophyll with spring, leeks are of the winter. It's one of those vegetables, like parsnips, that I resist until my options are more limited in late fall. When I have been lucky enough to have leeks in the garden, their greenness comes into the kitchen under piles of snow. The onions were pulled in from outside months ago, but the leeks wave their broad flag leaves through the winter winds.

It is a pain, to be sure, to go out and dig leeks after the snow has fallen. Like an iceberg, the majority of a leek's shaft is under the surface. They were planted that way in the spring; wispy starts plopped into a hole several inches deep in early April. Requiring little maintenance beyond a bit of weeding and some water throughout the summer, leeks grow out of that hole, putting up a shock of flat, torch-like leaves to take in the sun. The days shorten and cool, and around the time of year reserved for sweaters and soups, I harvest my first leeks. A digging fork loosens the soil about ten inches below ground level, and then with two hands I pull out the long stalk.

The cells of the leek's shaft are blanched white because of the lack of sunlight—the absence of activated chlorophyll. Nature's ombré shading white to pale green all the way to the blue green of the flags. Leeks never fail to remind me of Audrey Hepburn's cigarette holder from *Breakfast at Tiffany's*, Lincoln's top hat, or elbow-length opera gloves.

Despite their elegance, leeks are dirty buggers. While growing throughout the summer, they've sandwiched sand between their sheets. To wash leeks, cut the stalks and then soak in plenty of cold water, agitating a few times, allowing the sand to fall to the bottom of the bowl. Then lift the leeks from the water, scooping the leaves away from the dirt. If you pour the water over the leeks the sand will sneak its way back into the cut leeks, defeating the purpose. When leaving the leeks whole, separate the leaf layers and flush with running water to dislodge the dirt—like an underwater flip book. Letting them rest cut-side down allows the water in the layers to drip away.

Leeks lack the sugar present in both onions and garlic, so attempts to caramelize are futile. Instead, play upon the grassy notes that distinguish leeks from the others, pairing them with thyme and butter and cream or lemon and acid of all sorts. Although they are sturdy in the garden, be gentle with leeks. Browning them tends to produce bitterness. Allow that chlorophyll to shine through.

Leeks continue to be one of the most intimidating vegetables for most people. They are long and unwieldy and often very dirty. Remember that they are an onion. Think of them the same way you would a scallion or traditional onion. Cut away what you don't want to eat, and don't let them boss you around.

HOW TO BUY

- Leeks start to show up at market stalls in the late fall and persist through the winter months.
- Leeks in the spring have been over-wintered and tend to be a bit sweeter, though if the leek has started to sprout, the center could be a touch tough. But the surrounding layers will be delicate and tasty.
- Look for leeks that are rigid and don't bend easily.
- Look for leeks with the roots still intact, even if they are dirty, as they will store for longer when left uncut.
- I don't notice a taste difference between very thick leeks and more slender ones.

HOW TO STORE

- Leeks do not store as well as their storage onion cousins, so use them quickly once pulled from the ground.
- Store in a plastic bag with a moist paper towel around their roots in the refrigerator or other cold space.
- If you've bought leeks with their flag leaves still attached, be sure that those are also covered with plastic, or cut them away.

NOTES

- The coarser flag leaves are unpalatable but add flavor to stocks, soups, and poaching liquids.
- Leeks are often dirty, having pulled sand into their layers while growing.
- To trim the leeks: cut the roots from the bottom, cut away any tough green leaves from the top close to where the green and white meet, and peel away any battered or tough green leaves, exposing the center core. I leave as much green as I can without keeping any really stringy leaves. When in doubt, cut away more than you think, and reserve the trimmings for stock or poaching fish (page 23).
- To clean them, rinse away as much dirt as you can get at without tearing the layers. Then cut the leeks as you desire and immediately transfer them to a plentiful amount of cool water. Agitate the water, forcing the sand to drop to the bottom, and then lift the leeks from the water and allow to drain before cooking. Avoid pouring the water over the cut leeks to drain, because the sand will wiggle its way back into the crevices of the leaves, undoing all your work.

RAW

Like raw onions, uncooked leeks add a bite to any dish, functioning similarly to an acid element to balance rich foods. Unlike raw onions, the flavor is milder, with delicate green, grassy notes. But as with raw onions, the sulfurous bite can be minimized be rinsing or soaking in cold water. I like to play with the cut of the leek to achieve different textures. Long slender cuts the length of the stalk make delicate ribbons for a salad. Cutting them perpendicular to the stalk creates perfect rings or half-moons. There's no right answer, just how you want it to look and feel in your mouth.

marinated leek salad w/wheat berries, carrots, and seared salmon

Leeks in vinaigrette is a classic French dish that hasn't gained support in the States. The beauty of marinating leeks is balance. The technique allows the leeks to keep their punchy onion bite while tempering that bite with the flavors of the vinaigrette. They can soak for as little as 15 minutes or up to 3 or 4 days. I usually marinate in a tight-lidded container or a zip locking bag; just be sure that the marinade is touching all of the leeks. If it doesn't, shake or agitate to ensure contact.

This recipe is also great without the salmon or with everything tossed together into one big salad. It just depends on how you want to serve it. I like separating the components for a dinner party and serving as one big bowl for a potluck.

¾ cup (180 ml) olive oil, plus more for toasting wheat berries

1 cup (180 g) wheat berries

4 cups (1 L) water or stock

Salt

1 orange (3 fl oz | 90 ml), zest and juice

1 Tbsp (15 ml) apple cider vinegar

2 medium leeks (1 lb | 455 g), trimmed and cut into 1- to 2-inch-long (2.5- to 5-cm) thin strips or half-moons and cleaned well

4 salmon fillets (6 oz | 170 g each) or 1 full side (24 oz | 680 g)

4 carrots (12 oz | 340 g), shaved into ribbons with a vegetable peeler

½ bunch parsley (1.2 oz | ¾ cup | 34 g), roughly chopped

Heat a glug of olive oil in a medium saucepan. When hot, add the wheat berries and toast until fragrant and lightly toasty. Add the water and 2 big pinches of salt, bring to a boil, reduce to a simmer, and cook until the wheat berries are tender, about 45 minutes.

Combine the orange zest, juice, vinegar, olive oil, and a big pinch of salt and marinate the leeks.

Pat the skin of the salmon dry, sprinkle both sides liberally with salt, and sear (page 24).

While the salmon sears, combine the leek mixture with the carrots and parsley. Taste and adjust the seasoning and acidity.

Spread the wheat berries on a serving platter. Top with the fish and garnish with the salad.

variations

w/radish slaw + pork chops

2 leeks (1 lb | 455 g), cut into slices and cleaned well

1 <u>bunch</u> radishes (1 lb | 455 g), <u>shaved</u>

½ <u>bunch</u> parsley (1.2 oz | ¾ cup | 34 g), roughly chopped

½ cup (120 ml) apple cider vinaigrette (page 58)

4 pork chops, 8 to 10 oz (230 to 280 g) each

Salt and freshly ground black pepper

Combine the leeks, radishes, and parsley with the vinaigrette. Season the pork chops liberally with salt and pepper and sear in a large frying pan until cooked through, about 7 minutes each side (page 23). Allow the chops to rest for 7 minutes, and then top with the slaw or place alongside and serve.

w/lemon vinaigrette + fresh mozzarella

2 leeks (1 lb | 455 g), cut into <u>thin slices</u> and cleaned well

½ <u>bunch</u> parsley (1.2 oz | ¾ cup | 34 g), roughly chopped

½ cup (120 ml) lemon vinaigrette (page 58)

Salt and freshly ground black pepper

½ loaf sourdough bread, cut into slices

4 balls fresh mozzarella (2 lb | 910 g), each torn in half

Combine the leeks, parsley, and lemon vinaigrette with a big pinch each of salt and pepper. Toast the bread. Top the mozzarella with the marinated leeks and serve with toast on the side.

w/mustard vinaigrette, arugula + wild rice

2 leeks (1 lb | 455 g), cut into <u>thin slices</u> and cleaned well

½ cup (120 ml) mustard vinaigrette (page 58)

1 bag (4 oz | 115 g) arugula

2 cups (360 g) wild rice, cooked (page 43)

Salt and freshly ground black pepper

Dress the leeks with the mustard vinaigrette, combine with the arugula and wild rice, season, and serve.

W/EGG FRITTATA + GREENS

W/ROASTED POTATOES, SQUASH
+ RAW CARROTS

W/SEARED CHICKEN THIGHS + RICE

BRAISED

The counterbalance to the crisp bright acidity of raw leeks is the gentle sweetness and silken texture of braised leeks. This recipe can be served warm, allowed to cool to room temperature and served as a side to a larger meal, or gussied up with other ingredients as the variations suggest.

slow-cooked leeks w/thyme and cream

Here the caramely flavor from the sear blends well into the cream and chicken stock as they slowly soften.

Neutral oil

10 sprigs thyme

4 leeks (2 lb | 910 g), trimmed and sliced in half lengthwise with the core intact, cleaned well

½ cup (120 ml) white wine

1 lemon, peel cut into wide slices with a vegetable peeler

1½ cup (360 ml) chicken stock

½ tsp (3 g) salt

Several grinds black pepper

½ cup (120 ml) cream

Heat the oven to 300°F (150°C). In a large frying pan or Dutch oven, heat a glug of neutral oil. Briefly fry the thyme in the oil, then push to the side. Pat the leeks dry and sear them, cut-side down, letting them brown lightly. This may need to be done in batches to ensure even contact between the leeks and the frying pan. Flip to their round side. Add the wine and allow to reduce by half.

Add the lemon rind, chicken stock, salt, and pepper and bring to a boil.

Cover and braise in the oven until the leeks are tender, about 25 minutes. Remove from the oven, add the cream, and bring to a boil on a burner until the cream is reduced to the texture of creamed spinach, 3 to 5 minutes. Remove the lemon peel and thyme, and serve hot or warm.

variations

w/roasted potatoes, squash + raw carrots

10 small or fingerling potatoes (1 lb | 455 g), cut into wedges

1 small acorn or delicata squash (1 lb | 455 g), peeled and cut into wedges

Olive oil

Salt

3 carrots (9 oz | 255 g), cut into irregular pieces

1 bag (4 oz | 115 g) arugula

One recipe Slow-Cooked Leeks (page 281)

Heat the oven to 400°F (200°C). Toss the potatoes and squash with the olive oil and a big pinch of salt and roast until cooked through and crispy on the edges. Remove from the oven, toss with the carrots and arugula with another dash of olive oil, and serve with warm or room temperature leeks on the side.

w/egg frittata + greens

6 eggs

½ cup (120 ml) cream

½ tsp (3 g) salt

½ tsp (3 g) pepper

Olive oil

Any vegetables you want to add to the frittata (potatoes, peppers, tomatoes, and so on)

½ bag (2 oz | 55 g) arugula or salad greens

¼ cup (60 ml) apple cider vinaigrette (page 58)

One recipe Slow-Cooked Leeks (page 281)

Heat the oven to 350°F (180°C). Whisk the eggs with the cream, salt, and pepper. Heat a glug of olive oil in a frying pan and add any vegetables. Pour the egg mixture over them and let the bottom set in the frying pan. Transfer to the oven and let cook through, about 20 minutes. Dress the arugula with the vinaigrette. Remove the egg mixture from the oven and slice into wedges. Top with the braised leeks and dressed arugula.

w/seared chicken thighs + rice

4 to 6 seared chicken thighs (6 oz | 170 g each) (page 24)

Salt and freshly ground black pepper

2 cups (360 g) cooked rice (page 41)

½ bag (2 oz | 55 g) greens

¼ cup (60 ml) sherry vinaigrette (page 58)

One recipe Slow-Cooked Leeks (page 281)

onions

Every farmer I know has at least one plant they fawn over—their favorite to grow. I'm friends with a farmer who is fixated on onions. She loves onions because they take the whole season. Not like salad greens or radishes, in and out in a matter of weeks; onions start and end the season with her. She plants the little nigella-like seeds first thing in February. Little green wisps poke straight up from the soil block. Every time she walks by, a little pass of the hand to brush them back, strengthening their cells and releasing the faintest waft of the onion to come.

All of them start like this. The sweet Ailsa Craig, the strong Spanish storage onion, the disc-like Italian cipollini, the purple-fleshed shallot, the crimson red onion. They all stay in the greenhouse until the ground is fully thawed. Each one can take a bit of a frost, so they are less delicate than the bulk of spring green leaves.

Through spring and early summer, those little green whips grow and become like chives on steroids. The bulb grows above with a knot of roots reaching into the ground. It is this time of year that the onions require little attention from my farming friend. As long as they are kept free of weeds (mostly) and have enough water, they will wait happily while other crops take up her time.

The onions, before the summer solstice, absorb as much energy as possible to grow the bulb. In the plant's mind it is growing that bulb to store energy through the winter. After the solstice the plant senses that its opportunity to absorb solar energy is dwindling; it starts to cut off energy to the rest of the plant. The greens die back. Paper forms around the bulb, thickening its skin for the winter.

At this point the bulbs will not get much bigger. They are pulled from the ground and left to cure in a dry, cool, dark barn. The paper gets thicker and the greens shrivel. These onions are ready to be sold at market or stored throughout the winter.

All of this is true except for the sweet onions. Sweet onions contain roughly the same amount of sulfuric acid as storage onions, but they also house much more water in their cells, diluting the pungency associated with onions and leaving the impression that they are therefore sweet. That high water volume makes sweet onions less ideal for storage—more prone to rot. These onions are best eaten fresh in the middle of the summer. Some eat them like apples. I do not. I'll take them raw in a salad or battered for my once-a-year onion ring fry up. Also, please note that while you can use sweet onions to make caramelized onions, it will take longer (cooking out even more water) and be no more sweet (they don't have more sugar than "nonsweet" onions). That said, while not ideal, caramelizing and freezing are good ways to preserve sweet onions.

After the onion harvest and the days of curing, the onions simply wait patiently. They are steady friends to take to market each week. The corner of my friend's three-tent market stall is always dedicated to onions—a vast array of colors and shapes to cap end the stand.

While onions form the backbone of many dishes, they can also be stars in their own right. Fall is my favorite time to showcase them. By this time, I'm through with raw sweet onions. I've eaten enough salad for a while. My eyes turn toward long, slow-cooked dishes. I want something with a bit of fat, which always craves a jolt of acid to perk it up, dinner that will make me want to cuddle inside after a walk in the cold.

Onions can do this. My three go-to dishes all require a bit of time, but it is mostly inactive time, and so not likely to unduly sap my energy. Leaving enough space between starting the dish to completing it allows my mind to wander back to the February morning seed starting, the late March transplanting, the August harvest, and the fall markets. These onions have been along for the entire ride. My friend's ritual is to eat the last onion on the day the next season's onions are started, to say good-bye and hello simultaneously.

HOW TO BUY

- Look for onions that are firm when squeezed. If the ball is squishy, it won't cure well.
- The top of the onion should be fully cured and not have any greens or loose paper around the top; these indicate that the onion isn't well cured and more susceptible to decay.
- If you smell a terrible smell or notice any brown liquid dripping from the onions, walk away. Rotting onions have a smell that is hard to get out and very, very gross. Go to another stall.

HOW TO STORE

- Sweet onions should be stored in a plastic bag in the refrigerator because they are more volatile and prone to going bad.
- Storage onions should be stored in a cool dark place with few temperature fluctuations.
- Don't store potatoes and onions together, as this speeds the spoilage of both.
- If storing cut onions, wrap them in plastic or place in a plastic bag so the smell doesn't spread. Dairy products, including butter, absorb the sulfuric acid most quickly.

NOTES

- Sweet onions have no more sugar in their cells than storage onions. They have more water, which dilutes the sulfur and makes them seem sweeter.
- The greens from onions can be used like giant chives.
- Sometimes you will see onion whistles at the market; those are usually the second growth of onions and their flower. Use them like chives or scallions.

RAW

Onions provide an acidic bite to cut through rich dishes. Sweet onions are great to use raw. If the onions are stronger than you want for your dish, rinse in running water to wash away some of the sulfuric acid held in the cells.

shaved onion salad w/cucumber, yogurt, and mint over lamb chops

The testers of this book preferred this salad with a sweet onion. I like it with a storage or red onion. If you are not a red meat eater, this recipe pairs well with grilled fish, seared chicken, stewy black beans, or soft chickpeas.

½ tsp (1 to 2 g) cumin seed

2 Tbsp (15 ml) olive oil

1 garlic clove (0.2 oz | 14 g), minced

¼ cup (60 g) yogurt

Salt and freshly ground black pepper

3 to 4 lamb chops per person (or about 8 oz | 230 g per person)

1 small sweet onion (4 oz | ½ cup | 115 g), shaved thinly

1 cucumber (12 oz | 340 g), cut in half, seeds removed if large, then cut into half-moons

6 sprigs mint, stemmed, leaves kept whole

In a large frying pan, toast the cumin until fragrant.

Add it to the olive oil and garlic and allow to steep for 10 minutes.

Whisk the cumin oil into the yogurt with a big pinch of salt.

Pat the lamb chops dry and season liberally with salt and pepper

Roast or grill the lamb chops (page 23) to medium-rare, about 6 minutes on each side depending on thickness.

Remove the chops from the heat and let rest for 7 to 10 minutes

Meanwhile, toss the onion, cucumber, and most of the mint with the yogurt sauce.

Serve the chops with onion salad and the rest of the mint on top.

variations

w/tomato onion bread salad + herb oil

2 cups (80 g) croutons (page 48)

1 pint (1 lb | 455 g) cherry tomatoes, halved

1 or 2 large slicing tomatoes (½ lb | 230 g), cut into large pieces

1 onion (4 oz | ½ cup | 115 g), cut into thin slices

¼ cup (60 ml) herb oil (or combine fresh herbs such as mint, basil, and parsley with olive oil)

Salt and freshly ground black pepper

Combine everything together, and serve.

w/grilled pork loin, shaved carrots, onion + herb salad

2 lb (910 g) pork roast

1 bunch carrots (1½ lb | 4 cups | 680 g), shaved into long ribbons

1 onion (4 oz | ½ cup | 115 g), cut into thin slices

1 cup (55 g) assorted herb leaves (parsley, mint, basil, chives, tarragon, oregano)

Olive oil

Salt

Heat the oven to 350°F (180°C). Roast the pork loin to 155°F (68°C) internal temperature, about 45 minutes, then let rest for about 10 minutes. Toss the carrots, onions, herbs, a glug of olive oil, and pinch of salt. Slice the pork and top with the salad.

w/seared salmon, apricot, onion, mint + almond relish

6 oz (170 g) fillet of salmon per person

1 qt (1 lb | 455 g) apricots, halved

2 Tbsp (30 ml) apple cider vinegar

2 Tbsp (40 g) honey

1 onion (4 oz | ½ cup | 115 g), sliced thinly

½ cup (70 g) almonds, roughly chopped

5 sprigs mint, stemmed, leaves left whole

Sear the salmon (page 24) and cook to medium-rare, then let rest. Heat the frying pan until smoking and sear the apricots until blistered. Toss the apricots with the vinegar, honey, onion, almonds, and mint. Serve the salmon topped with the apricot relish.

BRAISED

Similar to other braises, these onions benefit from a hard sear as the first step of cooking. It is different from the other braises; using vinegar as the cooking liquid yields a delicate play between sweet and sour.

vinegar-braised onions w/seared whitefish and arugula

If you have excess onions, make a large batch of these. It takes no more time and they keep well in the refrigerator for weeks. When I have them on hand, these onions easily become part of a relish tray before a meal, to garnish a cheese course, or as the acidic pop for a salad. They go very well with roasted squash or root vegetables.

8 cipollini onions or shallots (1 lb | 455 g)	Salt and freshly ground black pepper	One 6-oz (170-g) fillet of whitefish per person
Neutral oil	½ cup (120 ml) red or white wine vinegar	1 bag (4 oz | 115 g) arugula
		¼ cup (60 ml) olive oil

Heat the oven to 325°F (165°C).

Clean the cipollini, removing the outer layers but leaving the root intact. Cut them in half (from top to bottom), bisecting the root.

Heat a glug of neutral oil in a medium, ovenproof frying pan until just about smoking. Sear the onions, cut-side down, until well charred. Flip and season with a hefty sprinkle of salt and pepper. Char the other, rounded side as best you can. As long as there is a good char on the cut side, you'll be good.

Remove from the heat and pour the vinegar over the onions, getting it into the petals of the onion (be aware it will spit as the vinegar hits the hot pan and will probably make you

cough). Cover with foil or parchment paper and place in the oven. Bake until the onions are tender, about 25 minutes.

In a large frying pan, heat a <u>glug</u> of neutral oil until smoking hot. Blot the whitefish skin dry, sprinkle with salt, and sear, skin-side down, about 5 minutes (page 24).

When the skin releases from the pan, place the whole pan in the already hot oven to cook through, about 4 minutes.

In a medium bowl, dress the arugula with the olive oil and a sprinkle of salt and pepper.

Serve the fish, skin-side up, topped with arugula and onions, spooning the onion liquid over the whole thing.

variations

w/goat cheese + raisin pecan toast

Toast slices of raisin pecan bread, schmear with 4 oz (115 g) goat cheese, and top with the vinegar-braised onions.

w/sausages + kale rice salad

Brown four to eight (4-oz | 115-g) sausages and cook through. Massage 1 <u>bunch</u> of kale (page 251) until tender, <u>toss</u> with 2 cups (360 g) cooked rice (page 41) and olive oil, and sprinkle with salt. Taste and adjust the seasoning. Top the rice salad with cooked sausages and the vinegar-braised onions.

w/cheddar, apples + greens

<u>Toss</u> **2 thinly sliced tart apples** with the vinegar-braised onions. Dress 1 bag (4 oz | 115 g) salad greens or spinach with ¼ cup (60 ml) olive oil and a sprinkle of salt and black pepper. Place the greens out on a serving platter, top with the apple and onion mixture, and garnish with 4 oz (115 g) Cheddar, cut into <u>ribbons</u> with a vegetable peeler.

CARAMELIZED

Caramelizing onions is not the quick affair that many cookbooks profess—it takes time. But that time is almost entirely hands-off time. And once completed the end result can be frozen and retrieved whenever needed.

The keys to success are to be sure the pot is uncovered, to allow the steam to escape and ensure caramelization of the sugars. The larger the surface area of the pot, the faster the whole project will be. The onions will stick to the bottom; that's what happens. Just add some water or wine and scrape the onions loose. If the onions won't budge even after forceful scraping, remove them from the heat and let the onions sit. The moisture in the onions themselves will slowly dissolve the burnt sugar, making it easier to lift them from the pan while achieving the dark rich color that makes caramelized onions truly flavorful.

caramelized onion and goat cheese toasts

This recipe is written for 5 lb (2.3 kg) of onions because that is a standard unit for a bag of onions, but caramelizing can be made with any amount of onions you have on hand. I generally caramelize onions in huge batches and use the food processor slicing blade to make quick work of getting the onion into slices. In general, the onions reduce to about one-fourth of their original volume. Read: if you start with 4 cups (640 g) of onions, expect to get about 1 cup (195 g) of caramelized onions.

Knob of butter or glug of oil

5 storage onions (3 to 5 lb | 1.4 to 2.3 kg), cut into thin slices

2 tsp (16 g) salt

1 cup (240 ml) white wine or hard cider

Slices of bread

1 oz (30 g) fresh goat cheese per person

Greens (arugula, parsley, spinach; optional)

In a large wide pan, heat the butter or oil over medium heat and add the onions and salt and stir to combine.

Cook until deep golden brown, scraping the <u>fond</u> from the bottom as you go. (I turn the heat down to low once the onions start to brown.)

Add the wine and allow to evaporate completely.

Toast the bread, schmear with goat cheese, and top with the caramelized onions and the greens (if using).

variations

french onion soup

Neutral oil	2 cups (390 g) caramelized onions	Sliced crusty bread
5 sprigs thyme	4 cups (1 L) chicken stock	4 oz (115 g) raclette or Swiss cheese, grated

Heat a **glug** of oil and fry the thyme leaves to make an herb oil. Remove the thyme from the oil and discard. Add the onions and stock and bring to a simmer. Taste and adjust the seasoning. Heat the oven to broil. Toast the bread. Ladle the soup into oven-proof soup bowls, float the toast on the soup, top with the cheese, melt the cheese in the oven until golden brown, and serve. If you don't have heatproof bowls, melt the cheese on the toast and then float in the warm soup.

w/cabbage + sausages

2 (4-oz | 115-g) sausages per person

¼ cup (49 g) caramelized onions per person

½ head (1½ lb | 680 g) cabbage, cut into <u>thin slices</u>

2 Tbsp (30 g) Dijon mustard

2 Tbsp (30 ml) olive oil

½ <u>bunch</u> parsley (1.2 oz | ¾ cup | 34 g), chopped

Heat the oven to 350°F (180°C). Brown the sausages in a frying pan. Transfer from the pan to a baking sheet and finish cooking in the oven, about 10 minutes. Warm the onions in the sausage frying pan. Combine the cabbage, mustard, olive oil, and parsley, and <u>toss</u> to coat. Remove the sausages from the oven and serve with the cabbage-onion salad.

french onion dip

1 cup (195 g) caramelized onions

1 cup (240 g) sour cream

½ tsp (3 g) smoked paprika

1 tsp (6 g) salt

2 garlic cloves (0.4 oz | 14 g), minced

Combine all ingredients and serve with dippers.

parsnips

Parsnips are prized here in the Midwest, where we must make full use of the summer to make do for the winter. Well, we do more than make do—we revel in the winter. Two sides of the same coin—the very full, long stomp of summer days balanced by the longer nights and shushing quiet of snow tread.

Parsnips need the summer. Planted in mid-June, the seed needs the warm soil and long days to grow thick tall greens, which feed energy to the long, carrot-like taproot below. But parsnips are meant for winter. In summer, the root is not firm and tastes exceptionally bitter. Bitterness is one form of defense for a plant—making itself unpalatable to bugs as well as animals like you and me.

Parsnips go a step further. They have a chemical in their cells, psoralen (precisely, a furocoumarin) that causes phytophoto-dermatitis—an inflammation (itis) of the skin (derm) induced by a plant (phyto) with the help of sunlight (photo). Literally, when the leaves are disturbed the plant secretes a chemical that absorbs UV light and burns the skin like a localized sunburn with blisters. Not cool, parsnips, not cool. Best to let sleeping dogs lie until after the first frost.

Then the leaves, and their chemical defenders, die back. The cold converts the starch in the cells to sugar as it buttons down for the long winter nap. If left in the ground, the parsnips will flower the next summer with a crown of yellow flowers clearly a cousin to the carrot family's Queen Anne's Lace. We snatch them up before they ever have the chance to flower and burn again. Parsnips are the last thing dug from the fall garden, preferably after several snows to ensure maximum sweetness.

Parsnips don't show up on my table until Thanksgiving, when they are oven roasted with other roots and drizzled with garlic mayo. Parsnips continue to hold court on the holiday table with other festive flavors—orange, star anise, blue cheese, and dried fruit. They see me through the dull light after the Christmas tree is down, when spicy flavors of chili and paprika mirror the effects of candlelight in the snow. The roots will get a bit spongier as the months tick past. Parsnips are easily around until early spring, when even the most winter-worthy of us are ready to thaw. Their sweet flavor is a nice balance to all of the green and grassy flavors of early spring—ramps, garlic chives, mint, even peas and bitter chicories.

Yes, it is true that in the Midwest we have fewer things to grow and a shorter amount of time in which to do it. Thankfully, the crops we grow are stalwart and adaptable enough to satisfy through several seasons.

HOW TO BUY

- Look for parsnips that are even in size. I don't prioritize either large or small, but like them to be the same size for ease of cutting and roasting.
- Avoid parsnips that feel spongy or strangely light, as they have probably lost some moisture.
- Parsnips are usually sold trimmed of their long rat tails and greens. Don't be put off by some browning at the point of being cut.

HOW TO STORE

- Parsnips are a storage crop and so can be kept for months if kept at a consistent cool temperature (between 35°F and 45°F [2°C and 7°C]).
- Avoid direct sunlight or swings in temperature, as warming after being cold will mimic springtime and encourage the roots to send up shoots.
- If storing in the fridge, keep in a paper bag in a plastic bag to keep moist but not wet.

NOTES

- Parsnips are in the same family as carrots and can be treated in a lot the same way.
- Parsnips have a low glycemic index and so are suitable for diabetics.
- Avoid touching parsnip greens with your bare hands, as they can cause a rash.

OVEN ROASTED

Parsnips are perfect for roasting because they are naturally a bit drier than carrots or sweet potatoes. I like to roast them pretty hard so that their little tips burn, foiling the natural sweetness of the root. As with all oven-roasted things, allow enough space between the pieces on the baking sheet; a convection oven will help develop that crispy exoskeleton on the veggie; and cook until the roots are tender when pierced with a knife.

roasted parsnips w/fresh goat cheese, pecans, and pickled apricots

Pickling dried fruit heightens its flavor by introducing a serious tang and a touch of salt. It breathes new life into a pretty standard pantry staple. It works with all dried fruit I've tried, though apple chips get weird and soggy. You can also pickle fresh fruit, though this will sometimes soften the flesh to mush, so be gentle with the heat.

I love this with basil, which is increasingly available from year-round growers. If you can't find good-looking basil, either drizzle with basil oil (page 56) from your freezer or use parsley or a mixture of parsley, tarragon, and/or mint.

10 parsnips (about 2 lb | 910 g), ends cut off, peeled and cut into <u>obliques</u>

¼ cup (60 ml) olive oil, plus more for cooking the parsnips

¼ tsp (2 g) salt, plus more for seasoning

Freshly ground black pepper

¼ cup (60 ml) apple cider vinegar

1 Tbsp (15 g) brown sugar

½ cup (90 g) dried apricots, cut into ¼-inch (6-mm) strips

4 oz (115 g) fresh goat cheese

1 cup (140 g) pecans, toasted (page 24)

6 leaves basil, torn

Heat the oven to 400°F (200°C). Toss the parsnips with a big glug of olive oil, 2 pinches of salt, and 2 grinds of black pepper. Transfer to a baking sheet and roast until the parsnips are tender and golden brown, 35 to 45 minutes.

Heat the vinegar, salt, and brown sugar to boiling. Pour this over the apricots and let them sit for 10 minutes (these will keep for weeks, so feel free to scale up and have some on hand).

Drain the apricots, reserving the liquid for a dressing or making a spritzer with soda water.

Remove the parsnips from the oven, toss with the ¼ cup (60 ml) olive oil, and let absorb for a couple of minutes. Place on a serving platter, dot with the goat cheese, scatter the pecans and apricots over them, garnish with torn pieces of basil, and serve.

variations

w/currants, walnuts, blue cheese + burnt honey

10 parsnips (2 lb | 910 g)	½ cup (70 g) currants	1 sprig rosemary, stripped and minced
⅓ cup (115 g) honey	½ cup (60 g) walnuts	
2 Tbsp (30 ml) water	4 oz (115 g) blue cheese	

After roasting the parsnips, remove from the oven and turn on the broiler. Combine the honey and water to thin. Drizzle the roasted parsnips with the honey mixture and slide under the broiler to char like a toasted marshmallow. Remove from the oven and transfer to a serving platter. Garnish with the currants (pickled as for the apricots, if you like), walnuts, blue cheese, and rosemary.

w/chili oil, parsley + lemon zest

10 parsnips (2 lb | 910 g)

¼ cup (60 ml) chili oil (page 55)

Zest of 2 lemons (their juice can be added to the chili oil)

1 bunch parsley (1.2 oz | ¾ cup | 34 g), stemmed, leaves left whole

Roast the parsnips and <u>toss</u> with the chili oil and lemon zest. Garnish with the parsley and serve.

w/other roots, garlic mayo + sage

Any and all of these roots, trimmed and peeled:

5 parsnips (1 lb | 455 g)

5 carrots (1 lb | 455 g)

1 celery root (½ lb | 230 g)

2 sweet potatoes (1 lb | 455 g)

5 sunchokes (½ lb | 230 g)

¾ cup (1 kg) garlic mayo (page 61)

3 sprigs sage, cut into <u>thin slices</u> or fried in oil until golden and crispy

Roast the roots, drizzle with the garlic mayo, and garnish with the sage.

PURÉED

I love vegetable purées. Generally, I make them fresh, but it is also a great way to repurpose vegetable leftovers. They are endlessly useful—everything from catching the sauce of a meal (the way mashed potatoes support gravy) to being a flavorful schmear on a sandwich or toast to being the base for a soup. They are also dead simple. It's true that you need to pull out the food processor, but you can scale them up and make a bunch and then freeze it.

parsnip purée w/duck breast, radicchio, and cranberry relish

This is one of my favorite dishes to make about a week after Thanksgiving when there's still some cranberry relish and we are all ready for some seriously Christmasy flavors. Feel free to substitute 1 cup (450 ml) of leftover relish if you have it. If you don't, follow these instructions and know that you can scale up the recipe as needed. This relish keeps for weeks, so don't be shy. The orange in the parsnip purée will go well with all of the variations that follow, but feel free to leave it out. If you can't find duck, substitute chicken breasts, thighs, or thick pieces of salmon.

12 oz (340 g) cranberries, washed and sorted

1 tart apple (½ lb | 230 g), cored and cut into large chunks

Zest and juice of 2 oranges

¼ cup (50 g) sugar

2 tsp (12 g) salt, plus more as needed

½ cup (120 ml) olive oil, plus more as needed

1 onion (½ lb | 1 cup | 230 g), cut into thin slices

1 cup (240 ml) white wine

8 to 10 parsnips (about 2 lb | 910 g), ends cut off, peeled and cut into chunks

1 cup (240 ml) cream

2 star anise (optional)

4 duck breasts (8 to 10 oz | 230 to 280 g each)

Freshly ground black pepper

1 head radicchio, cored and leaves cut into petals

In a food processor, combine the cranberries, apple, orange juice, sugar, and a big pinch of salt. Blend until still chunky but evenly sized. Allow to sit at room temperature for 1 hour.

In a medium saucepan, heat a glug of olive oil and sweat the onion until soft, 5 to 7 minutes. Add the wine and reduce until almost dry. Add the parsnip chunks and 2 tsp (12 g) of salt, and toss to coat.

Add the cream, ½ cup olive oil, and star anise (if using). Bring to a boil, reduce to a simmer, and cook until the parsnips are falling-apart tender, about 15 minutes. Remove the anise, transfer the parsnips (liquid and all) to a food processor, and blend until very smooth (this may need to be done in batches). Add the orange zest and set the parsnip purée aside.

Score the skin of the duck breasts; this allows the fat to render more easily from the meat. Season the duck liberally with salt and pepper.

Put the duck breast, skin-side down, in a cold, heavy-bottomed pan and turn the heat to medium. As the pan heats, it will slowly render the fat out of the duck, making the skin golden and crispy, about 12 minutes. (There will be a lot of fat; this can be saved and used to roast potatoes and such.)

When the skin is golden brown and crispy, flip the duck over to quickly sear the underside of the breast and cook to medium-rare, about 4 minutes. Transfer to a platter and let the duck rest for 5 minutes, skin-side up.

Dress the radicchio with a glug of olive oil and sprinkle of salt. Add any duck cooking juices to the cranberry sauce and stir to combine (optional).

Spoon some purée onto each serving plate, nestle the duck into the purée, top with a spoonful of the cranberry sauce, garnish with the radicchio, and serve.

PARSNIP PURÉE

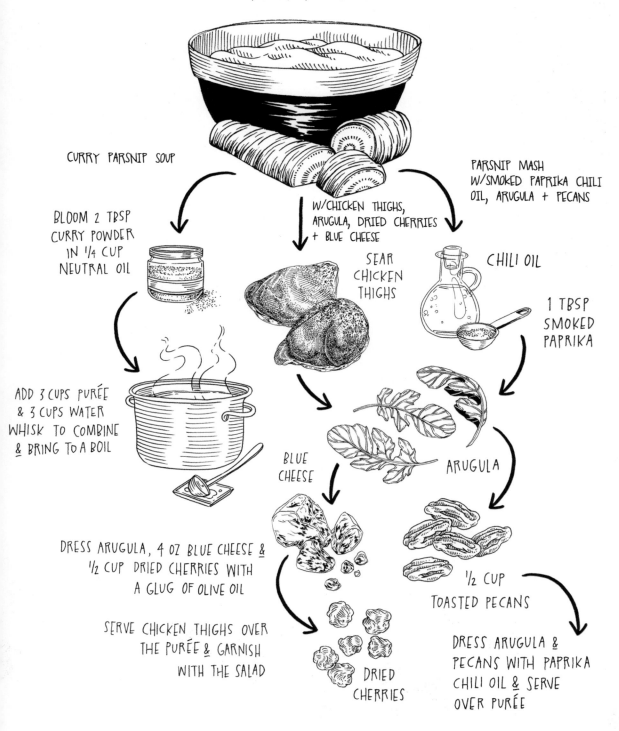

CURRY PARSNIP SOUP

PARSNIP MASH W/SMOKED PAPRIKA CHILI OIL, ARUGULA + PECANS

BLOOM 2 TBSP CURRY POWDER IN 1/4 CUP NEUTRAL OIL

W/CHICKEN THIGHS, ARUGULA, DRIED CHERRIES + BLUE CHEESE

SEAR CHICKEN THIGHS

CHILI OIL

1 TBSP SMOKED PAPRIKA

ADD 3 CUPS PURÉE & 3 CUPS WATER WHISK TO COMBINE & BRING TO A BOIL

BLUE CHEESE

ARUGULA

DRESS ARUGULA, 4 OZ BLUE CHEESE & 1/2 CUP DRIED CHERRIES WITH A GLUG OF OLIVE OIL

1/2 CUP TOASTED PECANS

SERVE CHICKEN THIGHS OVER THE PURÉE & GARNISH WITH THE SALAD

DRIED CHERRIES

DRESS ARUGULA & PECANS WITH PAPRIKA CHILI OIL & SERVE OVER PURÉE

peas

It feels like sacrilege to say, but I don't really like peas. I find them frustrating. Except for the shelled and frozen ones, which are incredibly consistent.

I have no feelings at all about snow peas. I'll eat them. I don't get excited about them. I like them stir-fried, but I almost never stir-fry myself, and so I rely on others to feed me snow peas. It's fine.

To me, snap peas are the worst. They look so good, they are so picturesque, and sometimes they taste amazing. Other times they are starchy and tough and the string gets caught in my teeth despite having already been stringed once. I truly can't be bothered.

The problem is that peas are one of the few things available during the hunger gap—the months of late April, May, and early June when Midwestern fields are planted but not producing and even I am hard pressed to get really, really excited about another parsnip.

Every year I buy peas. Every year I put them on the menu. Every year I either rejoice in the fact that they are good today or find a way to coax them into something tasty when they aren't the best pea I've ever had. The problem is, the flavor of a pea can change quickly as the sugar in the cells rapidly converts to starch after the pod is pulled from the plant.

By growing them yourself, the time from picking to eating will go down dramatically. Plus, they are important to grow. Peas are nitrogen fixers; the plant takes in nitrogen from the air and, with the help of *Rhizobia* bacteria, stores the nitrogen in nodules in its root structure. As the plant decomposes back into the soil, as plants are wont to do, the stored nitrogen is released into the soil for absorption by other plants next time. Nitrogen fixers are a key part of rotational farming. Think of how soy and corn are grown one year after the other on a lot of large-scale farms—soybeans are nitrogen fixers, corn is a big nitrogen feeder. It's a symbiotic relationship (though, to be clear, helped along with synthetic inputs unless grown organically). If you have space and want to do right by your soil, or at least have the best possible chance of getting a tasty pod, consider planting peas. They do well in the spring and fall but don't care much for the heat of high summer.

For my money, I generally buy shelled and frozen peas from as local a farmer as I can find. For fresh, I ask the growers I trust how they are tasting. (Please don't taste them yourself without asking. It's rude and, though small, it's theft.) Freezer peas model uniformity and dependability. They always taste the same. They can be counted on, which is not very romantic but has contributed to the success of our relationship.

The recipes in this chapter are meant for shelling peas, but you can substitute the podded others, except for the puréed. They are written to make good use of both the best of peas and the less wowing. I encourage you to use frozen shelling peas, which are more reliable than fresh and have better texture and flavor than canned. One of my goals for this book is for readers to feel confident cooking beyond the page and creating their own new variations on the dishes. I especially hope for that for peas, so that one of you kind souls will write to me and convince me to love peas. My DMs are open.

HOW TO BUY (MOVING BEYOND TREPIDATION)

- Look for bright green skin, free of intense veining or shriveling. The veining indicates the age of the pod before it was plucked from the plant and tends to parallel fibrous toughness. The shriveling shows how long since plucking, as the pod has lost its moisture and almost surely its sweetness, too.

- Look for plump but not swollen pods. If the peas inside are fully formed and bulging, they will almost certainly have converted all of their sugar into starch.

- Avoid yellowing peas, unless it is the yellow variety and the color is consistent.

HOW TO STORE

- Don't store them; eat them. Peas lose sweetness very quickly.

- If you must store them, get the peas into the cold as quickly as possible—the conversion of sugar to starch in the cells slows in cooler temperatures.

NOTES

- The three varieties listed here—shelling, snow, and snap—are three different varieties within the same family:
  - Shelling peas have fully formed seeds nestled in a fibrous pod.
  - Snow peas have immature seeds in a flat pod.
  - Snap peas have plump seeds in a rounded pod but should be tender enough to eat together.

- To string, snap the stem side of the pod down and unzip the pod's string all the way to the flower tip.

- I only string pods if the string is unpalatable.

- Peas take well to a quick boil in heavily salted water. Boil for 3 to 5 minutes, ensuring that they are tender but still bright green.

- In place of fresh peas, I vote for frozen peas over canned because they have less sodium and a better texture.

MARINATED

The first time I had marinated peas was at the now-shuttered Nightwood Restaurant in Chicago. We ate there not too long after it opened, and when the peas arrived I thought, *What a pity these are overcooked*, because they were the army green color of boiled-all-to-hell peas. Quite the contrary—the flavor was bright and acidic, the texture firm and surprising.

Marinated peas are more of a condiment (like a pickle) than a recipe in its own right. Add to any rich meal, or use less lemon to temper the tang, then serve as a side dish.

marinated peas w/yesterday's roast chicken, baby onions, and lettuce

This is one of my favorite ways to use up leftover roast chicken. I prefer the chicken at room temperature, but it can be served cold or warm as well. The result is a light, chopped salad good for lunch or early dinner. You could also turn this into a lettuce wrap, which a couple of recipe testers did with happy results.

2 cups (220 g) shelled peas

4 scallions, or 1 small red onion (2 oz | ¼ cup | 55 g), quartered or cut into thin slices

2 lemons (3 fl oz | 90 ml), zest and juice

½ cup (120 ml) olive oil, plus more as needed

½ tsp (3 g) salt

¼ tsp (1 g) chili flakes

2 cups (280 g) chicken meat picked from a roast chicken

4 sprigs mint, roughly chopped

½ bunch parsley (1.2 oz | ¾ cup | 34 g), roughly chopped

1 head (½ lb | 230 g) butter lettuce, leaves separated and torn into large pieces

Combine the peas, onions, lemon zest and juice, olive oil, salt, and chili flakes. Allow to marinate, refrigerated, for 20 minutes or up to three days.

Shred the chicken and allow it to come to room temperature.

Combine the chicken, peas, herbs, and lettuce and toss together. Taste and adjust the seasoning, adding an extra glug of olive oil if needed. Serve immediately as a hearty salad.

variations

w/salmon, radishes, parsley + rice

w/baby carrots, ricotta + chili oil (page 55)

w/pearl pasta, shaved asparagus, herbs + yogurt

PURÉED

As with most purées in this book, you can use day-old vegetables as a way to breathe new life into leftovers. It will be easier to blend and make a smoother purée if the peas are warm. Snap and snow peas will not blend well no matter what.

sweet pea toasts

There are very few dishes that my family asks for over and over again. This pea dip is one of them. It stores in the refrigerator and freezes well.

½ lb (2 cups | 230 g) peas

¼ tsp (1 g) chili flakes

½ tsp (3 g) salt

½ cup (120 ml) olive oil, plus more for drizzling

1 lemon (1½ fl oz | 45 ml), zest and juice

¼ cup (60 ml) cream

5 sprigs mint, roughly chopped

1 baguette or loaf of sourdough

Edible flowers (optional)

Bring a pot of salted water to a boil. Boil the peas until bright green, 3 to 5 minutes. Drain completely and transfer to a food processor. Add the chili flakes, salt, olive oil, and lemon zest and juice and blend until mostly smooth. Add the cream and blend to combine. Fold in the mint.

Slice and toast the bread, schmear with the pea purée, and garnish with a drizzle of olive oil and some edible flowers if you're feeling fancy.

variations

w/slow-cooked salmon + radish salad

4 salmon fillets (6-oz | 170-g each)

Salt and freshly ground black pepper

1 <u>bunch</u> radishes (1 lb | 455 g), <u>shaved</u>

1 bag (4 oz | 115 g) arugula

Olive oil

3 cups (720 ml) pea purée

Heat the oven to 300°F (150°C). Season the salmon liberally with salt and pepper and bake until medium-rare, 15 to 20 minutes. Combine the radishes, arugula, olive oil, a big pinch of salt, and several grinds of black pepper. Serve the salmon with a pool of the pea purée next to it and the radish arugula salad on top.

w/chicken thighs, morels + yogurt

Four 6-oz (170-g) chicken thighs

Salt and freshly ground black pepper

½ cup (120 ml) white wine or sherry

5 sprigs thyme

½ lb (230 g) morel mushrooms (or shiitake or cremini), cleaned and halved

½ cup (120 g) yogurt

3 cups (720 ml) pea purée

Heat the oven to 350°F (180°C). Season the chicken liberally with salt and pepper and pan sear (page 24). Transfer the pan to the oven to finish roasting, about 15 minutes. When the chicken is cooked through, remove from the oven and transfer the chicken to a plate to rest for 10 minutes. Add the wine and thyme to the frying pan and cook over medium heat, scraping up all the brown bits. When the wine is reduced, add the mushrooms and fry until golden brown and cooked through, about 10 minutes. Add the yogurt to the mushrooms to make a quick sauce. Divide the purée among the plates; top each with a chicken thigh and garnish with the saucy mushrooms (some herbs would be nice if you have them around).

on sandwiches w/spinach + baby turnips

1 bag (4 oz | 115 g) spinach

Olive oil

Salt and freshly ground black pepper

1 loaf sourdough bread

2 cups (480 ml) pea purée

1 bunch baby turnips (1 lb | 455 g), cut into thin slices

Dress the spinach with a glug of olive oil and salt and pepper. Slice the bread and toast, spread with the pea purée, top with the spinach and turnips, and serve.

PAN ROASTED

Peas take very little time to cook. The first recipe includes making a pan sauce, bringing chicken stock to a boil, and adding the butter in small pieces until it emulsifies, making the sauce thick and glossy. You can also skip this step and simply sauté the peas in fat until they are bright green and cooked through.

peas w/parsley, thyme, butter, and onions

You can combine the butter, parsley, and thyme into a compound butter or add all of the ingredients separately. These peas are a real treat just eaten out of a bowl by yourself with little ceremony. They can also be served alongside any protein or other veggies as you like. This is also one of my favorite things to combine with leftover rice from Chinese takeout. The sauce makes the rice creamy, and the rice makes the peas filling enough for a full dinner.

Neutral oil

1 small red onion (2 oz | ¼ cup | 55 g) or 3 scallions, sliced thinly

½ tsp (3 g) salt

½ cup (120 ml) white wine

1 cup (240 g) chicken stock

1 lb (4 cups | 455 g) shelling peas

4 Tbsp (55 g) butter

¼ bunch parsley (1.2 oz | ¾ cup | 34 g), roughly chopped

5 sprigs thyme, roughly chopped

Heat a glug of neutral oil in a large frying pan over medium heat. Add the onion and salt, and sweat until translucent. Add the wine and allow to reduce until almost dry.

Add the stock and bring to a boil. Add the peas and butter and cook until the stock reduces, the butter emulsifies, and the peas turn bright green. When the stock has thickened into a silky sauce, add the parsley and thyme. Taste and adjust the seasoning.

W/YOGURT + RADISHES UNDER CHICKEN THIGHS

W/RISOTTO, FRESH GOAT CHEESE, CHIVE + PARSLEY

W/LAMB, FROMAGE BLANC, MINT + CHILI FLAKES

variations

w/yogurt + radishes under chicken thighs

Replace the butter with ½ cup (120 g) of yogurt and swirl into the sauce at the very end, adding 1 <u>bunch</u> radishes, <u>shaved</u>, to the peas at the end of cooking. Serve with seared chicken thighs (page 24).

w/lamb, fromage blanc, mint + chili flakes

Neutral oil	Salt	Three 3-oz (85-g) lamb chops per person
¼ tsp (1 g) chili flakes	2 Tbsp (30 g) butter	2 oz (55 g) fromage blanc
2 cups (220 g) peas	5 sprigs mint	

Heat a <u>glug</u> of neutral oil in a frying pan. Add the chili flakes and briefly fry. Add the peas and a big pinch of salt and <u>toss</u> to coat and cook, then add the butter and mint and <u>toss</u> to combine. Serve next to grilled lamb and dot with the fromage blanc.

w/risotto, fresh goat cheese, chive + parsley

4 cups (800 g) risotto rice (page 42)	Pinch of salt	4 oz (115 g) fresh goat cheese
Neutral oil	10 sprigs chive, minced	
2 cups (220 g) peas	¼ <u>bunch</u> parsley (1 oz | ½ cup | 34 g), roughly chopped	

Make the risotto, following your favorite recipe. In a separate frying pan, heat a <u>glug</u> of neutral oil and pan roast the peas with the salt. <u>Toss</u> the peas with the chives and parsley, spoon over the risotto, and dot the entire thing with the goat cheese.

peppers, sweet

Why do I bother with this? is something I think on every single Fourth of July outing to watch the fireworks. I love fireworks, and I love Fourth of July.

I don't like spending hours talking about the best place to go to see the fireworks. I don't love discussing as a large group the best place to park for the fireworks that will balance the distance we have to walk to get to thus established perfect place and the ease with which we will be able to get the hell out of there at the end of the night. I don't love the nimrod sitting behind me screaming "Oohs and Ahhs" at the top of his lungs to drunkenly be the most patriotic in the vicinity. I don't love what it does to my dog's intestinal system. And I don't love thinking about what if these were actual bombs going off and what the noise must be doing to those who have witnessed war and the aftermath of them.

But we do it every year. At some point everyone just shuts up and watches the beauty; the cool evening air gives reprieve from the hot day and the hot dogs; I snuggle next to my man, our dog reassured between us, and I remember that the Fourth of July was a revolutionary act and from it came a remarkable nation that is still aspiring to its better angels.

Suddenly the crowds, even the eagle-cloaked fool behind me, feel united in spite of our differences. We came out, braving one another, to celebrate this nation. We have different ideas of how to make it a more perfect union, but somehow this feels like an act of solidarity. Tomorrow we can go back to arguing—hopefully productively.

This has nothing to do with sweet peppers except that once I told my husband that peppers remind me of the Fourth of July because they are a total pain, but in the end, I remember I love them. So there you go.

Peppers annoy me because they are hard to germinate into seedlings. They take forever to grow. Every time I get one about to turn from green to red, a bug or bird or tip rot helps itself, foiling my designs. They wilt at the slightest nip of frost. Everyone asks for them at the market all summer, and as soon as we have buckets full in September, those same people are asking for winter squash and Brussels sprouts.

All of this falls away when I char them on the grill until their skins are black and bursting. The smell of roasting peppers is intoxicating (despite not inducing you to shout "U-S-A!" in an outside voice). They are the perfect bridge to fall because they taste bright and acidic but pair well with stewy, warming dishes. The culinary equivalent of days where you work up a sweat in the sun followed by evenings cloaked in sweaters.

So, every year, I start a few seeds, complain about the germination, voice my opinion about the perfect park knoll to lay down a blanket, curse the birds and the bugs and the loudmouths, and then snuggle in and watch the show.

HOW TO BUY

- Look for peppers that are bright and shiny with taut skin.
- Wrinkles or collapsed sections are a sign of age or poor storage.
- Check the tip of the pepper for blemishes or rot—this is where it most often occurs.
- If there is damage to the pepper, consider asking for a discounted price. There is still good food there, but it won't store as long or yield as much.

HOW TO STORE

- Store at room temperature in a dark place.
- You can store in the refrigerator, but the cold will cause the cells to break down more quickly.

NOTES

- The variety of the pepper causes particular textures and shapes.
- The color indicates the stage of ripeness. Bell peppers ripen from green to yellow to orange to red.
- To peel peppers, char them on the grill or burner or under the broiler until the skin is dark and **blistered**. Transfer the charred peppers to a bowl and cover with plastic wrap to let steam. When the peppers are cool, slip the flesh from the skin and slide the seeds from the center. Strain the liquid, discarding the skin, stems, and seeds, and add it to whatever you are cooking.

GRILLED

This charring can be done either on a grill or over a stove burner. If burning inside, be sure to open your windows and/or turn on your hood fan because the good smells travel on a bit of smoke. This is also a time to truly hold your nerve: the skin should be fully black. The flesh will stay intact, but if not cooked through, the skin will cling to the flesh and be a hassle to peel. After charring, transfer to a bowl and cover with plastic wrap, letting the steam soften the peppers as they cool. When cool enough to touch, slip the pepper flesh from the charred skin and remove the seeds. I do this over the bowl to save any liquid that is released. Then I strain the skin and seeds from that liquid and use it on the final dish. This whole process can be done in large batches and then either frozen or pickled for future use.

grilled peppers w/eggplant and tomato over couscous

I like this dish with red, orange, and yellow bell peppers, though green will work well, too. You can make this dish more substantial by serving with a green salad or topped with kale or a poached egg (page 23).

4 bell peppers (1½ lb | 680 g), or about 2 cups skinned and seeded peppers

1 large eggplant (1 lb | 455 g), cut into medium cubes

½ cup (120 ml) olive oil, plus more for tossing

Salt and freshly ground black pepper

1½ cups (270 g) couscous (page 46) or pearl pasta

4 oz (115 g) feta (optional)

5 sprigs basil, parsley, or mint (or all three), torn or chopped roughly

1 pint (1 lb | 455 g) cherry tomatoes, halved

Heat the oven to 400°F (200°C). Prepare the peppers as previously described and cut into strips (ideally about ¼ inch [6 mm] thick).

Toss the eggplant with a glug of olive oil and salt and black pepper. Oil or spray a foil- or parchment-lined baking sheet, spread out the eggplant cubes, and roast until it is cooked through and golden brown, about 25 minutes.

Cook the couscous to the specs on the box and add the ½ cup (120 ml) olive oil, the feta (if using), and the herbs.

Toss the peppers, eggplant, and tomatoes with a pinch of salt and the pepper liquid.

Top the couscous with the vegetable relish and serve.

variations

w/roasted potatoes + garlic mayo

2 lb (910 g) baby potatoes	½ bunch parsley (1.2 oz | ¾ cup | 34 g), roughly chopped	¾ cup (180 ml) garlic mayo (page 61)
2 peppers (12 oz | 340 g) or 1 cup cooked peppers, cut into strips		Salt

Boil the potatoes in salted water and smash or cut into cubes.

Toss the potatoes, peppers, and parsley with the mayo and serve at room temp or cool. If serving cold, taste and adjust the seasoning with salt.

w/corn, soybeans + cherry tomatoes

3 ears corn, kernels
stripped (or 1½ cups |
210 g corn kernels)

½ cup (120 ml) olive oil,
plus more for the corn

Salt and freshly ground
black pepper

2 cups (370 g) soybeans,
shelled

2 or 3 bell peppers (12 oz |
340 g), cut into strips

1 pint (1 lb | 455 g) cherry
tomatoes, halved

1 bunch parsley or cilantro
(2.4 oz | 1½ cups |
68 g), roughly chopped

¼ cup (60 ml) vinegar
(I like sherry, but it
can be any kind except
balsamic)

Heat the oven to 400°F (200°C). Toss the corn kernels with a glug of olive oil and salt and black pepper. Roast on a baking sheet until cooked through and golden brown, about 12 to 15 minutes.

Blanch or microwave the soybeans until cooked through.

Toss the corn, soybeans, peppers, tomatoes, and parsley together with the ½ cup (120 ml) olive oil and the vinegar, and serve at room temperature.

w/fresh goat cheese + hazelnuts on toasts

½ cup (60 g) hazelnuts,
toasted (page 24)

4 raw peppers (24 oz |
680 g), cut into strips,
or 2 cups (425 g)
prepared

¼ cup (60 ml) olive oil

3 sprigs mint or oregano
(or parsley or basil),
roughly chopped
or torn

Pinch of salt

1 loaf crusty bread

4 oz (115 g) goat cheese

Smash the hazelnuts and combine with the peppers, oil, herbs, and salt.

Cut the bread into thick slices and toast. Schmear with the goat cheese, top with the pepper mixture, and serve.

BRAISED

I generally braise peppers with the skin still on because it doesn't bother me, and I don't always want to take the time to peel them. If you don't like the skin, feel free to prepare like the grilled peppers and then add in the skinned flesh to the dish. Truly up to you.

peperonata w/poached eggs and paprika potatoes

Peperonata is the base recipe here and can be turned into a million different things. It also freezes very well, so consider making a huge batch and freezing until the next season. I love this recipe with boiled potatoes, but as potatoes are so versatile, roasted or mashed would also be nice. If roasting, coat the potatoes with the paprika before roasting. If using mashed, spoon the paprika oil over the mash before serving.

½ cup (120 ml) neutral oil, plus more for the peppers

¼ tsp (1 g) chili flakes (optional)

1 large onion (½ lb | 1 cup | 230 g), cut into thin slices

3 garlic cloves (0.6 oz | 21 g), minced

1½ tsp (9 g) salt

1 Tbsp (15 g) tomato paste or ¼ cup (60 g) roasted cherry tomatoes

12 oz (340 g) crushed tomatoes or some sort of liquidy canned tomato product

4 red, yellow, or orange bell peppers (24 oz | 680 g), cut into strips

2 lb (910 g) fingerling or Yukon gold potatoes, about ½ lb (230 g) per person

2 Tbsp (14 g) smoked, sweet, and/or hot paprika

½ bunch parsley (1.2 oz | ¾ cup | 34 g), roughly chopped

2 quarts (2 L) water

¼ cup (60 ml) cheap vinegar

1 egg per person

To make the peperonata, in a medium Dutch oven or pot, heat a glug of neutral oil. Add the chili flakes to bloom the flavor. When they are fragrant, add the onion, garlic, and ½ tsp (3 g) salt and reduce the heat. Sweat the onions until soft, scraping up any brown bits. Add the tomato paste and fry with the onions. Add the crushed tomatoes and peppers and bring to a boil. Reduce to a simmer and let stew until the peppers are tender and the liquid is reduced and silky, 25 to 35 minutes. (This can also be done in the oven if you already have it on, though it will take a bit more time.)

Boil the potatoes in salted water until fork-tender. Drain and allow to cool.

Toast the paprika in a small frying pan; when fragrant, remove from the heat, add the ½ cup (120 ml) oil, and allow to steep for 10 minutes or so. Toss the potatoes with the paprika oil and parsley.

Combine the water, vinegar, and remaining 1 tsp (6 g) salt in a saucepan, and bring to a simmer.

Crack the egg into a bowl, slip the egg into the water, and poach the eggs until the whites are set but the yolk is soft (page 23).

Dish up the potatoes, top with the eggs and then the peperonata, and serve.

variations

w/seared salmon + rice

Per person:

One 6-oz (170-g) salmon fillet

1 cup (185 g) cooked rice (page 41)

Butter

½ cup (120 ml) peperonata

Sear the fish skin-side down (page 24). Warm the rice with a pat of butter (if you're feeling decadent). Top with the fish and then the peperonata.

w/peperonata over pork chops + greens

One (8- to 10-oz | 230- to 280-g) pork chop per person

½ bag (2 oz | 60 g) salad greens

Olive oil

¼ cup (60 ml) sherry vinaigrette (page 58)

Salt and freshly ground black pepper

½ cup (120 ml) peperonata

Grill the pork chops (page 23). Dress the greens with the olive oil, vinegar, and salt and pepper. Top each pork chop with peperonata and serve the salad on the side.

over ricotta toasts

1 loaf bread

2 oz (55 g) ricotta per person

¼ cup (60 ml) peperonata per person

Arugula (if you want something green)

Olive oil

Slice and toast the bread, schmear with the ricotta, and top with the peperonata.

Dress the greens with a dash of olive oil and scatter over the toasts.

Serve immediately (beware: these are a bit messy).

potatoes

The very first year of farming our running joke was, "Hey, this looks like something you could buy at a store!" We were surprised that we could produce something that could have been validated by the outside authority of a store—something professional, when we didn't feel like we were. I never thought much about it at the time—the power over our food that we've ceded to outside sources. It exemplifies the disconnection so many of us feel with our food.

Over time that thought (hoping our food would live up to what we saw at the grocery) transitioned to comparing the quality of what I can grow to what is on offer in the aisles. I saw the difference in what came from my garden over what was available on the shelves. I write "difference" deliberately. Sometimes it was better. Sometimes it was worse. Mostly it was truly just different.

Potatoes are the best way to describe that difference between homegrown and store-bought. (Note: I include what you can buy at a farmers' market or in your CSA in the homegrown category.) It always seemed like a potato was a potato was a potato.

Growing potatoes feels like a bit of agricultural witchcraft. In the spring, after the threat of frost has passed (mostly), you dig a hole or a trench, drop in an old potato from last year, cover it back up, and in the middle of summer dig them up. That one seed potato makes about a pound (in an average year) of new potatoes. There is a little maintenance along the way—weeding and mounding either with dirt or straw—but that is basically it. I will never forget the first day we dug potatoes. Red Norland was the variety. I had no idea what to expect, having never thought about how a potato grows before. On hands and knees, I pulled back the straw, lifted the plant by the stem, and then pawed at the soil, revealing a clutch of brand-new potatoes. The skin, an electric shade of magenta, was so tender that my finger pads could rub it away from the creamy white flesh if I was clumsy.

God as my witness, I never had that Scarlett O'Hara moment, but growing potatoes suddenly made me feel like I could always fend for and feed myself. That sunny, pleasant, summer day as I gleefully sank my hands into the soil, I was suddenly shaken by the reality of what it must have been like for the Irish to be clawing at the earth and finding only blighted rot under the ground. Potatoes can sustain life. You can live off of potatoes alone. Suddenly that lifeline for millions was cut. I had never thought much about the Great Potato Famine. I knew of it as a historic event that spurred immigration to our country, but that was about it.

I started to cry. It would be overly dramatic, or at least trite in a big way, to say that as a farmer I could feel the pain of the Irish poor. I was so far away from desperate on that afternoon, but I could sense it. I could imagine the feeling that comes after heartbreak, knowing that there is nothing and that that nothingness is going to spread. Potatoes remind me of what happens when suddenly that food runs out—when there's nothing on the shelves or in the ground for you. When society isn't strong enough to choose to feed the famished.

It is a privilege to have access to food, either homegrown or store-bought. Sometimes the ingredients are better; sometimes they are worse. Sometimes they are just different. But it is always a privilege to eat.

HOW TO BUY

- Look for potatoes with firm flesh. Squishiness indicates internal rot or poor storage.
- Avoid potatoes with green skin, caused by exposure to light. It is toxic in large quantities, which I don't actually worry about, but more importantly means they were stored in the sun, indicating other bad practices.
- Avoid potatoes with sprouted eyes. The eyes are the divots in the skin and normal. Sprouts mean that the potatoes were cooled and warmed, causing them to try to grow, which can yield a weirdly sweet and not stable flesh.
- If something smells rotten or if you notice brown liquid coming from under the potatoes, move on. Few smells stink worse than a rotten potato, and the smell sticks to hands, cars, and other potatoes.

HOW TO STORE

- Store potatoes in a cool dark place like a root cellar. If the potatoes are exposed to light, their skin will green up—nature's sunscreen. Just peel the green skins away; the flesh underneath is perfectly good.
- Do not refrigerate, because this mimics winter and causes the tubers to start to convert their starch to sugar, making the potato less stable.
- If buying potatoes with the dirt still attached, wash the potatoes only just before using. The less they are disturbed, the better they will store.
- Sprouts are the potato trying to put out roots for the spring. If the potatoes start to sprout they are still usable; just pull the sprouts off.

NOTES

- There are two types of flesh in potatoes: floury and waxy. Floury potatoes have fluffy interiors that fall apart when boiled (like russets). Waxy potatoes have denser flesh that will hold together (like Yukon gold).
- "New potatoes" technically refers to just-dug potatoes. Now that label is used to describe the size and shape—small and round potatoes. Also look for boiling potatoes or fingerling for smaller sizes.
- Potatoes also propagate by seed, but those seed pods are toxic. Potatoes also don't grow true from seed, so your best bet is to either save your own potatoes for seed or buy from a seed company.

W/ROASTED CHICKEN THIGHS

W/SEARED SALMON

W/KALE + BRAISED PEPPERS

W/SPINACH SALAD + SOFT-BOILED EGG

BOILED

Boiling potatoes is by no mean revolutionary, but the technique is so simple that it can be easily forgotten. Beyond serving as a side, boiled potatoes are a great way to get ahead of meal prep for the week. I like to boil them, smash them with my hands, cool them, and fry them for hash browns or crispy potatoes later on. They also make a fast potato salad or can be added to broth with a handful of greens to make a soup. Sky's the limit.

I generally boil potatoes whole so that they hold their shape. If the potatoes are very large, you can cut them in advance of boiling, but they will fall apart a touch.

simple boiled potatoes w/sweet butter and herbs

This is maybe the most boring recipe in this whole book, but boiled potatoes are the simplest of perfect treats. They feel revelatory when combined with an eye-popping array of fresh herbs, a good knob of well-salted butter, and a slick of olive oil to round out the flavor.

You can think of the herbs in one of two ways. One, use a million different herbs that give big jolts of surprising flavor, ranging from mint to rosemary to parsley to chervil and lemon verbena. Two, rely on one or two, but be sure to use them in copious amounts to enliven the potatoes. I rely on parsley and a bit of rosemary for this most often. Just be wary of basil; it tends to blacken when <u>tossed</u> with the hot potatoes. And then put the potatoes with whatever else you are cooking . . .

Serves 1 (but scales up like a dream)

½ lb (230 g) potatoes of any variety (I like the marble or fingerling potatoes for this)

Salt

2 Tbsp (30 g) butter

2 Tbsp (30 ml) olive oil

¼ cup (10 g) herbs, stemmed, leaves left whole, or roughly chopped if you're feeling it

Freshly ground black pepper

Wash the potatoes and place in a pot with enough water to cover. Add a big pinch of salt—I like to boil potatoes in water that is salty like for pasta.

Bring to a boil, reduce to a simmer, and cook until the potatoes are tender when pierced with a knife—the skins will start to split a bit (about 20 minutes for small potatoes, up to 40 minutes for whole large potatoes).

Drain the water away and <u>toss</u> with the butter, olive oil, and herbs, another pinch of salt, and several grinds of black pepper. Transfer to a warm serving bowl and serve with any of the items pictured on page 340. Use the leftovers to make a quick potato salad or good morning hash browns the next day.

OVEN ROASTED

The key to most roasted vegetables is to roast them a touch longer than you feel comfortable, so they get a crispy, crackly exterior and a soft, tender interior. If you have a convection feature on your oven it will help immensely. Also, if you line your baking sheets with foil that goes up over the edges, you can just lift it up off the tray—no need to wash the tray underneath (most of the time).

roasted potato salad w/egg, celery, herbs, and bread crumbs

This dish is what I like to call "New Midwestern." It is basically a potato salad but without the mayo and yellow mustard so commonly associated with that picnic staple. Instead, the egg is cooked separately, adding richness like in a mayo but also a soft texture to contrast the crunchy potatoes and garlic bread crumbs. This dish is my favorite to make with potatoes of all colors and sweet potatoes, highlighting the intense diversity of a vegetable with a banal reputation. Additionally, feel not only free but encouraged to add other veggies with the celery and onion. Shaved carrots, radishes, cauliflower, or broccoli would be perfectly at home here.

2 lb (910 g) potatoes—any type, or mix different colors, textures, even sweet potatoes—unpeeled and cut into wedges

Neutral oil

Salt and freshly ground black pepper

4 eggs

½ bunch parsley (1.2 oz | ¾ cup | 34 g), stemmed, leaves left whole (if the stems are tender, slice them as thinly as possible)

6 stalks (4 oz | 2 cups | 115 g) celery, cut into thin slices, leaves reserved

1 small onion (2 oz | ¼ cup | 55 g), any type, cut into thin slices

¼ cup (60 ml) olive oil

½ cup (70 g) garlic bread crumbs (page 48)

Heat the oven to 400°F (200°C). Toss the potatoes with a glug of neutral oil, big pinch of salt, and several grinds of pepper. Transfer to a baking sheet and spread in a single layer (it doesn't matter if the cut side is up or down, just be sure there's space between the pieces to allow the steam to escape). Roast until the outside is crispy and the inside is tender when poked with a paring knife, about 40 minutes.

Meanwhile, gently tap the fat side of the eggs on a hard surface to give them a slight crack (this helps them peel more easily). Place the hair-cracked eggs into a medium pot and add water to cover by 1 inch (2.5 cm). Bring to a boil, remove from the heat, cover, and let sit for 9 minutes. Drain the hot water and cool the eggs with cold water until they are cool to the touch.

Combine the parsley with the celery.

Peel the eggs and roughly chop or slice into rounds with one of those old-fashioned egg slicers.

When the potatoes are done, remove from the baking sheet. Either cool to room temperature and then finish assembling, or proceed and serve warm.

To assemble, toss the potatoes with the celery-parsley mixture, onion, and the olive oil. Transfer to a serving platter and top with egg rounds and the bread crumbs.

variations

w/caramelized onions, feta + thyme (could also use blue cheese if you like that stuff)

Season the potatoes with extra pepper (to balance the sweetness of the onions) and oven roast. Toss with caramelized onions (page 295) and thyme leaves, crumble feta over the top, and serve.

paprika potatoes w/garlic mayo

Season the potatoes with ½ tsp each smoked and sweet paprika and chili flakes, and a big pinch of salt, and roast. Put on a platter, drizzle with ½ cup (120 g) garlic mayo (page 61), and garnish with chopped parsley.

w/raclette + pickled beets

Follow the recipe for roasting the potatoes, sprinkle the roasted potatoes with 4 oz (115 g) raclette cheese (or Swiss, Cheddar, or Muenster) and return to the oven until the cheese melts, 1 to 2 minutes. Scatter pickled beets and chopped parsley around the cheesy potatoes and serve.

BRAISED

This is an unconventional braise because it is left open to allow the chicken stock and wine to evaporate, effectively steaming the chicken while cooking the potatoes. When searing the chicken thighs, you may need to cook them in batches to get an even nice browning on the skin. Feel free to replace the thighs with breasts if you prefer.

mustard braised potatoes w/chicken thighs

There is a longing in our times for fast, easy dinners that don't dirty up a bunch of dishes. This is my favorite dinner to meet all of those needs. Serve it with a green salad on the side or, if you want some cooked greens, fold 1 bunch of stripped and cut kale leaves into the potatoes. The variations use the same open cooked technique to allow the cooking liquid to evaporate off as the potatoes soften.

4 to 6 chicken thighs (6 oz | 170 g each), bone in and skin on

Salt and freshly ground black pepper

Neutral oil

3 sprigs thyme, left whole (optional)

2 Tbsp (30 g) mustard (whole-grain or Dijon or a mix)

1 cup (240 ml) white wine

1 onion (½ lb | 1 cup | 230 g), cut into thin slices

3 garlic cloves (0.6 oz | 21 g), minced (optional)

2 lb (910 g) fingerling potatoes or any sort of small potato, cut in half unless they are very small

1 cups (240 ml) chicken stock or water

½ bunch parsley (1.2 oz | ¾ cup | 34 g), roughly chopped

Heat the oven to 375°F (190°C).

Pat the chicken thighs dry and generously season with salt and pepper. Over high heat, add a glug of neutral oil to an ovenproof frying pan. Add the chicken, skin-side down, and brown the skin until golden and crispy, 5 to 7 minutes. Transfer to a plate without cooking the other side.

Add the thyme and mustard to the pan and briefly fry in the drippings, about 30 seconds. Deglaze the pan with the wine, scrapping up the drippings and allowing the wine to reduce by half, about 2 minutes. Add the onion and garlic, and sweat until tender, about 7 minutes. Add the potatoes and stock and a big pinch of salt. Place the thighs on top, skin-side up, and bring to a boil.

Transfer to the oven and bake, uncovered, until the thighs are cooked through and the potatoes are tender, about 25 minutes. Remove from the oven, garnish with the parsley, and serve, sauce and all.

variations

curry braised potatoes w/cauliflower, yogurt, parsley + mint

Neutral oil

2 Tbsp (12 g) curry powder

1 onion (½ lb | 1 cup | 230 g), cut into thin slices

5 garlic cloves (1 oz | 30 g), minced

2 lb (910 g) small potatoes

1 cup (240 ml) water or stock

Salt

1 head (2 lb | 910 g) cauliflower, shaved into ribbons

½ cup (70 g) golden raisins

½ bunch parsley (1.2 oz | ¾ cup | 34 g), roughly chopped

6 sprigs mint, roughly chopped

1 cup (240 g) yogurt

Heat a glug of oil in an ovenproof frying pan and bloom the curry powder. Add the onion and garlic and sweat until tender. Add the potatoes and water and a big pinch of salt. Braise until the potatoes are tender, about 25 minutes, then toss with the cauliflower, raisins, parsley, and mint. Top with the yogurt and serve.

w/bacon, thyme + cream

¼ lb (115 g) bacon, cut into ¼-inch (6-mm) bits

1 onion (½ lb | 1 cup | 230 g), cut into <u>thin slices</u>

3 garlic cloves (0.6 | 21 g), minced

5 sprigs thyme, stemmed, leaves left whole

Salt and freshly ground black pepper

1 cup (240 ml) white wine

2 lb (910 g) potatoes

1 cup (240 ml) chicken stock or water

½ cup (120 ml) cream

In a large frying pan, cook and render the bacon until crispy. Add the onion, garlic, and thyme with a big pinch of salt and pepper. Add the wine and reduce by half. Add the potatoes and stock and bring to a boil. Braise until tender, about 25 minutes. Remove from the oven and add the cream. Taste and adjust the seasoning as desired.

w/leeks, mushrooms + butter

Neutral oil

1 lb (455 g) mushrooms (any variety), torn or cut into pieces

½ cup (120 ml) white wine

2 long leeks or 4 little ones (1 lb | 455 g), thinly sliced into half-moons (float them in water to remove the grit)

2 lb (910 g) potatoes, cut into <u>chunks</u>

1 cup (240 ml) chicken stock or water

Salt and freshly ground black pepper

2 Tbsp (30 g) butter

Heat a <u>glug</u> of oil in an ovenproof frying pan and roast the mushrooms until crispy (page 24). Add the wine and leeks and <u>sweat</u> until soft. Add the potatoes and stock with a big pinch of salt and pepper. Bring to a boil and braise in the oven until the potatoes are tender, about 25 minutes. Swirl in the butter and serve.

BAKED

Baked, or jacket, potatoes are truly one of my perfect vessels for any sort of topping. They turn the weird salads that I make for dinner into a complete and filling meal. Every time I tell someone that's what we are having for dinner, I can see them picturing the steakhouse (or cafeteria buffet) baked potato—soggy, slathered in sour cream and butter, with some lame-ass, dried-out chives on top. This is not that.

The key to a great baked potato is the textural difference between the jacket (skin) and the creamy, fluffy interior. For that reason, I like to use floury potatoes such as russets—potatoes that fall apart when boiled and are much better suited to whole baking—and then top them with anything that provides a good crunch; maybe something cold to contrast with the hot interior, and surprising tang to balance all that starch. If you are feeling portion conscious, bake them, cut them in half, and serve only one side per person.

jacket potatoes w/shaved vegetable salad and tuna mayo

I love the richness that the tuna adds to the mayo, ensuring that you get a good amount of protein with your baked potato. I also love it because the mayo is salty enough to season both the potato and the vegetables in the salad. That said, I still sprinkle the potato with a pinch of salt before topping with the salad, because I like salt. If you aren't into tuna, feel free to omit and use plain or garlic mayo (page 61).

1 large russet potato (10 oz | 280 g) per person (the ingredients that follow are listed per potato)

1 cup (weight varies) <u>shaved</u> vegetables, whatever is in season or in your refrigerator; I love red cabbage, carrots, cauliflower, broccoli, radishes, kale, tomatoes, kohlrabi . . .

¼ cup (60 g) tuna mayo (page 61)

Salt

Handful of parsley, cilantro, and/or chives, roughly chopped

Heat the oven to 400°F (200°C). Prick the potatoes all over with the tip of a knife. Place on the oven rack and bake until tender when poked with a knife (they generally will hold their shape), about 40 minutes.

Dress the veggies with the tuna mayo and a big pinch of salt.

Taste and adjust as desired, return to the refrigerator (don't eat it all now, even though you could, or do as you like, and find another outlet for the potatoes).

Pull those hot potatoes from the oven and cut the length of the potato and 3 lines perpendicular to the center cut. Using potholders, squeeze the bottom of the potato, pushing the flesh up through the cuts (fluff with a fork if it doesn't lift up).

Season with a pinch of salt. Top with the vegetable salad. Sprinkle with the herbs and serve.

variations

w/bacon, kraut + caramelized onions

4 strips (4 oz | 115 g) bacon

¼ cup (60 g) caramelized onions (page 295)

¼ cup (36 g) sauerkraut

Baked potato

1 oz (30 g) Cheddar, grated

Cut the bacon into little strips (lardons) and render. Add the onions and stir to combine. Remove from the heat and add the kraut. Pile this mixture onto the potato, sprinkle with cheese, and return to the oven to melt.

w/massaged kale, cherry tomatoes + yogurt

6 leaves kale <u>midribs</u>
<u>stripped</u> out, cut into
<u>ribbons</u>

Salt

10 cherry tomatoes,
halved

¼ cup (60 g) yogurt

Olive oil

Baked potato

Sprinkle the kale with salt and massage until tender (page 251). <u>Toss</u> the kale, tomatoes, and yogurt together with a <u>glug</u> of olive oil. Top the potato with the little salad.

w/sausage, egg, spinach + sherry vinaigrette

2 oz (55 g) sausage (spicy
is nice)

Handful of spinach (two if
it is baby spinach)

1 Tbsp (15 ml) sherry
vinegar

2 Tbsp (30 ml) olive oil

1 egg

Salt and freshly ground
black pepper

Baked potato

Crumble and panfry the sausage until cooked through. Put the spinach in a bowl with the vinegar and oil, top with the sausage, and let the heat wilt the spinach. Crack the egg into the sausage frying pan, season with salt and pepper, and cook in the sausage fat until the white is set but the yolk is soft. <u>Toss</u> the spinach salad and pile it onto the potato. Slide the egg onto the very top and serve.

radishes

When I think of radishes I think, almost always, of farmers' markets in the spring.

People coming out either begrudgingly because it is pissing rain or gleefully because at least it is not snowing. Farmers standing in heavy sweaters and with green thermoses of coffee at the ready, offering kind smiles when customers mention the chill. They have been up since before dawn and working outside for weeks.

Tables and tables piled with greens—spinach, baby kale, salad leaves, maybe some bok choys, maybe some arugula. Next to those greens stands a stack of radishes blazing red. The color is always jarring, unnaturally bright, piercing the mist of such mornings. These little orbs demanding to be noticed. Demanding to be seen even when they are passed over for salad or asparagus.

There are reasons why radishes are some of the first crops for sale in the spring. Being a brassica, they prefer cool weather over hot. Similarly, they can take a bit of abuse from a frost. Radishes are heartier than the high-maintenance tomato. They grow quickly—traditionally it takes twenty-one to twenty-eight days from seeding to harvesting for most radish varieties—a boon when the ground is cold, but markets are starting soon. They are as much a part of the spring celebration as asparagus stalks or spinach leaves, but until we began selling at markets, I never felt that association.

That's why I go to farmers' markets (assuming it is a good market, where vendors grow what they sell, and not just a resale stop) to seek out what is truly in season in the area. There are lots of other reasons to shop at local markets—the community, your money stays in the local economy, they are generally lovely, you can usually bring your dog, you can wear your stripy sweater and eat a *pain au chocolat*—but it is the showcasing of what that region produces right then that is the perennial draw.

Admittedly, these other reasons can actually repel me from the markets. I like getting to see people in my life early in the morning. I love building a relationship with a farmer and learning from her. For example, I learned that the spice in a radish is the amount of mustard oil produced by the plant as a reaction to stress—generally high heat or drought—and that mustard oil is the plant's natural defense against pests that will prey upon it while it's in a weakened state. Plants rule.

But honestly, sometimes I can't be bothered. I don't always want to talk, I don't always want to learn, and it is all but impossible to go to a market without bumping into someone you know. (Unless you are blissfully in a strange town, and even then, the risk of it being "such a small world" is high.) Of course, I want my money to go directly to farmers, but there are more and more and more convenient options, like local groceries and co-ops that distribute for the same farmers and also sell toilet paper, avocados, and crackers that aren't $12 a bag, and sometimes I selfishly want the convenience.

And that is all OK, everyday choices, but the radishes never blaze quite the same as at a misty spring market.

HOW TO BUY

- Roots should be firm and not wrinkly.
- Greens should be perky and free of yellowing.
- Avoid ones with dark spots—a sign of root maggots.

HOW TO STORE

- If storing for a while, remove the tops.
- Store in the refrigerator wrapped in plastic.
- If they are getting limp, store in water to crisp.

NOTES

- French breakfast radishes are generally the most mild because of their high intercellular water content.
- The greens are also edible (though a bit hairy). Give them a quick sauté with garlic and eat like kale or collard greens.
- Watermelon, Beauty Heart, and black radishes are fall varieties and will store like turnips. I find them a bit "hotter" than regular red radishes and so either give them a soak in cool water to lessen their spice, or roast.
- Daikon radish can be used any way you'd use red radishes, just cut it into smaller pieces.

W/POACHED SALMON + WILD RICE

W/ASPARAGUS + HARD-COOKED EGG

W/GRILLED PORK LOIN + BABY POTATOES

PAN ROASTED

The key to the basic technique is to get a pan ripping hot. This is the biggest difference between restaurant kitchens and home kitchens—the size of our burners. To mimic the high heat of a restaurant burner, place your frying pan in the oven to warm for 10 to 15 minutes. Otherwise, just keep the frying pan on high heat until the oil starts to smoke. The other key is to not stir the radishes before they have developed a nicely browned skin. Be bold and let them cook in that hot pan.

roasted radishes w/their greens and white wine

Cooked radishes have gotten a bit more attention lately. The radish is transformed from a very crisp, slightly spicy refreshing vegetable to one characterized by a warming, golden exterior and creamy interior. Admittedly, I prefer a raw radish over a roasted one, but there are times for just about anything. I find myself roasting radishes most often in three situations. One, when the radishes are soft and not going to be best showcased in a salad. Two, when I have radishes coming out my ears and want to serve a lot of them in one fell swoop. Three, when the raw crunch would be distracting in the finished dish.

As a note, any radish can be roasted. French Breakfast radishes will leach out more water because they have more water in their cells. But just cook them longer—and to some extent a radish is a radish is a radish. If the greens are not lovely and appetizing, substitute kale or spinach or leaf (ha!) out altogether.

2 <u>bunches</u> radishes (2 lb | 910 g) with bright green leaves	Neutral oil Salt	¾ cup (180 ml) white wine 2 Tbsp (30 g) butter

Wash and dry the radishes and greens very well—the wetter they are, the more they will spit in the pan. Cut the radishes in half or into wedges.

Heat a large frying pan and heat a <u>glug</u> of neutral oil over high heat until smoking. Add the cut radishes and a big pinch of salt. Let them brown, undisturbed. When the radishes have a lovely brown crust, stir and let their other sides brown.

When both sides are well caramelized, add the wine and let it reduce by half. Add the radish greens and <u>toss</u> to wilt. Add the butter and a big pinch of salt, <u>toss</u> to coat, and serve immediately with any of the items pictured on page 356.

RAW

I've said this about a billion times. Most of these recipes call for radishes to be kept as wedges because it highlights their natural crunch and creates a bite with a bit more chew. That said, for dishes in which the radishes aren't the star, I <u>shave</u> them thinly. It is really up to you and how you want to showcase them.

radish wedges w/bagna cauda

This dish epitomizes the balance I strive for in a dish: the delight of raw, crisp, lightness of raw vegetables anchored by the fat and salt of the sauce. The variations here mimic that balance. Feel free to substitute any vegetables you have on hand for dipping in the "bath." Know too that the bagna cauda recipe will make more than you need for this recipe (I can't stand a half-used jar of anchovies in the refrigerator). Thankfully, it keeps in the refrigerator for basically forever and is delicious folded into boiled potatoes, dressing pasta, or to enrich a soup. This recipe could also be an appetizer if you serve the veggies and sauce separately and encourage people to dip to their Beauty Heart's content.

3 bunches radishes (2½ to 3 lb), greens reserved for another time if they are nice, roots cut into wedges

½ bunch parsley (1.2 oz | ¾ cup | 34 g), roughly chopped

¼ cup (60 ml) bagna cauda (page 60), warmed

Combine the radishes, parsley, and several big spoonfuls of the warm sauce, and toss. Taste and adjust the seasoning and acidity.

variations

w/chickpeas, cilantro, cumin, lime + red onion

2 cups (250 g) crispy chickpeas (page 45)

1 tsp (3 g) cumin seed

1 bunch radishes (1 lb | 455 g), cut into wedges or thin slices

1 bunch cilantro (1 oz | ½ cup | 34 g), roughly chopped

1 small red onion or shallot (2 oz | ¼ cup | 55 g), shaved

2 limes (2 fl oz | 60 ml), zest and juice

Salt

Combine the crispy chickpeas with the cumin, radishes, cilantro, onion, and lime zest and juice, and toss again. Taste and add salt, as needed.

w/spinach, smoked whitefish + dill yogurt

This is also good on top of greens or in lettuce cups if serving as an appetizer.

½ cup (120 g) plain yogurt

¼ cup (60 ml) olive oil, plus more for tossing

½ tsp (3 g) salt

6 sprigs dill, roughly chopped

1 bunch radishes (1 lb | 455 g), cut into wedges or thin slices

½ bag (2 oz | 55 g) spinach, washed and dried

4 oz (115 g) smoked whitefish, picked into large pieces, removing any bones and skin

Whisk the yogurt, olive oil, salt, and dill together. Toss the radishes, spinach, and whitefish together with a glug of olive oil and drizzle with the yogurt dressing.

w/romaine + ranch

1 head (12 oz | 340 g) romaine, base cut off, outer leaves discarded if gross

1 bunch radishes (1 lb | 455 g), cut into wedges

½ cup (120 ml) ranch dressing (page 60)

Freshly ground black pepper

Parmesan cheese, grated or shaved

On a large platter, stack the romaine leaves and the radish wedges, drizzle liberally with the ranch, season generously with pepper, and garnish with gratings or shavings of Parmesan.

POACHED

Poaching vegetables (or anything besides eggs, including chicken and fish, see page 23) has fallen a bit out of fashion but has become one of my favorite methods. It is a delicate way to coax flavor from vegetables and maintain a subtle crunch. You can poach in just about any liquid, so if you don't want to use the chicken stock, feel free to substitute water or a different broth. When serving, I include the very delicious liquid, or lift the radishes from the liquid and serve alone (saving the liquid for myself, to drink secretly in the kitchen).

poached radishes w/white wine, chicken stock, and butter

This dish is a nod to one of my mentors, Skye Gyngell. I was just out of cooking school when she welcomed me into her kitchen at London's Petersham Nurseries. I spent a month watching and learning over her shoulder. Every day we ate together as a staff, and I was included. One day, by the time Skye went to get her plate, all the staff meal was gone—gobbled up by the rest of us animals. She walked unfazed to the stove and pulled together this dish. She returned to our table with a bowl of silken pale pink radishes and a torn piece of crusty bread. As we talked through menu items and concerns about service, she dunked the pieces of bread in the bowl and eased my fears. She now owns Spring in London, and the furniture is the color of radish poaching liquid. She, like this dish, always reminds me to allow space for the suaveness of simple and pristine things.

2 bunches radishes (2 lb | 910 g), greens removed (if nice, reserve for another purpose)

¾ cup (180 ml) white wine

1 cup (240 ml) chicken stock

Salt and freshly ground black pepper

2 Tbsp (30 g) butter

1 lemon (1½ fl oz | 45 ml), zest and juice

If the radishes are vastly different sizes, halve or quarter the largest ones to be roughly the same size as the small ones. In a medium saucepan, combine the wine and stock with a big pinch of salt. When bubbling, add the radishes and reduce to a simmer; the liquid should just cover the radishes.

Cook until the radishes are just cooked through, about 6 minutes—they will be soft, with a touch of crispness still in the center. If the liquid is reduced and slightly syrupy, add the butter. If the liquid is still very thin, remove the radishes with a slotted spoon, bring the liquid to a boil, and reduce by half.

Add the butter and lemon zest and juice, let the butter melt, and spoon the liquid over the radishes. Serve with a big pinch of salt and grind of black pepper.

variations

w/roast chicken + celery salad

You could also make this a chicken salad by chopping the chicken and the radishes and combining all together.

Neutral oil

Four 6-oz (170-g) skin-on chicken breasts

Salt and freshly ground black pepper

6 stalks (4 oz | 2 cups | 115 g) celery, cut into thin slices

½ bunch parsley (1.2 oz | ¾ cup | 34 g), roughly chopped

¼ cup (60 ml) olive oil

1 lemon (1½ fl oz | 45 ml), zest and juice

One batch poached radishes, warm (page 23)

Pan sear the chicken breasts (page 24). Combine the celery, parsley, olive oil, lemon zest and juice, and 2 pinches of salt. When the chicken is cooked through, serve with the cold celery salad and warm poached radishes

w/spinach, lentils + goat cheese

1 bag (4 oz | 115 g) spinach

2 cups (400 g) cooked lentils (page 41)

One batch poached radishes with their warm liquid (page 23)

Salt and freshly ground black pepper

4 oz (115 g) goat cheese

Combine the spinach, lentils, and poached radishes and <u>toss</u>, allowing the warm liquid to gently wilt the spinach. Season with salt and pepper, and transfer to a serving dish. Dot with the goat cheese.

chilled w/dill cream cheese + pumpernickel toast

5 sprigs dill, roughly chopped

8 oz (230 g) cream cheese

Salt and freshly ground black pepper

Pumpernickel bread, 1 slice per person

One batch poached radishes, drained and chilled (page 23)

Work the dill into the cream cheese along with a big pinch of salt and pepper. Toast the bread, schmear with dill cream cheese, and top with chilled poached radishes.

ramps

For more and more of us, ramps (or wild leeks) are the harbingers of spring. Ramps are some of the first green leaves to pop out of the ground, sometimes even when there is still a light blanket of snow in the woods. After winter they are a welcome sign that, despite clouds and lasting frozen precipitation, things will grow again.

Members of the allium (onion) family, ramps share all the characteristics of that group. They differ from those cultivated varieties in their untamed smell and tender leaves—epitomizing both the intense flavor and the delicate texture found in the family.

They have a garlicky funk that is hard to describe or forget. I had never worked with ramps before cooking in Chicago—a town whose name is derived from the Native American word for ramp. My chef and I walked into "Rampfest," an annual fundraiser celebrating these foraged darlings; he looked at me and said, "Whoa, it smells like ramps in here." It smelled of wet soil after a rain mixed with an onion burp and somehow takeout food. That smell is fondly unmistakable, as is the classic "What's that smell?" the first time a ramp newbie walks into a room filled with them.

Ramps are available at the market or grocery store. But to harvest them yourself, you'll need a shovel and permission to go walking in the woods or other wild spaces. Search for long, ovate green leaves that look remarkably like those of lily of the valley. They often grow in circular crowns like a mushroom fairy circle.

With your shovel, push straight down next to the crown and gently wiggle the plants out of the ground, exposing their tender pink stalks—ideally lifting them from below their root system. With the crown lifted, bend down and pull no more than half of the ramps from the group.

Because ramps have such a short growing season, from first thaw until the trees leaf out, it takes them an average of seven years to regenerate. They propagate in two ways: one, at the end of their season they send up a pink flower that will send out seeds; two, like other alliums, they divide along their bulbs and regrow. This is why they are so often found in crowns. If you harvest the entire growth, there is no way for it to regenerate and no way for it to send out seeds. Leaving at least half ensures that that crown has a chance for next year.

When ramps come out of the ground, they are muddy and have a gelatinous sheath around the bulb. For the best storage, knock the dirt from the bulbs but leave the sheath to protect the plant's roots and keep the bulb hydrated.

To prepare them for cooking, soak the ramps in a good deal of cool water. Twist the roots from the bulb and slip the sheath from the base of the plant. This is a dirty process, so many people can't be bothered and instead buy them cleaned from the market (myself included, sometimes). Store in the refrigerator, loosely wrapped in a paper towel in a sealed zip locking bag. If you will not be able to cook them soon, cut the leaves from the bulb and store them separately. The leaves are very tender and will break down quickly, whereas the bulbs will store for weeks

In season, I will use ramps anywhere that scallions or even onions are called for. While their aroma mellows as it is cooked, ramps have a strong enough flavor to pair well with fats and can stand up to the smoke flavor of the grill.

According to our neighbor, Sharon, you should remember to pickle at least a **bunch** to garnish your martinis. The easiest way to do this is to simply warm up old pickle liquid saved from the end of a many a pickle jar, pour it over the bulbs, allow to cool, and refrigerate. Our other neighbor, Kathy, will simply pour vinegar and a good two pinches of salt into a jar filled with bulbs and preserve them that way.

HOW TO BUY

- The leaves, which resemble those of lily of the valley, should be free of bruising or mushiness.
- Natural yellowing of the leaves will occur later in the season.
- The bulbs have a pink tinge as they transition to the leaves.
- The bulbs will be more bulbous later in the season.

HOW TO STORE

- Cut the leaves from the bulb and store separately in a paper bag in a sealed plastic bag.
- The bulbs will store for weeks in a plastic bag in the refrigerator.
- Beware of storing loose ramps near any dairy products, which will pick up the oniony flavor.

NOTES

- Ramp season is from first thaw until the trees in the woods leaf out. Look for them in lower-lying areas with good drainage.
- When digging ramps, place your spade near the root base and step down.
- Remove only half of each cluster of ramps. The full life cycle of ramps is about seven years and removing the entire cluster will lead to decreased regrowth and overharvesting.
- Ramps are the plant that give Chicago its name. Native Americans called ramps *shikago*, and a lot of ramps grow in the Chicago region.

RAW

The ramp season is very, very short—generally about three weeks. At least one day out of those twenty-one I try to spend digging, cleaning, and preserving buckets of ramps. This is not a romantic affair; I generally do it begrudgingly. But in the middle of the summer, when I pop some ramp pesto out of the freezer for a very, very quick dinner, I always feel grateful to past Abra for making current Abra's life a lot easier. #treatyourfutureself

It might be very common practice at this point to freeze things like pesto in ice cube trays so that they are a manageable size when you want to use them. In practice, this ramp pesto needs a dedicated ice cube tray, as it will make your trays smell a good deal—not a problem when freezing other savory things, but not the best if you will ever be making ice cubes again.

ramp pesto w/seared chicken, radish, and bread salad

You can add garlic or cheese to this pesto if you like, but don't let not having those things prevent you from making the pesto. If you only have ramps, oil, and salt, you have enough to make a very flavorful sauce. Everything else is optional. There is really no point in using olive oil in this pesto, because the ramp flavor will obliterate any flavor nuance the olive oil brings—might as well stick to a cheaper neutral oil.

4 bunches ramps (2 lb | 4 cups | 910 g), leaves only, bulbs separated

2 Tbsp (20 g) sunflower seeds (optional)

½ cup (120 ml) neutral oil, plus more for searing

1 tsp (6 g) salt

2 garlic cloves (0.4 oz | 14 g)

¼ cup (8 g) grated Parmesan

4 to 6 chicken thighs (6 oz | 170 g), bone in and skin on

Salt and freshly ground black pepper

½ cup (120 ml) white wine

½ loaf sourdough bread, torn into 1-inch (2.5-cm) chunks

½ cup (120 ml) cream

1 cup (240 ml) chicken stock

1 bunch radishes (1 lb | 455 g), cut into thin slices

For the pesto: Roughly chop the ramp leaves, reserving the bulbs.

Toast the sunflower seeds (page 24) until golden and nutty.

In a blender, blend the oil, salt, sunflower seeds, garlic, and cheese. Turn off the blender and add the ramp leaves. Turn on the blender and whiz until the pesto is mostly smooth. Reserve ¼ cup (60 ml) for the dish and freeze the rest.

Heat the oven to 350°F (180°C). Season the chicken thighs liberally with salt and pepper

In a large ovenproof frying pan, heat a glug of oil and sear the chicken thighs until golden brown (page 24). Transfer to a plate.

Add the ramp bulbs and the wine to the pan with a pinch of salt and scrape up any brown bits in the pan. Cook and allow the wine to reduce. Add the sourdough chunks, cream, and stock and return the thighs (skin-side up) to the pan, resting on top of the bread nest.

Place the frying pan in the oven and roast until the thighs are cooked through (page 24).

Transfer the cooked thighs from the pan to a serving platter to rest. Toss the reserved pesto and radishes with the baked bread to coat. Add back the chicken thighs, dot with additional pesto, and serve.

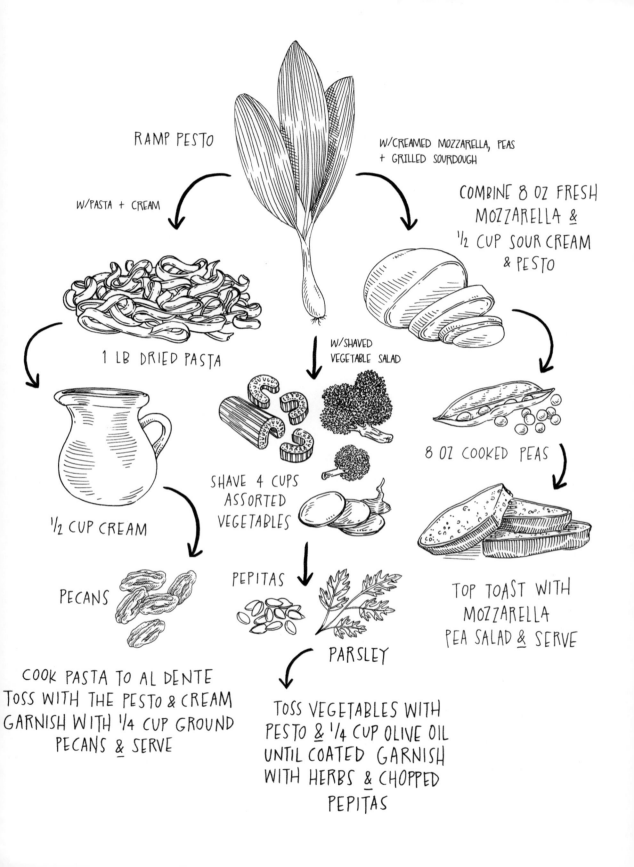

RAMP PESTO

W/PASTA + CREAM

W/CREAMED MOZZARELLA, PEAS + GRILLED SOURDOUGH

COMBINE 8 OZ FRESH MOZZARELLA & 1/2 CUP SOUR CREAM & PESTO

1 LB DRIED PASTA

W/SHAVED VEGETABLE SALAD

1/2 CUP CREAM

SHAVE 4 CUPS ASSORTED VEGETABLES

8 OZ COOKED PEAS

PECANS

PEPITAS

PARSLEY

TOP TOAST WITH MOZZARELLA PEA SALAD & SERVE

COOK PASTA TO AL DENTE TOSS WITH THE PESTO & CREAM GARNISH WITH 1/4 CUP GROUND PECANS & SERVE

TOSS VEGETABLES WITH PESTO & 1/4 CUP OLIVE OIL UNTIL COATED GARNISH WITH HERBS & CHOPPED PEPITAS

GRILLED

The pungency of ramps pairs well with grill-induced smoke. Plus, the preparation takes almost no time at all, which is nice when cleaning the damn things can take all afternoon. To showcase ramps at their most perfect and whole, I do nothing more than <u>toss</u> them in olive oil, salt, and pepper and cook on a hot grill. The leaves are nice with a good amount of char on them but will always take a fraction of the time of the bulbs to cook. Place the ramps perpendicular to the grill grates, with the bulbs over the hottest part and the leaves draped over a cooler part of the grill, and you're more likely to have a tender bulb and charred leaves in the same time frame.

Please note that any of these grilled recipes will also be wonderful with whole sautéed ramps if it is raining or you don't want to pull out the charcoal.

grilled ramps w/parsley, walnuts, and hard-boiled egg

The pounded walnut relish (page 63) is a pantry staple, with hard-boiled egg added for extra richness to balance the ramps. It is good on lots of things beyond ramps and will hold in your refrigerator for a couple of days before the walnuts get too soggy. If your oven isn't on, you can always toast the walnuts in a frying pan on the grill.

1 cup (120 g) walnuts

3 hard-boiled eggs (page 22)

1 bunch parsley (2.4 oz | 1½ cups | 68 g), roughly chopped

½ cup (120 ml) olive oil, plus more for the ramps

1 lemon (1½ fl oz | 45 ml) zest and juice

Salt and freshly ground black pepper

2 bunches ramps (1 lb | 455 g)

Heat the grill to medium-high. Toast the walnuts (page 24), either in a 350°F (180°C) oven or on the grill.

Grate the eggs on the widest tooth of a box grater.

While the walnuts are still warm, slightly smash the walnuts (I generally do this by putting them in a zip locking bag and bashing them with the bottom of a frying pan or rolling pin).

Combine the walnuts, parsley, grated egg, olive oil, lemon zest, juice, and 2 big pinches of salt, allowing the walnuts to soak up the acidity of the lemon as they cool.

Toss the ramps with a glug of oil and salt and pepper. Grill with the bulbs over the hottest part of the grill and the leaves over a cooler section. The ramp bulbs should be charred on the outside and slightly soft when touched; the leaves will singe a bit but not be frizzled completely to ash.

Transfer the ramps to a platter and spoon the walnut mixture over the top.

variations

w/tuna mayo

¼ cup (60 g) tuna mayo (page 61)

¼ cup (35 g) sunflower seeds (optional)

Grill the ramps, spoon tuna mayo over them, and garnish with sunflower seeds.

w/roasted cherry tomatoes + ricotta

½ cup (120 g) ricotta

¼ cup (60 ml) cream

1 lemon (1½ fl oz | 45 ml), zest and juice

Salt and freshly ground black pepper

1 cup (240 g) roasted cherry tomatoes (page 435)

Combine the ricotta with the cream, lemon zest and juice, and salt and pepper.

Spoon the ricotta onto a plate. Top with the ramps and dot with the roasted tomatoes.

w/yogurt + dukkah

Neutral oil

½ cup (120 g) yogurt

½ cup (60 g) dukkah (page 63)

Spoon the yogurt onto a platter, top with the grilled ramps, and spoon dukkah over the whole thing.

SAUTÉED

In the spring, ramps replace almost all other onions, and quickly cooking them in a hot pan is my most used technique. Ninety percent of the time I separate the leaves from the root, cook the roots first, and add the sliced leaves at the end. The other 10 percent of the time I will pan roast ramps whole and garnish them.

If sautéing whole, treat like a pan roast; add the ramp to the hot oil and don't turn or fiddle with it. Let the leaves take on a fried crispness and the bulbs will soften gently.

sautéed ramps w/morels, spinach, and cream on toast

The technique used here—gently wilting spinach with a hot sauce—is my way of preventing overcooked spinach globs. The hot sauce poured over the top and then left in place gently coaxes the leaves into a tender malleability.

Fresh morels need to be washed very well. If you detect a lot of creepy crawlies in the nooks and crannies, let the morels soak in very salty water for 10 minutes and then rinse.

1 bag (4 oz | 115 g) spinach

1 bunch ramps (½ lb | 230 g), bulbs and leaves separated, bulbs thinly sliced and leaves into ⅛-inch (12-mm) ribbons

1 bunch radishes (1 lb | 455 g), shaved, greens cut into ribbons if nice

Neutral oil

4 oz (115 g) morels or any other fresh mushroom, ends trimmed, well washed and dried

Salt

Butter

Freshly ground black pepper

¼ cup (60 ml) white wine

½ cup (120 ml) heavy cream

1 thick slice sourdough or multigrain bread per person

Combine the spinach with the ramp-leaf and radish-green ribbons, and set aside.

In a large frying pan, heat a <u>glug</u> of neutral oil until just about to smoke. Fry the mushrooms, seasoning with salt, until they are crispy and have released their moisture. Transfer to a paper towel–lined plate.

Wipe out the frying pan and add a knob of butter. When melted, add the sliced ramp bulbs and a big pinch of salt and pepper. Add the wine and let reduce until syrupy. Add the cream and bring to a bubble. When the cream is reduced by about half, stir in the mushrooms.

While the cream mixture is still very hot, pour it over the spinach and greens mixture. Allow the heat of the sauce to gently wilt the greens. <u>Toss</u> until evenly combined. Taste and adjust the salt and add pepper as desired.

Toast the bread. Top each toast with creamy spinach, scatter <u>shaved</u> radishes over it, and serve.

variations

w/peas + lettuce over rice

Separate the leaves and bulbs of 1 <u>bunch</u> of ramps. Sauté the bulbs, add 2 cups (240 g) fresh or frozen peas and ¼ cup (60 ml) wine. Reduce by half, pour over the ramp leaves and 4 oz (115 g) tender lettuce greens, and serve on top of cooked rice (page 41).

w/asparagus, lemon, chili flakes + wheat berries

Sauté 1 <u>bunch</u> <u>thinly sliced</u> ramps with 1 tsp (5 g) chili flakes. Add 1 cup (215 g) cooked wheat berries (page 43), and <u>toss</u> with the zest and juice of 1 lemon, ¼ cup (60 ml) olive oil, and 1 <u>bunch</u> <u>shaved</u> asparagus.

whole w/parmesan, lemon + bread crumbs

Combine 2 oz (55 g) Parmesan, zest of 1 lemon, and ½ cup (70 g) bread crumbs and set aside. Pan roast the ramps whole. Transfer to a platter and cover with the juice of 1 lemon, 2 Tbsp (30 ml) olive oil, and the bread crumb mixture.

squash, summer

Three things always come to mind when I think of zucchini.

One, the old saying that summer squash season is the only time of year when residents of small towns lock their car doors, for fear of the vegetable being left on their front seat by a gardening neighbor.

Two, after receiving our first big delivery of zucchini from the farmers' market at Zingerman's, my good friend (and then-boss) Rodger looking at it, saying, "Nature's Styrofoam," and walking away.

Three, how when we were growing up we used those monstrously large zucchini as bats in tomato baseball. Having your sister throw rotten tomatoes at you only to smash it with a giant zucchini is, to this day, far and away the most fun I've ever had with garden produce.

But all this illustrates that summer squash is a vegetable that everyone grows yet never seems to really love. It's a shame. I've come around on summer squash. Mostly because you can bend it to suit your needs by acknowledging the qualities of the squash, no matter the size.

The great big baseball bats are best suited to being grated and folded into a batter or dough. Me, I rely on marinating and grilling to work through volumes of squash. Grilled, because it is less likely to fall through the grates when sliced into wide planks, making me more willing to do large batches. Marinated, because it keeps in the refrigerator for a good long time, allowing me to work it into a bunch of different meals throughout the week.

On the other end of the spectrum are the skinny finger squash harvested very young from the plant. I find the interior flesh of these squash to be creamier and the skin thinner and more tender. Similar to cucumbers, the smaller the vegetable, the smaller the seeds, which are unpleasant when too large.

To embrace small squash, **shave** them thinly and serve them raw. This was a revelation to me as much as eating sushi for the first time—equally as implausible as it was delicious. The raw squash has a pleasant snap and delicate chew. Instead of resenting that creamy, Styrofoamy texture, I embrace it by playing against the blandness. I pair the squash with stronger flavors in the form of bright acid, cheesy salt, or spice.

This immediately turns nature's Styrofoam into a pop of brightness well suited for a hot summer night. The sort of night fit for a game of zucchini-tomato baseball.

HOW TO BUY

- Look for small-to medium-size summer squash. The larger the squash, the larger the seeds and the more water in the cells.

- Avoid squash with wrinkled or collapsed sections, which indicate age or poor growth.

- Check the flower end of the squash for blossom end rot.

HOW TO STORE

- Keep summer squash in a cool dark place.

- Do not store in the refrigerator, as it hurts the cells and facilitates decomposition, pitting the skin.

- Wash just before using because the fuzz and natural wax on the skin will help protect the flesh.

NOTES

- Zucchini and summer squash are mild, to say the least, in flavor. Pair them with bright acidic and punchy flavors.

- Delicata and acorn squash are technically summer squash with skins that cure more rigidly than zucchini. Cook them like a winter squash but eat the skin.

- The blossoms are edible and traditionally served stuffed or fried. Consider stuffing with fresh cheese and dipping in dukkah (page 63).

- Avoid salting the summer squash in advance of making a dish; the salt will leach water from the cells, making the dish watery and the texture of the squash rubbery.

- Salt the squash in advance if making fritters or zucchini cake, to remove excess water before folding into the batter. Be sure to wipe out before cooking.

RAW

To slice the squash thinly I generally use a mandoline, but a sharp knife also works well. I like to <u>shave</u> them into a variety of shapes— little rounds mixed with long thin planks running the length of the squash and wide ovals <u>cut obliquely</u>.

shaved summer squash w/parmesan, lots and lots of herbs, and olive oil

The key to this dish is a ton of herbs. Use as many different herbs as you like. I generally leave them whole if they are tender and mince any with woody stems. You can use just parsley, but don't skimp on the amount. Assume that for all raw recipes you want small- to medium-size squash. The bigger they are, the tougher the skin, the larger the seeds, and the even less exciting they become. I usually assume half a squash per person.

2 summer squash (20 oz | 4 cups | 570 g), <u>shaved</u> into ⅛-inch- (4-mm-) thick slices with a mandoline or a sharp knife

1 cup (25 g) assorted herb leaves

4 oz (115 g) Parmesan, peeled into <u>ribbons</u>

1 tsp (6 g) coarse salt

½ tsp (3 g) freshly ground black pepper

½ cup (120 ml) olive oil

Toss together the squash, herbs, Parmesan, and salt and pepper with ¼ cup (60 ml) of the olive oil.

Taste and adjust the seasoning, adding more olive oil as needed to make it well dressed and flavorful.

Serve within the next 30 minutes. If serving later, <u>shave</u> the zucchini in advance but dress just before serving.

variations

w/massaged kale, cherry tomatoes + walnuts

4 cups (20 oz | 570 g) shaved summer squash

1 bunch kale (½ lb | 4 cups | 230 g), cut into ribbons

1 pint (1 lb | 455 g) cherry tomatoes, halved

1 cup (120 g) walnuts, toasted (page 24) and roughly chopped

¼ cup (60 ml) olive oil

Salt and freshly ground black pepper

w/smoked lake trout, herbs + arugula

4 cups (20 oz | 570 g) shaved summer squash

6 oz (170 g) smoked trout, picked into large pieces, removing bones (or whitefish or canned tuna)

1 cup (25 g) assorted herbs

1 bag (4 oz | 115 g) arugula

¼ cup (60 ml) olive oil

Salt and freshly ground black pepper

w/goat cheese, pecans + charred oregano

6 sprigs oregano

4 cups (20 oz | 570 g) shaved summer squash

1 cup (120 g) pecans

¼ cup (60 ml) olive oil

4 oz (115 g) goat cheese

Lay the oregano on the grill over high heat until the leaves begin to singe. When cool, brush the leaves into a large bowl and crumble with your hands.

Toss the oregano together with the squash, pecans, and olive oil. Taste for seasoning and adjust. Transfer to a serving platter, dot with the goat cheese, and serve.

GRILLED

The spongy nature of summer squash soaks up oil, which is flavorful but can cause flare-ups when placed over the flame. I place the cut squash in a bowl and dress liberally with olive oil, salt, and pepper. Just before grilling, I squeeze the squash between two fingers (the way you'd move toothpaste to the top of the tube) and then grill. This allows the squash to soak up the oil but not so much that it blackens the creamy flesh (unlike when I cooked it for the shoot).

grilled zucchini planks w/white beans, olive oil, and rosemary

This is one of my favorite summer dishes because the beans are made well ahead. The summer squash can be grilled in advance and served room temperature or reheated in an oven just before serving. This dish isn't finicky and is exactly what I want on a hot summer night.

Neutral oil

6 garlic cloves (1.2 oz | 34 g), minced or cut into thin slices

3 sprigs rosemary, stemmed and minced

Two 12-oz (340-g) cans white beans, drained and rinsed (or cook your own)

¼ cup (60 ml) sherry vinegar or red wine vinegar

¼ cup (60 ml) olive oil to dress the beans, plus more for dressing

3 to 4 summer squash (40 oz | 1.2 kg), cut into ¼- to ½-inch- (6- to 12-mm-) thick planks

Salt and freshly ground black pepper

1 bag (4 oz | 115 g) arugula

In a frying pan, heat a glug of neutral oil and fry the garlic and rosemary until fragrant but not browned. Add the beans and sauté briefly. Add the vinegar and ¼ cup (60 ml) olive oil and remove the pan from the heat but keep at room temperature.

Season the squash liberally with salt and pepper and grill over medium-high heat.

Dress the arugula lightly with olive oil and a pinch of salt.

Spoon the beans onto a serving platter. Top with the squash and arugula and serve.

variations

w/poached salmon, cherry tomatoes, green beans + sunflower seeds

3 to 4 summer squash (40 oz | 1.2 kg) summer squash, grilled

1 pint (1 lb | 455 g) cherry tomatoes, halved

1 lb (455 g) green beans, blanched or grilled

¼ cup (35 g) sunflower seeds

4 to 6 salmon fillets (6 oz | 170 g each), poached (page 23)

Toss the squash, tomatoes, beans, and sunflower seeds together and serve with poached salmon.

w/grilled chicken, shaved red onion, mushrooms + massaged kale

6 to 8 oz (170 to 230 g) mushrooms, sliced

1 small (2 oz | ¼ cup | 55 g) red onion, shaved thinly

1 bunch kale (½ lb | 4 cups | 230 g), midribs stripped out, cut into ribbons

3 to 4 summer squash (40 oz | 1.2 kg), grilled

Olive oil

Salt and freshly ground black pepper

4 to 6 chicken breasts (6 oz | 170 g each), grilled

Roast the mushrooms (page 24) and toss with the onion, kale, grilled squash, a good glug of olive oil, and pinch of salt and pepper. Serve alongside the grilled chicken.

w/roasted eggplant, slab tomatoes + mozzarella

2 balls (1 lb | 455 g) fresh mozzarella, torn into chunks

¼ cup (60 g) yogurt or sour cream

1 lemon (1½ fl oz | 45 ml), zest and juice

1 eggplant (1 lb | 455 g), sliced into slabs, grilled

3 to 4 summer squash (40 oz | 1.2 kg), grilled

2 large (1 lb | 455 g) slicer tomatoes, sliced ¼ inch (6 mm) thick

Freshly ground black pepper

Dress the mozzarella with the yogurt and the lemon zest and juice.

Layer the vegetables with the dressed mozzarella and serve with a grating of fresh pepper over the top—also no one would complain if you added some basil or oregano to the mix, but it isn't necessary.

MARINATED

Escabèche is the Spanish technique for cooking something and then cooling it in a vinaigrette. As the cells cool, they absorb the acidity deep into their walls, yielding a flavor that is a richer version of a light pickle. Escabèching works well with fish and poultry, as well as vegetables, because the acidity in the marinade helps stave off bad bacteria for an extra few days. This summer squash version can be kept in the refrigerator for weeks and turned into myriad dishes.

summer squash escabèche w/mushrooms, arugula, and steak

The acidity of the marinated squash cuts through the richness of the meat. If you want to avoid stove work, cook the mushrooms and squash on the grill and proceed with the recipe as written.

Steak (any cut), 6 to 8 oz (170 to 230 g) per person

Salt and freshly ground black pepper

¼ cup (60 ml) apple cider vinegar

¼ cup (60 ml) olive oil, plus more for the arugula

1 Tbsp (15 g) brown sugar

½ tsp (3 g) salt

3 to 4 summer squash (40 oz | 1.2 kg) summer squash, cut into long planks or ¼-inch (6-mm) slices

6 oz (170 g) mushrooms (any variety), sliced

1 bag (4 oz | 115 g) arugula

Season the steak liberally with salt and pepper.

Whisk together the vinegar, oil, brown sugar, and salt.

Panfry the summer squash until golden brown (this will mostly likely need to be done in batches). When the squash is cooked, immediately dress with some of the vinegar mixture and allow to cool.

Panfry the mushrooms until crispy.

Grill the steak to your desired doneness.

Dress the arugula lightly with olive oil and a pinch of salt.

Combine the squash and mushrooms. Serve the steak topped with the squash mixture and the arugula.

variations

w/oven-roasted eggplant, tomato + parmesan ribbons

1 large (1 lb | 455 g) eggplant, cut into rounds	½ cup (70 g) bread crumbs	2 large slicing tomatoes (1 lb | 455 g), cut into thick slabs
¼ cup (60 g) mayo (page 61)	Summer squash escabèche	4 oz (115 g) Parmesan, peeled into ribbons

Heat the oven to 400°F (200°C). Brush the eggplant slices with mayo and press them into the bread crumbs. Bake until the eggplant is cooked through and crispy, about 35 minutes. On a serving platter, alternate squash, eggplant, and tomato, until it is all used up. Top the whole thing with the Parmesan ribbons.

w/poached lake trout, cucumbers, dill + yogurt

Summer squash escabèche	5 sprigs dill, roughly chopped	½ cup (120 g) yogurt
1 cucumber (10 oz | 280 g), cut into half-moons	Salt and freshly ground black pepper	6 oz (170 g) trout per person, poached (page 23)

Combine the squash, cucumbers, and dill, and season with salt and pepper. Schmear yogurt over the serving platter, place the trout on top, and top with the salad.

w/goat cheese, chard + pecans on toast

1 bunch chard (½ lb | 4 cups | 230 g), cut into ribbons and massaged if too tough

Olive oil

Salt

1 thick slice of bread per person

4 oz (115 g) fresh goat cheese

Summer squash escabèche

½ cup (60 g) pecans

Dress the chard with a glug of olive oil and a pinch of salt. Toast the bread and schmear with goat cheese. Top with squash, chard, and pecans.

squash, winter

I fall victim to the winter blues, especially when Erik is on the road. It starts as just wanting to curl up on a warm sofa and watch the snow falling outside. It devolves into not wanting to go out at all. Then on to realizing that there is no fresh food in the house and finally removing a frozen pizza from the depths of the freezer and eating it by myself, standing over the sink.

To combat these tendencies, I've tried different things, but none as successful as getting up, going to the market, and buying the biggest, weirdest winter squash I can find. This works for me for three reasons.

One, large squashes are so, so much food, so to eat all of it, I need to have friends over for dinner. Friends don't just bring big appetites; they also bring conviviality; they socialize with me, creating the secondary benefit of mitigating my cold weather hermit crabbiness.

Two, when I'm feeling daunted by the winter blues, it takes a lot to work up the energy to cook. I will make grand plans to make an elaborate meal, and as soon as I'm done writing the prep list, I am suddenly confronted by a feeling of *Meh, I can't be bothered*. But with a squash, my favorite way to cook it is to crack it in half (explained shortly), scoop out the seeds, and roast (cut-side down) until the flesh is fully tender. Even in my most sedentary state, I can achieve that. By the time I feel immovable, the sweet smell of caramelized squash is filling the kitchen and encouraging me to make something else. Just like that, I'm moving, and momentum is working in my favor.

Three, the leftovers are incredibly easy to repurpose into different meals after my friends are gone.

Simply carrying such a squash home from the market, cradling it in my arms like a baby, fills me with the anticipation of people over and the oven on. Additionally, buying the biggest, weirdest looking ones makes farmers happy. The bane of the fall market season is hauling one's strangely shaped squash darlings back and forth, as such cucurbits rarely get love from market goers. True, they are big and unruly and, if priced by the pound, cost more than people usually tend to spend. They are worth every penny because the flavor is deep and intense, not to mention there is so much food and cooking efficiency underneath that bumpy skin.

My favorite varieties are blue Hubbard, Sibley (or Pike's Peak), red Kuri, Buttercup, Galeux D'eysines, and Pink Banana. They all taste slightly different, but all have a drier flesh than the always-favored butternut. These are also mostly heritage seeds that help ensure that we are not on a road to an acorn squash monocrop apocalypse.

No matter the type of squash you chose—including spaghetti squash, even though that squash yields a different result—the basic technique is the same.

Heat the oven to anywhere between 325°F and 400°F (165°C to 200°C). The higher the temperature, the faster it will cook. There is little danger of burning the squash, because the skin will protect it, but it is possible, so keep an eye out.

Cut the squash in half and remove the seeds. It can be a trick to get a small knife through a big squash, so use the longest knife you have. I will sometimes cut off a bit of one side to create a flat side to rest on the cutting board, making the squash far more cooperative. Then just start slicing. If the knife gets stuck, lift the squash, with one hand on the side of the squash and the other on the knife handle, and whack it on the cutting board while applying downward pressure on the knife. It is loud and a bit nerve-wracking, but it will help to cause the squash to literally crack in half. Don't worry if the edges aren't even; it will all look the same after the squash is cooked.

At this point you can save the seeds to roast for a snack if you like. For me, sometimes adding that step makes the day feel too full, so I've been known to add the seeds to the compost and not look back. You do you.

Rub the squash with a bit of oil and place cut-side down on a foil-lined baking sheet. Bake until the flesh collapses underneath a prodding finger or spoon. At this point the squash will be golden brown and bubbling around the sides. It should look inviting and yield easily when poked.

Remove from the oven and allow to cool. Scoop the flesh away from the skin and then choose your own adventure for what is next. More often than not, I blend that flesh with some brown butter to make a silky smooth purée and serve it with something spicy or salty. It is a show stopper that replaces grits or mashed potatoes at many a wintry dinner party.

The warmth of that conviviality will temper the seemingly unavoidable "alone over the sink" nights. Converting the leftovers into a soup or a schmear for sandwiches will stave off the sad meals lurking in the back of the freezer.

HOW TO BUY

- Look for squash that are free of bruises, soft spots, gashes, or scabs.
- Avoid squash without the stem still attached, unless you will be using it soon. The loss of a stem creates a chink in the squash's armor and can be a place for bad bacteria to get in.
- Avoid squash that have strange round marks, especially green on a yellow or orange squash. That is usually a virus, and those squash don't seem to store for as long.
- Look for squash that are heavy in the hand. The lighter the squash, the less moisture is in the flesh.

HOW TO STORE

- Keep in a cool, dark place.
- Avoid temperature fluctuations and freezing.
- Once the squash is cut, store wrapped in the refrigerator.

NOTES

- Delicata and acorn squashes are technically summer squash with a skin that cures like winter squash. It stores well but not as well as other traditional winter squashes.
- The seeds are edible and tasty roasted. Soak them overnight in salty water and then pull the squash flesh away from the seeds. Dry the seeds and **toss** them with oil and any spices you like and roast at 400°F (200°C) until golden and crispy.
- Winter squash is also tasty raw, though I don't like it as much as cooked, so I haven't included recipes here. If you'd like to try this, cut away the skin, **shave** the flesh into thin **ribbons**, and **toss** it into any salad as you would raw summer squash or apples.

PAN ROASTED

I like browning the squash in the pan to get good caramelization on the cut sides. If the oven is already on, feel free to finish cooking the squash there to free up a burner. Also note that if you cut the squash into large pieces (more than 1 inch [2.5 cm] thick) you will need to finish the squash in the oven after the initial sear because it will never cook all the way through without burning.

delicata squash w/dukkah, ricotta, and dried cherries

Delicata, festival, and acorn squash are my favorite types of squash because they have a thin enough rind that it can be eaten, skin and all. If using a thicker-skinned squash like butternut, peel the skin away with a vegetable peeler or knife and continue as described.

I started making this dish with quark, the German fresh cheese. Quark is available in the most unlikely of places—like Amish stores or places with German or Dutch populations. Ricotta is much more ubiquitous and has the same fresh, creamy, slightly grainy texture.

Neutral oil

2 medium (2 lb | 910 g) delicata, acorn, or festival squash, cut in half lengthwise, seeded, and cut into half-moons or claws 1 to 2 inches (2.5 to 5 cm) thick

Salt and freshly ground black pepper

½ cup (60 g) dukkah (page 63)

½ cup (70 g) dried cherries, tart or sweet

1 bunch parsley (2.4 oz | 1½ cups | 68 g), stemmed, leaves left whole

4 oz (115 g) ricotta or quark

Heat a glug of neutral oil in a large frying pan over high heat. When smoking hot, add the squash in a single layer, sprinkle with salt and pepper, and allow to brown. When brown, flip, add an additional glug of oil, and brown the other side. Do this in batches; if there is too much in the pan, the squash will steam and not brown evenly.

When the squash is tender and golden brown, transfer it to a large bowl and toss with the dukkah, cherries, and parsley. Transfer the squash mixture to a serving platter. Dot with the ricotta and serve.

variations

w/roasted cherry tomatoes, goat cheese + herbs

2 medium (2 lb | 910 g) squash, cut in half lengthwise, seeded, and cut into half-moons

Olive oil

Salt and freshly ground black pepper

1 cup (240 g) roasted cherry tomatoes

4 oz (115 g) goat cheese

Any and all herbs you have (parsley, cilantro, mint, sage, thyme, rosemary, oregano)

Roast the squash, transfer to a serving platter, and dot with tomatoes and goat cheese. Scatter with the herbs and serve.

w/arugula salad, mushrooms + parmesan

6 oz (170 g) mushrooms, sliced

2 medium (2 lb | 910 g) delicata squash, cut in half lengthwise, seeded, and cut into half-moons

1 bag (4 oz | 115 g) arugula

Olive oil

Salt and freshly ground black pepper

2 oz (55 g) Parmesan, grated or peeled into ribbons

Pan roast the mushrooms (page 24). Remove from the pan and reserve. Roast the squash. <u>Toss</u> the roasted squash with the mushrooms and arugula. Dress with a <u>glug</u> of olive oil and pinches of salt and black pepper. Garnish with the Parmesan and serve.

w/mustard vinaigrette, chard + salmon

2 medium (2 lb | 910 g) delicata squash, cut in half lengthwise, seeded, and cut into half-moons

1 <u>bunch</u> chard (½ lb | 4 cups | 230 g), cut into <u>ribbons</u>

¼ cup (60 g) Dijon mustard

¼ cup (60 ml) olive oil

1 Tbsp (15 ml) red wine vinegar

Salt

6 oz (170 g) salmon per person

Roast the squash and transfer it from the pan (reserve the pan) to layer on the chard, wilting it. Add the mustard, olive oil, vinegar, and a big pinch of salt. Sear the salmon (page 24) in the squash frying pan. When fully cooked, <u>toss</u> the squash and chard to make the salad. Serve with the seared salmon.

OVEN ROASTED

My friend Leandra Forman at FoodChain in Lexington, Kentucky, processes thousands of pounds of gleaned squash every winter and turns it into frozen squash purée. She then uses the purée to make soups, sauce for macaroni and cheese, the base for bread stuffing at Thanksgiving, and pumpkin bread for the dinners and cooking classes hosted at FoodChain's community kitchen. I always thought I was a fanatic for squash, but I've never cooked eight thousand pounds in just a few months. Hats off to the team at FoodChain. You, your work, and your squash are an inspiration.

winter squash and brown butter purée

This recipe calls for some brown butter. No matter how you use this purée, the brown butter adds a toasty, nutty richness. But you can easily swap it out for regular butter, olive oil, or coconut oil. You can also skip the fat, but the purée will never get quite as silky.

1 large winter squash (about 3 lb | 1.4 kg)	Neutral oil (optional) 4 oz (115 g) butter	1 to 2 tsp (6 to 12 g) salt

Heat the oven to between 325°F and 400°F (165°C and 200°C)—the hotter the oven, the faster it will cook.

Cut the squash in half lengthwise (see page 396 for technique and tips). Scoop out the seeds. Toss with oil, if using, and place the squash cut-side down on a lined baking sheet. Roast until the flesh collapses. Remove from the oven and cool.

In a saucepan or frying pan, heat the butter until it browns (it will first get foamy, then settle, and the milk proteins will brown). Remove from the heat and scrape up the browned bits to loosen.

When the squash is cool enough to handle, scoop the flesh from the skin. Put in a food processor and add salt to taste. Blend, adding in the brown butter as you go.

SQUASH & BROWN BUTTER PURÉE

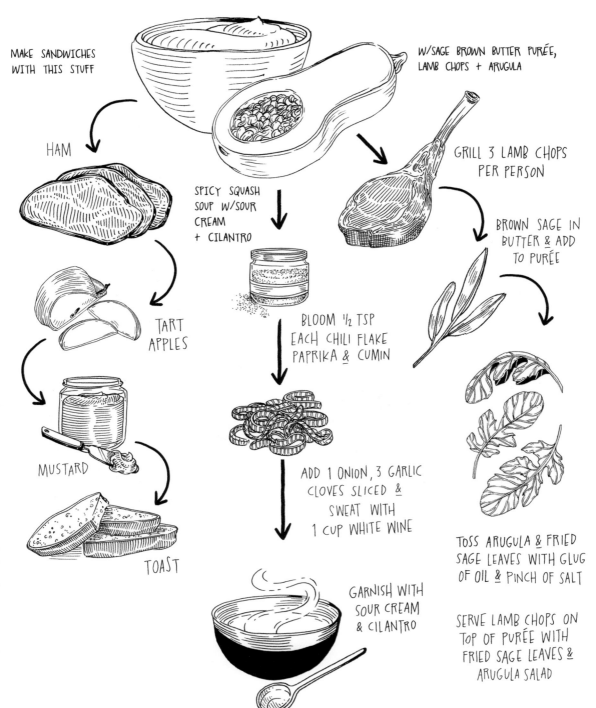

MAKE SANDWICHES WITH THIS STUFF

W/SAGE BROWN BUTTER PURÉE, LAMB CHOPS + ARUGULA

HAM

SPICY SQUASH SOUP W/SOUR CREAM + CILANTRO

GRILL 3 LAMB CHOPS PER PERSON

BROWN SAGE IN BUTTER & ADD TO PURÉE

TART APPLES

BLOOM ½ TSP EACH CHILI FLAKE PAPRIKA & CUMIN

MUSTARD

ADD 1 ONION, 3 GARLIC CLOVES SLICED & SWEAT WITH 1 CUP WHITE WINE

TOAST

GARNISH WITH SOUR CREAM & CILANTRO

TOSS ARUGULA & FRIED SAGE LEAVES WITH GLUG OF OIL & PINCH OF SALT

SERVE LAMB CHOPS ON TOP OF PURÉE WITH FRIED SAGE LEAVES & ARUGULA SALAD

sunchokes

Sunchokes (aka Jerusalem artichokes) are the tuberous root of a variety of sunflower. They grow similarly to a potato. In early fall the leaves and flowers die back, having put all their energy into the crown of creamy brown, knobby roots beneath the soil. These roots are packed with micronutrients and inulin, a starch that has a low glycemic index so it won't screw with blood sugar levels and therefore is suitable for diabetics. Inulin also promotes good gut health by feeding the flora of our digestive system—a good dinner choice after a round of antibiotics. But buyer beware: the positive effects of this flora feeding have also led to an apt nickname, fartichokes.

When Jess and I started Bare Knuckle Farm, we chose varieties and planted seeds mostly according to his know-how and my favorite things to eat. Each selection felt like an adventure—bright and full of potential. That was the height of my personal sunchoke craze; I mentioned again and again that we should grow them.

That fall, Jess finally relented and ordered 50 lb (23 kg) from Johnny's Selected Seed out of Maine. They were shipped to Michigan, but sadly they arrived two days after Jess had had his mail forwarded to Brooklyn, where he would be living for the winter. So the New York mail-lady lugged them up three flights of steps to this new address, but Jess' name wasn't on the box, and so she didn't leave them. Then the sunchokes went back on the route three days in a row. On day three, they were finally just abandoned on his door. They arrived limp and browned. He put them in his refrigerator and by February, they went from withered to shriveled, and he threw them out. I laughed for about an hour at the telling of this story, while confident he would never agree to grow them after it.

That spring in the doorway of our hoop house was a plastic grocery bag with a few pounds of sunchoke tubers starting to sprout and a note: "Thought maybe you'd like to plant these. xo, Julia."

The Julia is Julia Branbanec, our then-eighty-five-year-old neighbor who still maintains a large garden, small orchard, and twenty-year-old asparagus patch. She and her husband John moved to Leelanau County from downstate Michigan to start growing tree fruit organically. They were pioneers in our area, specializing in hand-pruned and -picked peaches and apples. She is one of those women who might very well be a wood sprite. She loves nature and is a part of it. Slight in stature but hawk-like in her attention to detail. We would go walking and she would point out the wild parsnips and the remnants of an older orchard that was there before she and John bought the land. She never knew the previous farmers' names or what their story was, but she liked feeling their presence there just the same. After every afternoon together, I feel like she might vanish like the poof of a dandelion cloud, leaving perfect berry patches and knowledge behind her.

In our case, it was a trail of sunchokes. We took her tubers and planted them in the lowest-lying part of our newest field—naming it Julia's Garden. The sunchokes are still there, dug up and replanted each year. Beyond their indelicate nickname, sunchokes have a pushy reputation—they are known for taking over garden spaces. They will regrow from the smallest nub left in the ground over winter.

Several years later, I told Julia this story—the sunchokes in the mail, them taking up half a refrigerator all winter, her magical delivery. She laughed and said, "That's funny, because I really just needed to thin my patch and had run out of people who would take them."

For a lot of reasons, we closed Bare Knuckle Farm. It can be a bittersweet thing, having your life evolve and needing to abandon paths you thought you'd walk for a lifetime. I don't keep in good contact with Julia, but I always imagine that even if no farming ever happens on that land again, her sunchokes will sprout up each spring—a marker that someone was here before.

HOW TO BUY

- Look for sunchokes that are firm and not squishy.
- Avoid sunchokes with damaged or brown tips, unless you are OK with cutting that part away.
- Avoid sunchokes that have started to sprout.
- The more knobby the sunchoke, the more soil lodged between the branches, and the more cleaning required.

HOW TO STORE

- Store in a cool dark place.
- Avoid temperature fluctuations and freezing.
- No need to store in the refrigerator unless the chokes have gotten very cold.

NOTES

- Sunchokes are packed with a carbohydrate called inulin that promotes good gut health. They are especially good after a round of antibiotics to help regrow the beneficial bacteria in the GI tract.
- The inulin also gives sunchokes a low glycemic index, making them a good option for diabetics.
- Sunchokes oxidize quickly. Soak cut pieces in **acidulated water** to prevent unpleasant browning.
- Sunchokes regrow very, very easily and have lovely tall foliage. To grow your own, plant one tuber in a hole 4 inches (10 cm) deep and 12 inches (30.5 cm) apart. Be warned, sunchokes are hard to control, so consider growing in deep pots to be sure you keep them where you want them.

RAW

Sunchokes are delicious raw and add a nice water chestnut–style crunch to winter dishes. The key is to <u>shave</u> them very thinly. I generally use a mandoline to shave wafer-thin pieces, but a sharp knife and deft hand will work just as well. For serving raw, look for very firm roots, and be sure to scrub between all of the little knobs where the dirt hides. I never bother to peel a sunchoke, making a good scrub even more necessary. Don't hesitate to pull out an old toothbrush; it may feel unduly meticulous but makes quick work of that nitty-gritty.

shaved sunchokes w/mustard vinaigrette and parsley

The creamy, mild flavor and crunchy texture of raw sunchokes pairs perfectly with aggressive flavors. Don't be shy with the vinegar in this recipe or the variations.

10 large sunchokes (about 2 lb | 910 g), <u>shaved</u> into thin wafers varying from circles to long sheets

1 small (2 oz | ¼ cup | 55 g) red onion or shallot, minced

¼ cup (60 g) whole-grain or Dijon mustard

¼ cup (60 ml) apple cider vinegar

1 Tbsp (20 g) honey

1 tsp (6 g) salt

½ cup (120 ml) olive oil

1 <u>bunch</u> parsley (2.4 oz | 1½ cups | 68 g), stemmed, leaves left whole

Submerge the sunchokes into <u>acidulated water</u>.

In a large mixing bowl, combine the onion, mustard, vinegar, honey, salt, and oil.

Drain the sunchokes, add to the bowl along with the parsley, and <u>toss</u>. Taste and adjust the seasoning. Serve immediately.

variations

w/shaved radishes, yogurt + dill

½ cup (120 g) plain yogurt

1 lemon (1½ fl oz | 45 ml), zest and juice

¼ cup (60 ml) olive oil

Salt and freshly ground black pepper

10 sunchokes (about 2 lb | 910 g), shaved

1 bunch radishes (1 lb | 455 g), shaved, greens reserved if in good shape

10 sprigs dill, minced

Whisk together the yogurt, lemon zest and juice, olive oil, and a big pinch of salt and pepper. Add to the sunchokes and radishes (including any good radish greens) and toss. Taste and adjust the seasoning. Garnish with the dill and serve

w/peas, mint, parsley + apple cider vinaigrette

10 sunchokes (about 2 lb | 910 g), shaved

1 cup (120 g) fresh or thawed shelled peas

5 springs mint, roughly chopped

½ bunch parsley (1.2 oz | ¾ cup | 34 g), roughly chopped

⅓ cup (80 ml) apple cider vinegar

2 Tbsp (40 g) honey

½ tsp (2 g) chili flakes

⅓ cup (80 ml) olive oil

Salt

Put the sunchokes, peas, mint, and parsley in a salad bowl. Combine the vinegar, honey, chili flakes, olive oil, and a big pinch of salt. Pour over the vegetables and toss. Taste and adjust the seasoning and serve.

w/cumin, garlic + lemon vinaigrette

⅓ cup (80 ml) olive oil

½ tsp (2 g) cumin

4 garlic cloves (0.8 oz | 28 g), minced

3 lemons (4.5 fl oz | 135 ml), zest and juice

½ tsp (3 g) salt

10 sunchokes (about 2 lb | 910 g), shaved

1 bunch cilantro (1 oz | ½ cup | 30 g), roughly chopped

Heat the olive oil, then remove from the heat. Add the cumin and let bloom. Add the garlic to the warm oil. When cool, combine with the lemon zest and juice and salt. Pour over the vegetables and herbs, and toss. Taste and adjust the seasoning and serve.

PURÉED

This is something I'll make regularly when I have a bunch of sun-chokes that need to get used up. This purée will be darker than those with celery root or parsnip because of the sunchoke skins—if you want it pure white, give them a peel.

sunchoke purée w/cream and white wine

I love Riesling wine, especially the incredibly flavorful and bone-dry versions being made in Northern Michigan. We have also been experimenting with nonlocal boxed wine—I haven't found a Riesling I like very much among them, though they do make great cooking wine. The fruity almost-sweetness goes well with the nuttiness of the chokes. Everything has a home somewhere.

Butter

2 onions (2 lb | 910 g), cut into thin slices

Salt

1 cup (240 ml) dry white wine

10 (about 2 lb | 910 g or as many as you like) sunchokes, cut into 1-inch (2.5-cm) chunks

1 cup (240 ml) cream

1 cup (240 ml) stock or water

1 tsp (6 g) salt

Pinch of ground nutmeg (totally optional and something I'm only starting to really like)

Heat a knob of butter in a medium saucepan until melted and foamy. Add the onions and salt, and sweat until tender. Add the wine and cook until evaporated. Add the sunchokes, cream, and stock. Bring to a boil and reduce to a simmer. Cover with a cartouche until the sunchokes are tender, about 35 minutes. Remove from the heat and blend in a food processor until very smooth. Taste and adjust the seasoning.

variations

w/venison, spinach + dried cherries

¾ cup (230 g) dried cherries

¼ cup (60 ml) hot water

¼ cup (60 ml) balsamic vinegar

12 venison chops (3 oz | 85 g each) or 1 tenderloin (about 3 lb | 1.4 kg) (feel free to substitute beef, lamb, or duck)

Salt and freshly ground black pepper

2 to 3 cups (480 to 720 ml) sunchoke purée

1 bag (4 oz | 115 g) spinach

Olive oil

Combine the cherries with the hot water and vinegar and let sit for 10 minutes. Season and grill the chops (page 23) to medium or as you like it. Spoon the purée over serving plates. Dress the spinach with a glug of olive oil and a sprinkle of salt and pepper. Slice the meat (or leave the chops whole) and put it on the purée, top with the balsamic cherries and the spinach, and serve.

turkey sandwiches w/sunchoke purée + cranberry relish

Make a sandwich with this stuff! Or anything else you have in the refrigerator. Mushrooms are good with it, too, or even eggplant.

smooth, creamy sunchoke soup

Whisk enough water or stock into 2 to 3 cups (480 to 720 ml) of purée to make a thin but creamy soup. Taste and adjust the seasoning.

OVEN ROASTED

One of the nice things about roasting roots is that you can do them in advance. Just roast them slightly less than completely done—I look for a fully tender root but with little to no caramelization on the skin. Let them cool completely, then store until you are ready to make dinner. Then spread them out on the baking sheet as you would if you were roasting them for the first time and reheat at 375°F (190°C). Know that you can reheat (or roast for that matter) at different temperatures if you already have the oven on for something else, making your oven do double duty. Just remember, the hotter the oven the faster the food will cook (read: burn), so don't abandon it.

roasted sunchokes w/massaged kale and brown butter vinaigrette

This vinaigrette is one of my favorite sauces. For the record, this dressing can go on almost anything and make it delicious, but it pairs really well with other veggies like parsnips, carrots, and squash. I also generally spike it with a bit of chili flakes to play some spice against the sweet, but this is not necessary.

10 sunchokes (about 2 lb | 910 g), cut into 1-inch (2.5-cm) pieces

Olive oil

1 tsp (5 g) chili flakes

Salt

½ cup (120 ml) brown butter vinaigrette (page 59)

1 bunch kale (½ lb | 4 cups | 230 g), midribs stripped out, cut into ribbons

4 oz (115 g) quark or ricotta (optional)

Heat the oven to 400°F (200°C). Toss the sunchokes with a glug of olive oil, chili flakes, and a big pinch of salt. Spread on a baking sheet, allowing some space between the pieces, and roast until tender, about 25 minutes.

Warm the dressing and set aside in a warm place; if it gets too cold, it will congeal.

If the kale is too tough to chew easily, sprinkle with salt and massage until tender (page 251).

Remove the chokes from the oven and <u>toss</u> with the kale and ½ cup (120 ml) of the vinaigrette, adding more as needed. Dot with the quark (if using) and serve warm.

variations

w/spinach, goat cheese + pecans

10 sunchokes (about 2 lb | 910 g), cut into 1-inch (2.5-cm) pieces	1 bag (4 oz | 115 g) spinach Olive oil	1 cup (120 g) pecans, toasted (page 24) 4 oz (115 g) goat cheese

After roasting the sunchokes, <u>toss</u> with the spinach and a big <u>glug</u> of olive oil, and transfer to a serving platter. Sprinkle with the pecans and dots of goat cheese, and serve.

w/slow-roasted salmon, oranges + arugula

10 sunchokes (about 2 lb | 910 g), cut into 1-inch (2.5-cm) pieces	Salt and freshly ground black pepper	3 oranges, zested, peeled, and segmented or cut into pinwheel slices
4 salmon fillets (6 oz | 170 g each) or 1 side salmon (24 oz | 680 g)	Olive oil ½ tsp (2 g) chili flakes	1 bag (4 oz | 115 g) arugula

After roasting the sunchokes, lower the heat to 300°F (150°C). Season the fish with salt and pepper and bake until just cooked through—about 35 minutes for a side, 12 minutes for fillets. Meanwhile, add a <u>glug</u> of olive oil and the chili flakes to the oranges, stir gently, and let rest. <u>Toss</u> the sunchokes with the arugula and the orange mixture. Transfer the cooked salmon to a platter, top with the sunchoke salad, and serve.

root bake w/lemon-caper mayo

These root vegetables are my favorites, but you can use any old mix of random root veggies you have around.

5 sunchokes (about 1 lb | 455 g), cut into 1-inch (2.5-cm) pieces

4 carrots (about 1 lb | 455 g), cut into 1-inch (2.5-cm) pieces

1 celery root (about 1 lb | 455 g), cut into 1-inch (2.5-cm) pieces

6 fingerling potatoes (about ½ lb | 230 g)

2 parsnips (about ½ lb | 230 g), cut into 1-inch (2.5-cm) pieces

½ bunch parsley (1 oz | ½ cup | 30 g), stemmed, leaves left whole

¾ cup (180 g) lemon-caper mayo (page 61)

After roasting the vegetables, toss the roasted roots with the parsley and dollop the mayo over the whole thing.

BRAISED

In its most simple form, braising means slowly cooking something in a bit of liquid at a low temperature. I'm fairly sure that the strict definition requires searing first and then cooking in liquid, which doesn't happen here, and so maybe this is more of a stewing. But that doesn't sound as nice unless you're English, which sadly I am not.

The benefits are a silky, yielding tuber in a rich sauce thickened by the natural starch in the flesh, and almost no active time required of the cook, as the stove does the bulk of the work.

braised sunchokes w/almonds, cream, sherry, parsley, and duck breast

In this recipe you can add almonds to the braise, which softens them like the sunchokes. I prefer leaving them crispy and <u>tossing</u> them with the parsley as a salad on top of the duck breast. I leave this up to you. If you don't have sweet sherry on hand, you can substitute ½ cup (120 ml) white wine with 2 Tbsp (30 ml) of bourbon or brandy.

Butter

1 onion (½ lb | 1 cup | 230 g), cut into <u>thin slices</u>

Salt and freshly ground black pepper

½ cup (120 ml) sweet sherry

10 to 15 sunchokes (2 to 2½ lb | 910 g to 1.2 kg), cut into 1-inch (2.5-cm) pieces

1 cup (240 ml) cream

1 cup (240 ml) stock or water

4 duck breasts (10 oz | 280 g each)

½ <u>bunch</u> parsley (1 oz | ½ cup | 30 g), stemmed, leaves left whole

½ cup (75 g) almonds, roughly chopped

1 orange (3 fl oz | 90 ml), zest and juice

1 lemon (1½ fl oz | 45 ml), zest and juice

Olive oil

Heat the oven to 300°F (150°C). In a Dutch oven or large ovenproof saucepan, heat a knob of butter until melted. Add the onion with a big pinch of salt and pepper and <u>sweat</u> until soft, about 7 minutes. Add the sherry and cook until almost dry.

Add the sunchokes and <u>toss</u> to combine. Add the cream and stock and bring to a boil. Cover with a lid or foil and braise in the oven until the sunchokes are fork-tender, about 25 minutes.

Score the duck breast by making cuts along the skin. In a frying pan, place the duck breast skin-side down and turn the heat to medium. Slowly render the fat and cook the duck breast until the skin is crispy and golden brown and the meat is medium rare, about 12 minutes, flipping to just cook the underside, 3 to 5 minutes. Let the duck rest for 7 to 10 minutes and then slice into ¼-inch (6-mm) pieces.

When the sunchokes are done, taste the sauce and adjust the seasoning.

Combine the parsley, almonds, citrus zest and juice, a **glug** of olive oil, and a pinch of salt.

Spoon the sunchokes and sauce onto the plates and top with the duck breast slices. Garnish with the parsley salad mixture and serve.

variations

w/bacon, mushrooms + chicken thighs

4 to 6 chicken thighs (6 oz | 170 g each)

Salt and freshly ground black pepper

½ lb (230 g) bacon, sliced into lardons

1 onion (1 lb | 1 cup | 455 g), cut into <u>thin slices</u>

4 garlic cloves (0.8 oz | 28 g), cut into <u>thin slices</u>

6 oz (170 g) mushrooms, left whole or cut into halves

10 sunchokes (about 2 lb | 910 g), cut into 1-inch (2.5-cm) pieces

1 cup (240 ml) red wine or white wine or sherry

1 bag (4 oz | 115 g) arugula or spinach or other tender greens

Olive oil

Heat the oven to 350°F (180°C). Pan sear the chicken thighs (page 24). Remove the chicken, add the bacon, and cook until crisp. Add the onion, garlic, and mushrooms, and <u>sweat</u>. Add the sunchokes and wine, and bring to a boil. Nestle in the chicken, skin-side up, and bake in the oven until the sunchokes are tender and the chicken is cooked through, about 35 minutes. Lightly dress the arugula with olive oil and a pinch of salt, and serve with the chicken dish.

sunchoke chowder w/sausage, tomatoes + cream

Neutral oil

½ lb (230 g) spicy sausage, or ½ lb (230 g) ground pork with 2 tsp (12 g) salt and ½ tsp (2 g) chili flakes

2 onions (2 lb | 2 cups | 910 g), cut into <u>thin slices</u>

4 garlic cloves (0.8 oz | 28 g), cut into <u>thin slices</u>

Salt and freshly ground black pepper

1 cup (240 ml) light beer

1 pint (1 lb | 455 g) cherry tomatoes, halved

10 sunchokes (about 2 lb | 910 g), cut into 1-inch (2.5-cm) pieces

1 cup (240 ml) cream

3 cups (720 ml) stock or water

Chopped parsley, or basil oil (page 56) (optional)

In a soup pot, heat a <u>glug</u> of oil and brown the sausage. Add the onions and garlic and a big pinch of salt and pepper and <u>sweat</u>. Add the beer and cook until evaporated. Add the tomatoes and sunchokes, and <u>toss</u> to combine. Add the cream and stock, and bring to a boil. Reduce to a simmer and cook until the sunchokes are tender, about 35 minutes. Taste and adjust the seasoning. Garnish with a handful of parsley or a spoonful of basil oil, if desired.

w/dill, sour cream + seared salmon

Neutral oil

1 onion (1 lb | 1 cup | 455 g), cut into <u>thin slices</u>

½ cup (120 ml) white wine

10 sunchokes (about 2 lb | 910 g), cut into 1-inch (2.5-cm) pieces

1 cup (240 g) sour cream

½ cup (120 ml) water or stock

4 salmon fillets (6 oz | 170 g each)

5 sprigs dill, minced

Heat the oven to 350°F (180°C). In a Dutch oven, heat a <u>glug</u> of oil and <u>sweat</u> the onion. Add the wine and cook until almost dry. Add the sunchokes, sour cream, and water, and stir to combine. Cover with a lid or foil, and cook in the oven until the sunchokes are tender, about 25 minutes. Sear the salmon (page 24) skin-side down until medium-rare. Remove from the heat and flip to gently cook the underside. Transfer the cooked sunchokes to a plate, top with the salmon, and garnish with the dill.

tomatoes

The best tomato I've ever eaten was not an heirloom.

It was a Sungold. An orange orb of joy **tossed** with olive oil, lemon thyme, salt, and pepper resting next to a piece of creamy mozzarella.

Sungolds are a modern hybrid tomato. Their thin skin and juicy interior make them prone to splitting, meaning that Sungolds are very rarely grown far away and sent on a cross-country journey to our tables. They are often raised by local farmers, picked when ripe, and eaten within a couple of days. In my mind, this is what makes for great flavor in a tomato—being raised well, harvested just ripe, and eaten quickly. I prioritize flavor above all else in a tomato (and most other things for that matter).

In the last couple of years, the term "heirloom tomato" has entered the daily market-going lexicon. Every tomato that is gently set out on a farmers' market table is now called an "heirloom." I don't always know what people are asking for when they insist on an heirloom. I think that they mean a tomato that is grown locally, often funny looking, not always red-n-round, and never tasting of cardboard.

An heirloom tomato by definition is an open-pollinated plant whose seeds have been passed down through the years. There is no consensus on how many generations' hands need to have touched the seed to give it family jewels status. There is no law, in letter or spirit, that heirlooms need to be grown locally. By contrast, hybrids are plants that have been bred to showcase the different characteristics of different parents in an attempt to select the best traits from each. There is also no guarantee that hybrids will grow true from their seed, so they are no good for seed, making growers reliant on the seed companies to provide them.

Hybrids get a bad rap from people who mistake them for genetically modified foods (where scientists splice traits into the genetic material of the plant). GMOs are common among commodity crops, developed for a trait not found in nature—resistance to synthetic herbicides, for example. As of this writing, the Flavr Savr is the only GMO tomato on the market.

With the advent of cross-country refrigerated shipping, tomatoes could be grown in the dead of winter, picked with the slightest blush of red, ripened with ethylene gas, and placed on supermarket shelves looking glossy and bright.

Large farms needed a way to standardize and consolidate their tomato harvest, so tomatoes were bred to produce fruit all at one time, determinate varieties (which grow to a certain size and stop; indeterminates just keep growing and producing). They were bred to produce fruit that will withstand being jostled for lots and lots of miles on their way to those shelves. They were bred to be big, round slicers. They were bred for lots of reasons besides flavor.

Heirloom tomatoes have regained favor as shoppers seek out flavorful tomatoes with a variety of looks. Similarly, there are lots of tomatoes that have been grown for flavor—like the Sungolds. These modern hybrids do not have the storied historical legacy of some of the best-known heirlooms like Brandywine, Cherokee Purple, and Aunt Ruby's German Green. But hybrids taste great and provide a modern option for selecting the best tomato for your growing environment.

I encourage you to go to your farmers' market and talk to your farmer. Ask her for the tomato that she thinks tastes the best, heirloom or not. Then pick out a couple that are so funny looking that they will tickle your fancy and your tongue.

HOW TO BUY

- Look for tomatoes that are heavy in the hand and fragrant.
- Please don't squeeze tomatoes at farmers' markets. It bruises them.
- I still buy tomatoes with small blemishes because there is so much food around the bruise, but be aware that they won't store as long.

HOW TO STORE

- Store on the counter in a cool place.
- Do not store tomatoes in the refrigerator; the cold kills the flavor volatiles.
- If you want to ripen the tomatoes, store them in a paper bag to trap the naturally occurring ethylene gas.

NOTES

- Tomato seeds are known to irritate diverticulitis; if you have a guest who suffers, consider removing the seeds in advance of dinner.
- Plum tomatoes, or sauce tomatoes, have less water in their internal cells, making them better candidates for canning because there is less water to evaporate before jarring. You can preserve any type of tomato by canning as long as the pH is acidic enough to combat bad bacteria.
- Tomato blight is a fungal disease in the soil that can cut short a tomato's season. If you're growing your own, avoid splashing ground water on the leaves, which can aid in spreading the blight.

RAW

Raw tomatoes come in and go out of my life. No matter how carefully I select my tomatoes, there are times when they just aren't knock-your-socks-off great. When that's the case, cut the tomatoes (in half for cherries or wedges for big girls) and season with a healthy pinch of salt and let sit for 10 to 15 minutes. Salt is hydroscopic and will pull excess water from the cells, doing the double duty of concentrating the remaining flavor and creating a light brine on the tomatoes. The salinity of the brine will penetrate the tomato, increasing the flavor throughout. And #realtalk, I buy fresh tomatoes in the winter now and again. The salt technique works on them, too.

tomato panzanella w/corn, cucumbers, and herb salad

This salad can be made with any other vegetables you have on hand. The key is to get a nice balance of crispy bread, soft tomato, and bright punchy herbs. This is another recipe where a good mixture of herbs will enliven the salad, but if you have only basil or parsley, it will still be great. To maintain the crunch, I <u>toss</u> the croutons with the tomatoes only a few minutes before serving. If they sit together for long it will slowly soften the bread, which is still delicious, making it a great (if slightly soggy) salad for summer picnics or other buffet settings.

4 ears corn (2 cups | 280 g), fresh or frozen kernels (page 162)

¼ cup (60 ml) olive oil

Salt and freshly ground black pepper

½ loaf crusty bread

2 Tbsp (30 g) butter (optional but delightful)

1 qt cherry tomatoes (about 2 lb | 910 g), halved, or 3 to 4 large slicing tomatoes, cut into large dice

1 cucumber (8 oz | 230 g), cut into half-moons (removing the seeds if large)

2 cups (70 g) herbs (basil, parsley, mint, chives, lemon balm, borage, mint, chervil, tarragon, lemon thyme, rosemary), stemmed, leaves left whole

Heat the oven to 400°F (200°C). Toss the corn with a glug of olive oil, sprinkle of salt, and grind of pepper. Spread the dressed corn out on a baking sheet and bake until cooked through and caramely, 12 to 15 minutes.

Cut or tear the bread into pieces and toss with a large glug of olive oil and salt and pepper. Bake the bread pieces until golden brown, about 10 minutes.

Toss the hot croutons with the butter so it melts and coats them.

Toss the croutons with the roasted corn, tomatoes, cucumbers, and herbs and a bit of salt and pepper. Taste the seasoning and adjust the salt (or add a splash of vinegar).

variations

w/spinach + delicata squash

1 medium delicata squash (about 2 lb | 910 g), cut into half-moons

1 qt (about 2 lb | 910 g) cherry tomatoes, halved

1 bag (4 oz | 115 g) spinach

Olive oil

Salt and freshly ground black pepper

Roast the squash until cooked through and lightly browned. Toss the roasted squash, tomatoes, and spinach with olive oil, salt, and pepper, and serve.

w/herbs, lemon + tuna mayo

1 qt (about 2 lb | 910 g) cherry tomatoes, halved

5 sprigs mint, stemmed, leaves left whole

5 sprigs basil, stemmed, leaves left whole

½ bunch parsley (1 oz | ½ cup | 30 g), stemmed, leaves left whole

Olive oil

1 Tbsp (9 g) white or black sesame seeds (optional)

1 lemon (1½ fl oz | 45 ml), zest and juice

Pinch of salt

½ cup (120 g) tuna mayo (page 61)

Toss the tomatoes and herbs together with a glug of olive oil, the sesame seeds (if using), lemon zest and juice, and the salt. Schmear half the tuna mayo on a serving platter and top with the tomato salad. Dot the rest of the tuna mayo over the salad.

w/fresh mozzarella + bread crumbs

2 balls fresh mozzarella (1 lb | 455 g), torn into chunks

¼ cup (60 g) sour cream

1 lemon (1½ fl oz | 45 ml), zest and juice

3 large slicer tomatoes (ideally of various colors) (about 2 lb | 910 g), cut into ½-inch- (12-mm-) thick slices

¼ cup (35 g) toasted bread crumbs

Any herbs you like (optional)

Toss the mozzarella with the sour cream and lemon juice and zest. Top the tomato slabs with the mozzarella. Top the whole thing with the bread crumbs and herbs, if you like, and serve.

STUFFED

I love party food from the 1970s, and all stuffed foods fall into that category for me. I love stuffing peppers and acorn squash. My favorite stuffable vegetable is tomatoes. The juice from the center mixes well with the filling, making a juicy, savory dinner. They are silly yet extremely practical. You can make them a day or two ahead and reheat them for your party.

tomatoes stuffed w/lentils and goat cheese

Stuffed tomatoes are always juicy—and therefore extremely hot when removed from the oven. Let them cool for a few minutes—ideally to room temperature—before diving in. I like them at all temperatures except cold. Serve alone or with a green salad and a thick piece of toast to soak up the juice.

3 to 4 large slicing tomatoes (about 2 lb | 910 g), cored

2 cups (400 g) cooked lentils (page 41)

4 oz (115 g) fresh goat cheese

1 medium onion (½ lb | ½ cup | 230 g), <u>diced</u>

1 tsp (3 g) smoked paprika

2 Tbsp (30 ml) balsamic vinegar

½ <u>bunch</u> parsley (1 oz | ½ cup | 30 g), stemmed, leaves left whole

¼ cup (35 g) bread crumbs (not toasted)

Heat the oven to 350°F (180°C).

Scoop out and reserve the center flesh of the tomatoes, leaving a thick lining of flesh.

Combine the lentils, goat cheese, onion, tomato flesh, paprika, vinegar, and parsley and mix to make a filling. Fill the hollowed tomatoes with the filling. Top with the bread crumbs just before baking. Bake until the filling is warm and the outer walls of the tomato have softened slightly, about 20 minutes. Allow to cool some and serve hot or at room temperature.

STUFFED TOMATO

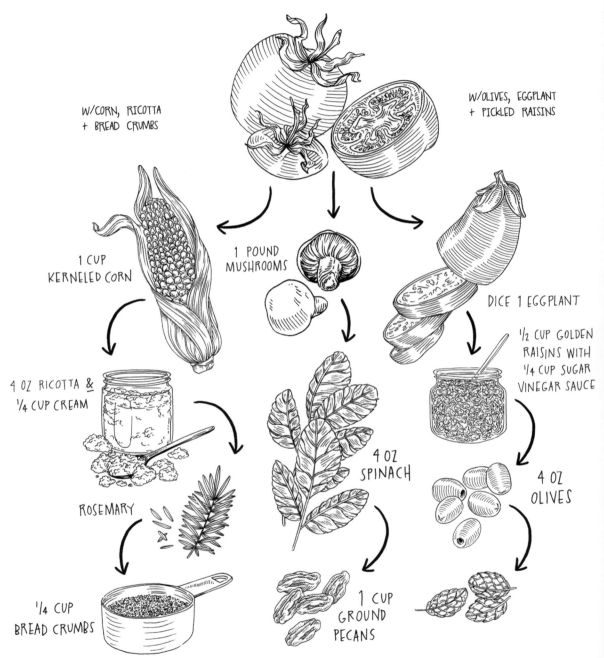

W/CORN, RICOTTA + BREAD CRUMBS

1 CUP KERNELED CORN

4 OZ RICOTTA & 1/4 CUP CREAM

ROSEMARY

1/4 CUP BREAD CRUMBS

COMBINE ALL WITH 2 SPRIGS ROSEMARY & FILL TOMATOES THEN BAKE

1 POUND MUSHROOMS

4 OZ SPINACH

1 CUP GROUND PECANS

COMBINE ALL & STUFF TOMATOES & BAKE

W/MUSHROOM, SPINACH + PECANS

W/OLIVES, EGGPLANT + PICKLED RAISINS

DICE 1 EGGPLANT

1/2 CUP GOLDEN RAISINS WITH 1/4 CUP SUGAR VINEGAR SAUCE

4 OZ OLIVES

COMBINE ALL WITH 2 GARLIC CLOVES & ZEST & JUICE OF 1 LEMON. ROUGHLY CHOP. STUFF TOMATOES & BAKE.

OVEN ROASTED

This is the only time that you can roast without needing space between the vegetables. The more tomatoes you have in the pan, the longer it will take to get the liquid to reduce, but go ahead and fill up your baking dish.

oven-roasted tomatoes

These are good fresh from the oven or cooled and then frozen and used months later. The roasting evaporates the water in the tomatoes and concentrates the sugar. Feel free to add garlic, chili flakes, or oregano.

As many cherry tomatoes as you can get your hands on

Big glug of olive oil

Sprinkle of salt and freshly ground black pepper

Heat the oven to anywhere between 300°F and 400°F (150°C and 200°C)—the higher the temp, the more often you'll need to stir. Toss together the tomatoes, olive oil, and salt and pepper. Put in an ovenproof baking dish and bake, stirring occasionally, until the tomatoes burst, and the juice is reduced to a thick syrup, 30 to 45 minutes. The mixture should be thick enough to leave a trail when a spatula is dragged across the pan—nappé, baby. Remove from the oven and let cool.

things to put these tomatoes on/in

toast w/cheese, pasta w/cream + basil (oil), roasted eggplant, stuffed peppers, stuffed squash, top-seared fish or roasted chicken, butter for slathering on steak, more, more, more . . .

turnips and rutabaga

Myrtle Allen started Ballymaloe House as a second form of income to support her family's farm. She once told me that she relied on the food that she knew, the food of farmers who both cherish and are spoiled by what they grow. I asked her what she meant by spoiled. She said, "A farmer won't suffer a bad swede," which didn't really answer my question.

Turns out a swede is a rutabaga, and rutabaga was bred from a turnip and cabbage cross. What I've come to infer from her answer is that a farmer will suffer crappy weather, physically taxing work, little money, and the whims of Mother Nature, but won't stomach bad food. It doesn't have to be fancy, probably better if it's not, but it has to be fresh and well grown.

Our current conversation about local and seasonal produce tends to focus on the delicate stars—greens, berries, tomatoes—but it always stuck with me that Myrtle emphasized the rutabaga. Turnips and rutabaga feel more like sustenance food. The point I think she was making is that a food with even the coarsest reputation can be suave in the right place and in the right hands. The best version of the least refined food is better than a mediocre version of the most genteel. Myrtle taught herself how to coax fine dining from a lowly swede.

Members of the brassica family, turnips grow well in cold climates, store well, and are dense with an unending list of micro-nutrients—vitamins C, A, K, folate, calcium, and lutein, to name a few. They are evocative of rough, weather-beaten hands and never seem to claim elegance among their descriptors. For many, during the famines of war these were the food of last resort and still carry that reputation of hardship. Pity, that, because turnips and ruta-baga are incredibly versatile and nourishing to share over a table. Their flavor and textures span a spectrum, with age and variety most affecting the taste.

Salad turnips are the thin-skinned, small-rooted ones. These look a good deal like white radishes but lack the spice because they contain less mustard oil and sulfur. Their greens are tender and verdant without a hint of prickly fuzz. You're most likely to see salad turnips in the spring and the fall because they, like most brassicas, don't like the heat and take the least amount of time from seed to full size.

Rutabaga has less diversity in variety than the turnips but shares most other characteristics—edible leaves and a sulfuric bite. Until I grew them myself, I had only ever seen them in the Upper Peninsula of Michigan, where they are pronounced "rootabagey" and are essential in the traditional Cornish-style pasty. It was a shock to see the sheer volume of leaves on each plant. We clipped the greens and used them like collards. The roots were tender and sweet, instantly becoming a favorite for a raw root vegetable salad in the spring and the fall.

Both turnips and rutabaga work well raw or cooked, though the older the plant is—either since being planted or since being harvested—the stronger the flavor. Brassicas contain sulfur, the same compound that can make water smell like rotten eggs. The sulfur density increases as the plant ages and pulls it from the soil to aid in biosynthesis. It is good for you but not always the most polite of flavors.

Myrtle Allen taught and created a space for Darina Allen, who founded the Ballymaloe Cookery School, where I was lucky enough to train. These women (and the many more who teach there now) cultivated within me a nascent love of good produce. As the years have gone on I think of Myrtle's answer—"A farmer won't suffer a bad swede"—and am inspired to cajole grace from even the least refined vegetables and prioritize them over the fanci-est of foods that arrive in a mediocre state.

HOW TO BUY

- Look for turnips and rutabaga with even, tight skin.
- Pock marks and extensive browning are signs of age or pest damage.
- If possible, buy with the greens still attached and then treat like kale or chard—*cima di rapa* is an Italian turnip green, used in a popular dish of sautéed greens with a bit of garlic and white wine.

HOW TO STORE

- Separate the greens (if present) from the roots unless you'll be using them quickly.
- Store the thin-skinned salad turnips in the refrigerator.
- Larger storage turnips and rutabaga will do fine in the refrigerator or root cellar—just don't let them freeze.

NOTES

- The sulfuric bite of these brassicas can be lessened by soaking in cool water to dilute the sulfuric acid.
- Rutabagas are a hybrid between cabbage and turnips.
- Rutabaga are one of the few necessary ingredients in the Upper Peninsula's famous Cornish-style pasty.
- Turnips come in a variety of colors ranging from white to yellow to red to purple topped. Instead of peeling the turnips, simply scrub them with a vegetable brush or scruffy part of a sponge, leaving the color intact.
- The greens tend to be bitter and a bit spicy, like their cousin broccoli rabe, and pair well against the sweet of the root.

RAW

Both turnips and rutabaga are great raw, though the larger and more mature roots tend to have more sulfuric acid and so taste hotter and stronger. Taste a piece, and if it is too intensely cabbagey, give the rest a soak in cool water (which also crisps them) for 10 to 20 minutes. It has the secondary benefit of crisping the root.

matchstick salad: turnip, carrots, kohlrabi, w/lemon, parmesan, and parsley

I like this salad to have similar shaped vegetables. It doesn't have to be matchsticks; could be wedges or half-moons, or a mix. Bottom line: don't let the knife work dissuade you from making the salad. As long as you get the vegetables into bite-size units, you'll be good.

For the variations, you can use the same proportion of vegetables or stick with only turnip or rutabaga. The key is to have a nice dose of fat and brightness to balance the brassica flavor.

1 bunch salad turnips (1 lb | 455 g), cut into matchsticks

3 medium turnips or 1 large rutabaga (1 lb | 455 g), ends trimmed, peeled, cut into matchsticks

4 carrots (various colors are nice) (1 lb | 455 g), cut into matchsticks

2 kohlrabi (1 lb | 455 g), ends trimmed, peeled, cut into matchsticks

1 or 2 apples (1 lb | 455 g), unpeeled, cut into matchsticks

2 lemons (3 fl oz | 90 ml), zest and juice

½ cup (120 ml) olive oil

Big pinch of salt

1 bunch parsley (1.2 oz | ¾ cup | 34 g), roughly chopped

2 oz (55 g) Parmesan, shaved with a vegetable peeler or grater

Dress the vegetables and apples with the lemon zest and juice, olive oil, and salt. Toss all together, and let sit for 10 minutes to lightly marinate. Taste and adjust the seasoning. Add the parsley to the salad, garnish with the Parmesan shavings, and serve.

variations

pickle liquid dressing (page 58) + parsley

w/leeks + anchovy vinaigrette (page 59)

w/tuna mayo (page 61) + bread crumbs

OVEN ROASTED

When roasting turnips or rutabaga, the strong sulfury brassica flavor is diminished as its water content is wicked away and the sugars are concentrated. If your turnips or rutabaga are particularly strong, you can rinse the sulfur away (as with the raw) but be sure to pat the pieces dry before roasting, or they won't get crispy. Salad turnips are great pan-fried as well as in the oven.

roasted turnip, apple, rosemary, w/pork loin and spinach

The apples in this recipe marry the salt of the pork, the funk of the rutabaga, and the herb of the rosemary all together with a hit of sweet and tang. I love roasting meats on a bed of vegetables, because not only is everything in one big pan, but also the drippings add flavor to the veggies and vice versa. This recipe can also be done with any sort of meat, especially chicken or a gamier fish. If roasting everything together feels daunting, feel free to roast the meat and vegetables separately. If the protein is done first, it can rest while the vegetables finish up, and vice versa. The veggies also work well on their own as a hearty side.

5 sprigs rosemary

1 pork loin (assume about ¾ lb | 340 g per person)

¼ cup (60 g) Dijon mustard

2 Tbsp (30 ml) olive oil

1 tsp (6 g) salt, plus more for seasoning

1 tsp (6 g) freshly ground black pepper, plus more for seasoning

4 turnips or rutabaga (2 lb | 910 g), cut into large chunks

4 potatoes (2 lb | 910 g), cut into large chunks

3 apples (1½ lb | 680 g), cored and cut into large chunks

1 onion (1 lb | 1 cup | 455 g), sliced into petals

Neutral oil

½ tsp (1 g) caraway seeds (optional)

½ cup (120 ml) white wine or hard cider

½ bag (2 oz | 55 g) spinach

Olive oil

Heat the oven to 375°F (190°C). Tuck 3 of the 5 rosemary sprigs along the ties of the pork loin or just near the loin.

Whisk together the mustard, olive oil, salt, and pepper. Rub it all over the pork loin and set aside for 10 minutes or so.

Toss the roots, apples, onion, and remaining 2 rosemary sprigs with a glug of neutral oil, the caraway seeds, salt, and pepper.

In a large Dutch oven, heat a glug of neutral oil over medium heat. Sear the pork loin on all sides, then remove from the pan. Add the white wine to the pan and deglaze, then reduce to almost dry. Add the vegetables to the Dutch oven and toss to coat.

Nestle the pork roast onto the vegetables and roast until the pork is cooked medium-well or reaches an internal temperature of 150°F (65°C), 45 to 60 minutes (or about 20 minutes per 1 lb | 455 g). Transfer the pork from the vegetables to a platter, cover it loosely with foil, and let rest for 10 minutes.

Transfer the vegetables to a serving platter.

Dress the spinach with a glug of olive oil, big pinch of salt and several turns of black pepper.

Slice the pork roast and lay the slices over the vegetables on the serving platter. Top with the spinach and serve.

variations

w/dill yogurt + lake trout

Same mixture of turnip, rutabaga, potato, and apple, or just turnip and rutabaga

1 side of lake trout or salmon, skin on, left whole or cut into 4 fillets (about 6 oz | 170 g each)

1 cup (240 g) yogurt

1 lemon (1½ fl oz | 45 ml), zest and juice

Salt

1 bunch dill (10 sprigs), roughly chopped

Roast the veggies. Pan sear the fish so the skin is crispy (page 24). Whisk together the yogurt and lemon zest and juice with a pinch of salt. Serve the fish skin-side up next to the roasted vegetables. Drizzle both with the yogurt dressing and sprinkle with the chopped dill.

w/paprika, parsley, cream + chicken thighs

4 chicken thighs (6 oz | 170 g each)	Same mixture of turnip, rutabaga, potato, and apple, or just turnip and rutabaga	½ tsp (2 g) smoked paprika
Salt and freshly ground black pepper		½ tsp (2 g) sweet paprika
		¼ cup (60 ml) white wine
		1 cup (240 ml) cream

Season the chicken thighs with salt and pepper. Toss the veg with the paprikas and spread in a baking dish. Pour the wine and cream over the veg, put the chicken thighs on top of the vegetables, and bake until the chicken and the vegetables are cooked through, about 40 minutes.

w/kale + garlic mayo

4 turnips or rutabagas (about 2 lb | 910 g), ends trimmed, peeled, cut into 2-inch (5-cm) pieces	Salt and freshly ground black pepper	1 bunch kale (½ lb | 4 cups | 230 g), midribs stripped out, cut into ribbons
Olive oil	½ cup (120 g) garlic mayo (page 61)	¼ cup (35 g) sunflower seeds, toasted (page 24)

Heat the oven to 400°F (200°C). Toss the vegetables with a glug of olive oil and salt and pepper. Roast until cooked through and crispy, about 40 minutes. Combine them with the mayo. Toss the cooked roots with the kale, drizzle with the mayo, and top with the sunflower seeds.

BRAISED

The addition of liquid and a touch of acid to stewing these roots makes a magical potage in which the liquid absorbs and reduces as the veggie stews, yielding a slightly thickened and sumptuous sauce.

turnip and potato mash w/chicken legs, orange, vanilla vinaigrette, and radicchio

This recipe involves lightly smashing the turnips and potatoes with the braising liquid, making a rough mash. Feel free to leave them in chunks if you like the stewy nature of the sauce. Also feel free to use all turnip or rutabaga instead of adding potatoes, though the potatoes lend a bit of starch to the finished sauce. This recipe is also perfect with duck legs if you want something richer than chicken.

4 chicken legs (about 10 oz | 280 g)

Salt and freshly ground black pepper

Neutral oil

½ cup (120 ml) white wine

1 onion (½ lb | 1 cup | 230 g), cut into thin slices

1 tsp (6 g) salt

3 turnips or rutabaga (1½ lb | 680 g), ends trimmed, peeled, cut into large chunks

3 to 6 potatoes (1½ lb | 680 g), Yukon gold or red-skinned, cut into large chunks

1 cup (240 ml) stock or water

2 oranges, zest and segments or half-moons

½ tsp (3 ml) vanilla paste or extract

2 Tbsp (30 ml) sherry or apple cider vinegar

¼ cup (60 ml) olive oil

2 heads radicchio (1 lb | 455 g), cored and cut into petals

Heat the oven to 400°F (200°C). Pat the chicken legs dry and season all over with salt and pepper. In a medium Dutch oven, heat a glug of neutral oil over medium heat and sear the chicken legs until golden brown, about 12 minutes (page 24). Transfer the chicken legs to a plate to hold. Deglaze the pan with the wine. Add the onion and salt, and reduce the heat to medium-low to sweat until tender, about 7 minutes. Add the roots and stock, and bring to a boil. Place the chicken legs on top of the roots.

Cover and slow cook in the oven until the roots are tender and the sauce slightly reduced, 30 to 45 minutes.

Make the vinaigrette by combining the orange zest, vanilla, vinegar, and olive oil with a big pinch of salt.

Remove the pan from the oven. Remove the chicken legs from the pan. With a potato masher or heavy spoon, gently smash the cooked roots, working the liquid in to make a loose mash.

<u>Toss</u> the radicchio with the vanilla vinaigrette. Top the mash with the chicken legs, then the radicchio, and finally the orange segments. Alternatively, serve the mash, chicken legs, and salad separately, whichever works best for you.

variations

w/pork chops, arugula, dried cranberry + pecans

Same vegetables as for the braise	½ cup (70 g) dried cranberries	Olive oil
		Salt
Pork chops, 1 or 2 per person (8 to 10 oz | 230 to 280 g)	2 Tbsp (30 ml) balsamic vinegar	½ cup (60 g) pecans, toasted (page 24)
	1 bag (4 oz | 115 g) arugula	

Braise the vegetables in the same way. Sear the pork chops and finish in the oven (page 23), reserving the fat. <u>Toss</u> the dried cranberries with the balsamic vinegar. Stir the pork fat into the braised roots and put on a platter. Place the pork chops on the braise. Dress the arugula with a <u>glug</u> of olive oil and a pinch of salt. Top with the arugula, marinated cranberries, and pecans, and serve.

w/salmon, spinach, turnip, sherry vinaigrette

4 salmon fillets (6 oz | 170 g each)	Salt and freshly ground black pepper	¼ cup (60 ml) sherry or red wine vinegar
	1 bag (4 oz | 115 g) spinach	½ cup (120 ml) olive oil

Braise the vegetables in the same way. Season the salmon with salt and pepper and sear, skin-side down, until crispy (page 24) and cook to medium-rare. Dress the spinach with the vinegar, oil, and salt and pepper. Serve the salmon, crispy skin-side up, on the braise, topped with the spinach.

w/mustard, white wine, cream under chard, kale + mushrooms

Same vegetables as for the braise	1 bunch chard or kale (½ lb | 4 cups | 230 g), kale midribs stripped out, chard stems cut into thin slices, leaves cut into ribbons	4 hard-boiled eggs (page 22), roughly chopped
2 Tbsp (30 g) Dijon or whole-grain mustard		Olive oil
1 cup (240 ml) cream		Salt and freshly ground black pepper
8 oz (230 g) mushrooms of any sort, sliced thinly		

Add the mustard and cream to the braising liquid and braise as in the master recipe. Panfry the mushrooms until crispy and well-browned. Toss the chard leaves, stems, mushrooms, and chopped egg with a glug of olive oil and salt and pepper. Top the braise with the chard-mushroom salad and serve.

acknowledgments

A kindly old woman was walking through the land when she came upon a village. As she entered, the villagers moved toward their homes, locking doors and windows. The stranger smiled and asked, "Why are you all so frightened? I am a simple traveler, looking for a soft place to stay for the night and a warm place for a meal."

"There's not a bite to eat in the whole province," they told her. "We are weak, and our children are starving. Better keep moving on."

"Oh, I have everything I need," she said. "In fact, I was thinking of making some stone soup to share with all of you." She pulled an iron cauldron from her cloak, filled it with water, and began to build a fire under it.

Then, with great ceremony, she drew an ordinary-looking stone from a silken bag and dropped it into the water. By now, hearing the rumor of food, most of the villagers had come out of their homes or watched from their windows. As the stranger sniffed the "broth" and licked her lips in anticipation, hunger began to overcome their fear.

"Ah," the stranger said to herself rather loudly, "I do like a tasty stone soup. Of course, stone soup with cabbage—that's hard to beat."

Soon a villager approached hesitantly, holding a small cabbage he'd retrieved from its hiding place, and added it to the pot.

"Wonderful!" cried the stranger. "You know, I once had stone soup with cabbage and a bit of salt beef as well, and it was fit for a king."

The village butcher managed to find some salt beef . . . And so, it went, through potatoes, onions, carrots, mushrooms, and so on, until there was indeed a delicious meal for everyone in the village to share.

The village elder offered the stranger a great deal of money for the magic stone, but she refused to sell it and traveled on the next day. As she left, the stranger came upon a group of village children standing near the road. She gave the silken bag containing the stone to the youngest child, whispering to the group, "It was not the stone, but the villagers, that had performed the magic."

This book has been made, and made immeasurably better, because it passed through the hands and minds of the following capable women (and a few men). In a lot of ways, I feel like I tricked them all into making this literary stone soup, but, my goodness, they sure did perform a lot of magic.

Kari Stuart held the beat (beet!) for this entire book from inception to the copy you are holding in your hands. The first conversation we ever had about this book, I was standing outside the restaurant where I worked, between the parking lot and the dumpsters, and I felt about as couth as my venue, doubtful of putting pen to page. From there she added her know-how, her smarts, her grace, and her all-around savvy to this book and to the process. If it takes a village, Kari is the mayor.

Sarah Billingsley was the first townsperson to add to the soup, but instead of approaching hesitantly, she leapt from her house, bringing a skilled crew of talent to the party. Her enthusiasm and vision made this book possible and readable, given my deficiencies as a first-time author. Chronicle is lucky to have her, and I'm grateful that she wanted to work with me.

Emily Berger can make a jar of markers look interesting and beautiful. Thankfully, she instead turned her lens to the food in this book and made the images drip from the page. It should also be noted that Emily's use of natural light to harness the glory of everyday scenes is a rare and appreciated talent.

Lucy Engelman stepped up to the challenge of how to make hundreds of dish ideas graphic, interesting, and understandable. I know almost nothing about illustrations and had a vague cloud of an idea about how they would work with these recipes. Lucy brought the pens and mad talent to the page, breathing life into the possibilities of this soup.

Mollie Hayward styled the food in the way Coco Chanel dressed herself—always take one thing off before you leave the house. Her talents in the kitchen and behind the camera made this book more composed than I ever could have imagined. She is the salt in this soup.

Sara Schneider, through her talented design work, refined my ragtag collage of ideas into a cohesive and subtle work. Thank you for knowing how a book should look when I could see it only in my mind. Thank you to the rest of the team at Chronicle, specifically Brooke Johnson, Tera Killip, and Magnolia Molcan.

Kristi Hein, copyeditor, is the reason these recipes and essays read like real recipes and not the notes from a cook's workbook, all shorthand and lists.

Allison Scott read every page and honed the book by lending her brain and friendship to the page, all while chasing a toddler and registering hundreds of people to vote.

Francis Lam, thanks for feeding me chard for the first time, just before I jumped in a lake in Maine. Since then you have been a beacon in this world. Can I have some more kiddo pictures, please?

I wanted to be sure that this book really worked for readers with no training in food or access to industrial kitchens. Thank you to everyone (and they are a village full) who tested these recipes—Rick Alverson, Joseph Arendt, Betty Barnes, Jared Batson, Sally Berens, Jennifer Breckner, Katie Burdett, Jamie Citron, Anne Dannhausen, Penny Duff, Hayley Edwards, Emily Elert, Meghan Fishstix-Kinney, Courtney Hall, Jennifer Jackson, Heidi Joynt, Colin Kerr, Ritchie King, Quin Kirchner, Molly Kobelt, Lizzie Kucich, Nikki Ladapolous, Maddie LaKind, Jamie Lausch, Erika Lund, Megan MacDonald, Anya Maziak, Patrick Mills, Rose Perez, Barbara Piskor, Heather Radke, Emilie Rex, Jamie Saltsman, Michael Slaboch, Sarah Splietoff, Emily Spurlin, Anthea Stolz, Karl Sturk, Marianne Sundquist, Devin Ulery, Matt Ulery, Izaak Vanderbroek, Kathleen Williams, Caroline Woods, and Jill Yeomans. With special gratitude to Rose Hollander, Colleen Ciampa, Kelsey Coday, and Marsha Fitzgibbons for doing the heavy lifting of testing multiple chapters.

No recipe is worth anything without quality ingredients. Thank you to all the farmers and producers out there. Thanks to Jess Piskor and our years at Bare Knuckle. We learned so much together, and I wouldn't be the same person without him and those years in the field. Special thanks to the incredible team at Granor Farm because I'm no farmer and you all are. Katie Burdett, Wesley Rieth, Jose Olivera, Alfredo Olivera, Rob Buono, and Liz Cicchelli, thank you for growing such beautiful food, building a venue to share that food with our community, and letting me show off your produce in this book.

It takes know-how to turn even the best ingredients into a dish. Thank you to Rodger Bowser for teaching me how to cook and sending me to Ballymaloe, where I would learn even more. Thank you to Darina Allen and Skye Gyngell for training me and being #ladybosses to the highest degree. Thank you to Paul Virant for the years of paying me to learn at his apron strings. My food would be dramatically less me without having learned from him. Thank you to Allison Batdorff of the Record Eagle and Barb Tholin of Edible Grande Traverse for being willing to publish an untested author—you inadvertently started this process.

Thank you to Lee Berens for providing the bowls (and plates and platters and glasses) to hold all this soup.

Finally, stone soup wouldn't be what it is without the magic stone. In my case, Tim Mazurek is that rock. One day, at a low point in my confidence and career, he told me that he wanted me to contribute a recipe to something he was working on. I scoffed at the idea because I had never thought of myself as a chef, let alone one who could publish something. Here we are. Since that time, he has been one of the most important voices in my life, simultaneously encouraging and challenging me while wrapping me in friendship and feminism. And he had the good sense to marry Bryan, so I could be friends with him, too.

So, so many hands touch a book before it is published, and only two of them were mine. Thank you. Dear reader, you are in very good hands.

index